The World-Famous
Alaska
Highway

A Guide to the Alcan
& Other Wilderness Roads of the North

TRICIA BROWN

Fulcrum Publishing
Golden, Colorado

For Jennifer, the first and the fairest

Text and photographs copyright © 2000 Tricia Brown

The World-Famous Alaska Highway provides many safety tips about weather and travel, but good decision-making and sound judgment are the responsibility of the individual. Neither the publisher nor the author assumes any liability for injury that may arise from the use of this book.

Library of Congress Cataloging-in-Publication Data

Brown, Tricia.
  The world-famous Alaska Highway : a guide to the Alcan and other wilderness roads of the North / Tricia Brown.
        p. cm.
Includes index.
  ISBN 1-55591-446-2
  1. Alaska Highway—Guidebooks. 2. Automobile travel—Northwest, Canadian—Guidebooks. 3. Automobile travel—Alaska Highway—Guidebooks. 4. Northwest, Canadian—Guidebooks. 5. Alaska—Guidebooks. I. Title.
    F1060.92 .B79 2000
    917.9804'52—dc21   00-009197

Printed in China
0 9 8 7 6 5 4 3 2 1

Editorial: Don Graydon, Daniel Forrest-Bank
Design: Michelle Taverniti
Maps: Marge Mueller, Gray Mouse Graphics
Front cover image: Motorhome on road, on the south side of Denali National Park in
    southcentral Alaska, copyright © 2000 Clark James Mischler/AlaskaStock.com.
Back cover images: TOP—A yellow cab rests outside the Arctic Brotherhood Hall, established
in 1899, in Skagway. BOTTOM—A bear sculpture adorns the exterior of a gift shop in
downtown Anchorage. Photographs by Tricia Brown

Fulcrum Publishing
16100 Table Mountain Parkway, Suite 300
Golden, Colorado 80403
(800) 992-2908 • (303) 277-1623
www.fulcrum-books.com

Acknowledgments

Thanks, Marlene Blessing, for inviting me to hit the highway once again. Special thanks to Bob Calderone and the rest of the folks at Cruise America, who helped make our travels exceptionally comfortable, and to Perry, who always pulled over without waiting for a please. To all the counter people at all of the visitor centers throughout the northland, the museum volunteers, the friendly clerks in gift shops, the coach drivers, the railroad dining car servers, the concierge staff, the tour reservation operators—you do a great service to your state or province. Your love for the place you live is contagious. Continue to share it with enthusiasm, knowing that for most people, this is a once-and-only trip of a lifetime.

Unimproved portions of the Alaska Highway are becoming more rare, but do expect construction.

Crossing into Alaska usually involves a stop for picture taking at this magnificent sign.

A deer feeds at roadside just outside Hudson's Hope city limits in British Columbia.

A distinctive geological feature, Folded Mountain is about 410 miles north of Dawson Creek.

Contents

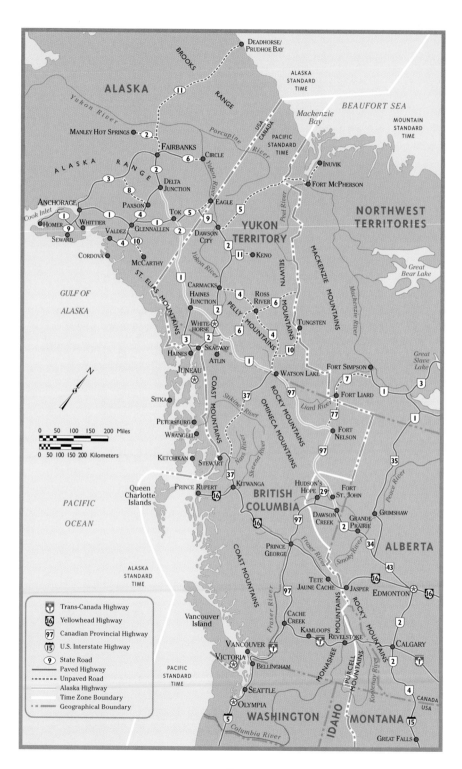

The Road to Hell?

*Winding in
and winding out
fills my mind
with serious doubt,
as to whether the lout
who planned this route,
was going to hell
or coming out.*

The author of that old rhyme remains anonymous, but his message still echoes from earlier days of driving North America's best-known wilderness road. Labeled the Alcan during its construction through Canada and Alaska's backcountry, the Alaska Highway began as a World War II supply line from the continental United States to its far-off territory. At war's end, after the road opened to the public, the civilian world learned what the military already knew: This two-lane gravel road was a beast, known for its twists, miry stretches, and burdensome length, yet adorned by fabulous beauty that dared you to take your eyes off the road.

After decades of improvements, the route has matured into a destination unto itself, and those who travel its length never forget the journey. Now well past its 50th birthday, the Alaska Highway has been surveyed, straightened, graded, rerouted, paved, and populated in some places, but it remains a wild thing that's only somewhat tamed. This route through some of the most uncivilized parts of the continent still embodies the romance and challenge that adventure travelers seek. For some, it's not the getting to Alaska that matters anymore—although Alaska is a lifetime dream for many—it's having driven the road. Bumper stickers, postcards, key chains, T-shirts, all the souvenirs you can carry will spout the news: "I drove the Alaska Highway...and survived!"

The "before" shot of our homemade trailer, back in 1978.

Our pre-schoolers watch as more repairs are underway. The note on the back of this photo reads: "It was a better mud flap than it was a trailer."

Going to hell or coming out? Looking back more than 20 years, I remember asking myself that question. On my first trip up the Alaska Highway, most of the road was unpaved, dangerously gooey in the rain and dust-choked in the sun. More miles were crooked than straight, and washboard had developed on nearly every turn. A person could get seasick hundreds of miles from the ocean. I remember dark thoughts drumming through my head one day as I kicked 3 inches of muck off our bumper while my then-husband shinnied under the trailer to see about a broken axle. Our two toddlers were crying, their play having turned to fight. We had stopped asking ourselves if we were doing the right thing, and were on a tight-lipped march to our finish line in Fairbanks.

A new life in the Last Frontier awaited there, 4,000 miles from our home in northern Illinois. Modern pioneers in a 1978 Chevrolet Blazer, we towed a little trailer intended for snowmobiles, not the hulking plywood box that carried all of our worldly goods. I had painted a colorful emancipation proclamation on the side: "Alaskabound." It looked like a clown car. The trailer generated lots of goodwill, waves, and blessings. But somehow Alaskabound didn't look so jaunty when it was propped up at a weird angle along the road. Turns out the thing was so weighty that tire blowouts were a daily occurrence. We stocked up on spares in every town we came across, knowing we'd be changing tires as often as we changed our socks. Our total came to 12 flats. A broken trailer tongue and the busted axle topped off the tally, and repairs slowed us by days. We crept along with help from good people along the way and discovered the meaning of northern hospitality. Meanwhile, we solemnly drank in mountainscapes that we flatlanders had seen only in books and movies. Did we know what we were getting into when we left? No. We were young and blessed with excessive hope.

Living in Alaska for 20-plus years, I have driven every highway on its limited state road system. I've picnicked above the Arctic Circle, trundled down the only road into Denali National Park, and retraced the pioneering route of the Valdez-to-Fairbanks Trail, now the Richardson Highway. In one 10-year span, I put nearly 200,000 miles on my vehicle—all of them Alaska miles. But I never drove the Alaska Highway again. Oh, friends and relatives made the trip up without incident, arriving with glowing reports of moose and bear sightings, serene lakeside campgrounds, and awesome scenery. "The road's great!" they proclaimed. "It's almost completely paved now. You wouldn't recognize it." But I had vowed long ago, like a fist-shaking Scarlett O'Hara of the North: *As God is my witness, I shall never drive that road again!*

I laughed when I was asked to write this book, then found myself breaking my own promise. But I had to do it, to see for myself what the Alaska Highway has become. Maybe it's the same urge for that firsthand experience that has you captivated, too, and you feel you must go. With the assistance of some great folks at Cruise America, my husband and I loaded our things into one of their Tioga motor homes, and we headed out, learning as much about land cruising as we did about the people and places along the highway.

In this book, I'll introduce you to roadside history, geography, Native cultures, and recreational opportunities in Alberta, British Columbia, the Yukon, and Alaska, covering miles well beyond the Alaska Highway itself. I've included details about attractions, restaurants, hotels, and campgrounds. You'll also meet some of the colorful characters who make the northland so memorable, and get tips from road warriors we met along the way. I hope this guide enhances your travels. We had a ball, and you will, too.

Remember this, though: The Alcan, with all of its history, romance, and wonder, is not just about driving. It's a passageway to places you've only dreamed about: the stomping grounds of the gold rush stampeders and pioneers. Land that's steeped in centuries of Native culture. Crystalline streams, jade-colored lakes, wild animals, snowy mountain peaks, and spruce forests. You'll meet new friends who are on the same journey, and those who live along the way. The beauty will linger in your mind well beyond the boundaries of your trip, indelible pictures that you'll carry yet lack words to express. You, too, will find that until you've experienced the Alaska Highway for yourself, it's kind of hard to explain it. Welcome to the club.

Chapter 1

Getting Ready

Planning for months, traveling for weeks, remembering for a lifetime. Those are the pleasures of a road trip to the far north. On the road to Alaska, you'll wend through farms and prairies and vast acres of pristine forest; you'll climb the Canadian Rockies and breach the continental divide. You will head for the Yukon, a place-name that still rings with the promise of gold, as it did a century ago during the Klondike Gold Rush. And you'll view the famous Yukon River, so broad and unspoiled. The road leads farther north, into Alaska, where you'll explore a state highway system that, measured to scale against this landscape, is nothing more than a dozen pieces of thread thrown against a fabulous, multicolored king-size quilt.

This is more than just a trip—this is an unparalleled adventure.

Any experienced traveler knows the importance of researching a place before embarking on a trip. Next in line is packing smart. Not too much, not too little. This chapter outlines in detail how to prepare for weeks on the road.

Your Travel Timeline

Time is the issue that separates the two types of highway travelers: those who just want to get to a place, and those who know that the journey can be as enjoyable as the destination. The first and best rule of thumb is: Take your time. This is not a race. Stop for ice cream. Read the historical signs. Try not to think about making good time. Most of all, be mindful that posted speed limits are not suggestions but law. The laws of physics aren't flexible either. Some Alaskans (mostly male, for some reason) claim special bragging rights to having made their personal best time in covering the Alaska Highway. "Why, we went from Seattle to Fairbanks in 72 hours. 'Course, we never stopped. We traded off on driving." This is no great achievement, but rather an expression of recklessness, not only for themselves and their passengers, but also for others on the road. The Alaska Highway as yet is no superhighway.

What to Pack

It's an old joke, but it holds true in the northland. If you don't like this weather, just wait a few minutes, particularly in the summer months. So be ready with a little of everything, and if it turns chilly, put it all on!

The length of the Alaska Highway crosses several microclimates, and within

ALASKA AND THE YUKON

HERE is a tremendous country scenically, an intensely interesting country historically, with a superb summer climate, and splendid transportation facilities by rail and boat—still left an almost virgin field for the tourist. But the lure of this Land of the Midnight Sun, of Northern Lights—this land made famous by the great "Klondike" rush for gold—is rapidly bringing it into its own.

Hundreds every summer are taking the marvelously beautiful "Inner Passage" trip to Skaguay, and from there, traveling amid scenes of unrivaled magnificence into the very heart mysterious of the great "Northland."

WHITE PASS & YUKON ROUTE

Travel advertising from an earlier day is on display in the White Pass & Yukon Route railway depot, Skagway.

Alaska you'll find even more. It can be 55°F at Mount McKinley while it's 80°F in Fairbanks, just 2 hours away.

Beauty salons or barber shops are easy to find in most towns. Make an appointment, or walk in. Usually it's not a problem. Pharmacies likewise are not difficult to find.

The benefits of the midnight sun are many, including the growth of unnaturally large cabbages and squash, and excessive energy in human beings. But for those who have trouble getting to sleep in the daylight, bring along a sleep mask.

Following is a packing checklist to help you get started. You decide how many of each item to bring, remembering that there will be no shortage of self-service laundries, so less is better.

Clothing

Underwear
Short-sleeved shirt
Long-sleeved shirt
Lightweight pants or shorts
Pants for chilly weather
Hooded sweatshirt or sweater
Windbreaker
Raincoat
Bathing suit
Towel

Jacket with zip-in lining for extra warmth
Comfortable walking shoes (soft soles for grip in slippery places)
Dress clothes (just in case)
Dress shoes
Socks and stockings
Slippers
Lightweight gloves
Knit hat or baseball cap

Other Items

Sunglasses
Toiletries
Hair dryer
Curling iron
Prescription drugs and refill prescriptions
Mosquito repellent
Identification
Emergency medical information
Contact numbers

First-aid kit
Plastic grocery bag
Zip-closure plastic bags
Film, tapes, and batteries for your cameras
One or two bottles of water
Your pet's health certificate (for border crossings)
Cash
Bank card/ATM card

What Not to Bring

Leave your fanciest clothes and jewelry at home. Alaska and the Canadian north are places where informality reigns. Although you can dress up for a night on the town if you like, at any given event or restaurant you'll find people in all kinds of clothes, from cocktail dresses to jeans. Men, pack a jacket and tie if you plan to dine at a four-star restaurant in Calgary, Edmonton, or Anchorage. Ladies, a simple dress will do.

Don't bring guns. Unless you're headed into the backcountry on your own, you won't need one, and unless you know how to use it, you're probably more dangerous to yourself than that charging grizzly bear is. Hire a guide to take you backcountry hiking or fishing; he or she likely will carry a protective weapon. Canada is explicit and firm about the transport of firearms across its borders (see the section on Guns/Ammo in Chapter 2, What You Need to Know).

Don't bring extra luggage for bulky or weighty souvenirs. You can have anything shipped home, from a chainsaw carving of a brown bear to a new parka, a hunk of jade, a piece of etched baleen, even your children's book collection—one for every child and grandchild in the family! Don't weigh yourself down. Insure the expensive stuff and ship it. I vote for mailing home all the paper you pick up at visitor centers, too—brochures, travel magazines, postcards, note cards, everything. It's so much better to travel light.

Preparing Your Vehicle

Make sure your vehicle is at its best before you leave home. If you're not mechanically oriented, take it to your mechanic for a once-over, or use this checklist to ensure that you don't overlook any of the automotive essentials:

Tires in good condition	Belts/seals/hoses
Spare tire, fully inflated	Brakes/bearings
Jack, and knowledge of how to use it	Exhaust system
Tune-up	Windshield wipers
Oil change	Air-conditioning (yes, it may be needed)
Fluids	Radiator

Also, carry the following emergency equipment:

First-aid kit	Pencil and paper
Tow cable	Bottles of drinking water
Toolbox	Paper towels
Road flares/reflectors	Nylon rope
Flashlight and fresh batteries	Squeegee (for muddy windows)
Jumper cable	Spare headlight
Matches in a sealed container, like a film canister	Gas can
Candles	Cell phone (even though it may not work in some remote regions)

If you're a U.S. resident, check with your insurance company about claims from within Canada and what will be provided for you in case you need assistance. Read your policy and understand it well, then ride on that security. Don't worry. Accidents are not commonplace. If you're a member of an auto club, familiarize yourself with their procedures in case of an emergency. Keep your membership number handy.

Windshields are sometimes nicked or chipped by flying gravel. If you're concerned about your windshield, headlights, or paint job, consider attaching a screen to your vehicle's front end for extra protection.

There was a day when long-distance travelers carried many gallons of extra gas. That's really not necessary anymore, unless you're on Alaska's Dalton Highway or one of Canada's more remote unpaved roads that have not yet developed routine roadside services. Throughout the length of the Alcan and along most of Alaska's state highways, you'll find gas stations at regular intervals. An informal rule of thumb: Never let the tank get below the halfway mark. Top it off before you leave a community.

Traveling by RV

Like many people who drive the Alaska Highway, my uncle and aunt, Gerald and Lillian Stinson, bought a camper upon retirement and set out for their new life as Alaskan snowbirds. They head south to Michigan about the time that the folks in Michigan are pointing toward Arizona. Christmas is spent in Florida, then it's back to the Midwest for spring, then on to Alaska for the summer. I guess they've driven the Alaska Highway 25 times or more. (Actually, they should be writing this book, not me.) They're so accustomed to preparing for travel that they can pack up their camper and be ready for the road in a matter of hours, without making notes. They have a system, and it works. It's figuring out the system that can be painful.

Everyone who has ever spent a weekend or more in an RV knows the practice of living in a moving motel has its pluses and minuses. It's wonderful to have everything in its place, to unpack only one time, to fix a meal when you're hungry, and to slip between familiar sheets at night. But other matters must be considered, such as: Who is driving and who is navigating? Can he/she be trusted with the task? Is a different person responsible for meals, even if it wasn't his or her responsibility at home? Could you at least get your feet out of the way when I'm carrying a hot dish? Like naughty children thrown together in a room to have it out and then get along, traveling companions usually work these things out, and comfortable patterns emerge.

If you're already a regular RV traveler, you'll have shortcuts and camping methods of your own, and likely have traded ideas with others in campgrounds across the country. That's another great thing about RV travel—making new friends and comparing notes about travel experiences and opportunities.

We learned that some people lighten their load by keeping the freshwater tank empty. They bring bottled water for cooking and drinking, and hook up only occasionally for dishwashing and showers (or use the shower house). Others believe that carrying the extra weight is less of a problem than finding a campsite with full hookups.

RV campgrounds with full hookups are not always available, so empty your gray water and sewer tanks every day or two, and keep the fresh water topped off in case you decide to switch to the generator and take hot showers. Often, just electricity is available. Hot showers commonly are available at campgrounds that don't offer full hookups. Pull-throughs, those campsites that allow RVers to pull in at one end and go out the other, may be at a premium late in the day, so consider settling in before dinner.

"Dry camping" is a common option, and not a bad one if there's a shortage of space. That can be the case in June, July, and early August. The more spontaneous types don't mind driving into the unknown of "where shall we stay tonight?" Others prefer a smartly choreographed itinerary with reservations in place, from one end of the country to the other, before leaving home. That doesn't leave much room for the winds of chance, but offers a lot of security. You'll find lists of campgrounds, some of which accept reservations, in the chapters that follow. And don't forget that, even in Alaska, superstores like Kmart and Wal-Mart have an open-parking-lot policy for wandering folks like you. This is not recommended for the best camping experience, but it sure works for a middle-of-the-night, sleepy-driver emergency.

Own or Rent? Packing the RV is dependent upon your travel timeline and on whether you own the RV or are renting. Owners normally keep a second set of everything in their campers, road-trip ready. RV renters can arrange one-way or round-trip packages. Everything you need for the kitchen is available for an extra fee. One-way travelers can bring along the basics with an eye toward shipping it all back home or throwing it in an extra suitcase for the homeward flight.

My husband, Perry, and I chose a rental RV with Cruise America, a company with offices all over the United States and Canada. Painted in its distinctive colors and logo, our vehicle was a rolling billboard for the company's 800 number, and we waved whenever we saw others like us on the road. Check the Yellow Pages for your choice of company, or look in your local newspaper's classified section for private owners who will rent their recreational vehicles. It's extremely important to pay close attention or even take notes when the RV company representative or owner is explaining how everything works.

Recommended packing for the extra-light traveler: For each person, bring one dish, one cup, one glass, one bowl, one set of silverware, two bath towels, a washcloth, and a hand towel. Linens should include one set of sheets, two blankets and pillows, and two dishtowels and dishcloths. For the kitchen, find a small screw-top container for dish soap rather than bringing the full-size bottle. Buy disposable salt-and-pepper containers and pack minimal other spices. Bring two sizes of cooking pots and lids, one pan and lid, spatula, large plastic spoon, slotted spoon, ladle, and manual can opener. Bring along a broom and, if you can, a small, electric-powered Dirt Devil (especially good for dog fur on upholstery). I threw in a sample-size piece of leftover carpet as a doormat—you really do need one, so buy one if you have to. Buy chemicals for the toilet; bring soap, shampoo, and other basic toiletries.

We decided to premeasure laundry soap into plastic bags so we wouldn't have to deal with a big carton. I also preground my coffee beans and left my coffeepot at home, figuring that I'd just pour hot water through a one-cup filter holder (which I then forgot). I improvised by cutting holes in the bottom of a plastic margarine container, and felt immensely clever.

Motorists often create homemade protective screens for their grill and headlights.

It really did feel like playing in a dollhouse. Within a day or two, it was easy to make a meal, wash the dishes, sweep up, and be ready to roll in record time. The routine took on its own familiarity even though we were far from home.

If you're like us, at the end of each day you will be road-weary and yearning for a quiet place, so keep a wary eye out for the location of a busy road or railroad tracks before you choose a campsite. We cruised the campgrounds to check out the party sites before we picked the one farthest away. In most cases, however, people were extremely respectful of each other, and the noise level went down around 10 P.M. Parents with children likewise were understanding of those who are not accustomed to noisy play, and they made sure the kids were in tow by evening.

At the end of the day, we walked, read, and played cards, and I sewed while he studied maps and made notes. I created a travel journal and kept track of our daily mileage, too, and I urge you to start your own travel journal for your notes and remembrances. It's also a great place to write down information about the photographs you took that day. What seems indelible in your mind today will become blurred without notes, believe me.

All in all, traveling by RV was extremely satisfying—it allowed the security of familiar surroundings as we entered the larger picture of a world to explore together.

Cameras

Oh, the photos that were never taken because the battery died at that moment! Or you ran out of film. Alas, it could have been a *National Geographic* cover. So be forewarned and pack plenty of film and an extra camera battery. Even if you have a rechargeable battery for your video camera, think about bringing backup. You won't always have access to power for recharging, and after all, this is your trip of a lifetime.

Driving on unpaved roads poses a dust concern, so keep your electronics in their tote bags unless you're shooting pictures.

Winter travelers need to consider the effect of static electricity on film that's rewinding. If your photos come back with white veins on the negatives, you're a victim. If you rewind by hand, go slowly. If your camera is auto rewind, consider saving that last shot for indoors, in a room with higher humidity. Here's the test: If you can scoot your feet across the carpet and shake hands without shocking somebody, you'll be all right.

A few shooting tips: First and foremost, don't harass the wildlife. That means don't

Canada geese and fireweed are symbolic of northern latitudes.

creep up too close for their comfort and your safety. The best wildlife photographers choose a spot and wait for their shot. If you don't have time for that, then buy a bigger lens, or risk a ticket from an Alaska Fish and Wildlife Protection officer.

Secondly, watch for groups of vehicles that have pulled over. That's a sure sign that something big and hairy, or feathery, or furry, is near the edge of the road and will be the subject of many vacation photographs. Pull off the road completely and stop your vehicle before you begin shooting. Alaskans have seen it a million times—people standing in the middle of the road with their cameras stuck to their faces and no clue that an oncoming Winnebago is about to make a significant impact on their lives.

Videographers, remember to spend a few seconds shooting pictures of identifying signs to help establish where you are. Or while you're taping, have a traveling companion read from a travel guide, brochure, or informational sign as you capture the scene. It's better than relying on memory later.

And one more tip for good measure: Don't forget the people in your trip. Shots of beautiful scenery and wildlife are important vacation remembrances, but 10 or 20 years from now, or more, it will be the photos of the people with you, and the people you meet along the way, that will cause you to ooh and aah.

Strategy for Medical Needs

The greatest disruption on a vacation is getting sick. Worse still is not having the medicine you need to feel better. So bring along the basics, and make sure your prescription medications have been filled just before you leave. Ask for a refill slip from your doctor if you expect to be gone for long.

Make a see-through zipper bag your first-aid kit. For its contents, buy travel-size containers to keep it from becoming unwieldy. Drop in your vitamins, adhesive bandages of various sizes, first-aid ointment, aspirin or other pain reliever, alcohol swabs, hydrogen peroxide, an Ace bandage, muscle ache ointment, cotton balls, a few safety pins, hand sanitizer, cold-medicine tablets, chewable tablets for indigestion, and throat lozenges, along with prescription drugs that you don't normally carry with you. You might keep your prescriptions for refills in the first-aid kit, too.

In your purse or wallet, along with your identification and insurance card, carry a written statement of any medical conditions, allergies or other health alerts, and medicines that you're currently taking. List the name and number of your family doctor and of the person to call in case of an emergency.

Driving in Winter

Winter driving is possible, and some people actually prefer it, claiming that the road is better with fewer vehicles in front of them and a good layer of compacted snow under them. But extra care must be taken to pack smart. I remember the winter my father and brother slid off the road on a lonely stretch near the Alaska-Canada border. It was −40°F. They bundled up, then Dad built a fire and climbed back up to the road to flag down help, which happily did arrive before either of them suffered frostbite. They had packed emergency gear such as extra warm clothes, sleeping bags, and matches. Even though the car was totaled, in the end they were merely banged up, but it easily could have gone another way had they not been prepared. It's a good idea to equip your vehicle with these extras:

Studded snow tires or chains	Shovel
Ice scraper/brush	Blanket or sleeping bag
Nonperishable snack foods	Extra parka, snow pants, warm boots,
Heavy-duty extension cord	mitts
(see next paragraph)	Chemical-pack hand-warmers
Sandbag or kitty litter, for extra	CB radio (if you want an extra measure
traction should you become stuck	of security)

The farther north you drive, the colder it gets. So before you leave home, ask your mechanic to use 5-30W motor oil in your car. And have the shop install an engine-block heater or, at the least, an oil-pan heater, so the oil will not become so thick that you can't turn the engine over. With either heater under the hood, you will end up with a short, three-pronged electric cord sticking out of the grill. Buy a 15- to 20-foot heavy-duty extension cord so you can access power when you turn the car off for 2 or more hours, or when you park it for the night.

In the far north, outdoor electric outlets are common; in Fairbanks or Dawson City, you'll see them at the heads of parking spaces in public lots. Ask about where to plug in when you check in at your motel. If you haven't plugged in all night, do so an hour or so before you plan to leave. Plugging in at 10°F or colder is a good idea. It means less wear and tear on your engine and less drain on your battery, not to mention a reassuring sound when the engine turns over effortlessly. And the sooner the engine heats up, the sooner you'll have warm air coming out of your interior blower.

Another trick among winter drivers of the north has to do with a quick-and-cheap addition to your front end: a large piece of corrugated cardboard. Wedge the flattened piece between your grill and radiator to prevent super-cold air from passing through the radiator. The engine will get warm and stay warm much faster, and in the end, your interior heater will be much more effective.

Remember that winter days in the north are extremely short. You'll be driving in dim light or darkness, even if you limit your driving time to daytime, so working headlights are especially important. Snowstorms can surprise you, too, so check your radio dial and ask the locals about the forecast when you stop, or request a number to call for recorded messages on road conditions.

Sharing the road with tractor-trailers can be a challenge, because they tend to kick up a blinding snow shower, so back off rather than pass them. Vision is critical, so make sure your windshield wipers are in good shape. Use common sense for safe snow driving: Bring down your speed a notch, never jam on the brakes, and as your driver's ed teacher told you, steer in the direction of the slide.

And, at the risk of nagging, we'll say it again: Take your time.

Dog mushing is Alaska's state sport.

Chapter 2

What You Need to Know, A to Z

Alaska-speak. English is spoken in Canada and the United States, but occasionally a regional term can trip you up. Here's a quick list of words in the Alaskan vocabulary:

Outside. Anywhere not in Alaska
Cheechako. A greenhorn, a newcomer
Wanigan. Lean-to, usually in add-a-room style attached to a cabin
Carhartts. Brand of warm, durable clothing commonly worn in winter; the Alaska tuxedo
Bunny boots. Large, usually white, rubber boots with a built-in vapor barrier for extra insulation; boomed in use during construction of the trans-Alaska oil pipeline during the 1970s; still very popular
Breakup. Spring season when ice breaks up and moves out from the rivers
Termination dust. First snow that dusts the mountaintops; signals the termination of summer
Kuspuk. Brightly colored shirt-dress worn by Native Alaskan women
Native Alaskan. Person of ancient heritage—Eskimo, Indian, or Aleut descent
native Alaskan. Person of any race who was born and raised in Alaska
Sourdough. An old-timer, a pioneer Alaskan
Rondy. Anchorage Fur Rendezvous, the biggest winter carnival in the country
PFD check. Annual payment mailed by the state to every eligible resident; portion of interest dividends and capital gains on state's oil revenues. In 1999, the amount was about $1,700 per person.

Alaska State Troopers

Not every town on the Alaska road system has its own police force. Alaska State Troopers enforce the law along the miles and miles of highway. Dialing 911 remains the universal call for help throughout the state, but Trooper offices may be found in the following communities along the highways: Glennallen, Trapper Creek, Nenana, Tok, Cantwell, Palmer, Anchorage, Montana Creek, Talkeetna, Healy, Fairbanks, North Pole, Cordova, Girdwood, Seward, Soldotna, Kenai, and Homer.

The Municipality of Anchorage extends from the Knik River Bridge on the Glenn Highway to the town of Girdwood on the Seward Highway, and a host of police officers patrols the highways in this vast area, with support from the Alaska State Troopers.

Other road-system cities with their own police force include Wasilla, Palmer, Valdez, Homer, Soldotna, Kenai, Seward, and Fairbanks. In the remote, off-road villages, law enforcement is handled by a VPSO, a Village Public Safety Officer. State Troopers fly into villages when a VPSO needs assistance.

Alaska Fish and Wildlife Protection officers serve in a special branch of the State Troopers. Even though they are sworn to enforce fish-and-game laws, they can and will issue traffic tickets and pursue other criminal activity.

Alaska has no counties, so there are no sheriffs or deputies.

Alcoholic Beverages

Alcohol is not sold in grocery stores in Alaska, and liquor stores will not sell to individuals younger than 21. Drinking-and-driving laws are tough, so stop for the night before you crack open that beer. Some Alaska villages are dry; some are damp. Just to be sure, don't fly into a village with alcohol in your suitcase.

U.S. citizens who are 19 or older may transport alcoholic beverages over the U.S.–Canada border in these quantities: 40 ounces (1.14 liters) of spirits or wine, or 288 ounces (8.5 liters) of beer or ale.

Border Crossings

At the border, have your identification and vehicle registration ready. A passport is not necessary to pass between the United States and Canada, but it may be used for your identification. Most crossings are fairly routine. You will be asked a dozen questions or more, and allowed to continue on your journey.

Occasionally, officials ask permission to look around inside a car or camper. Every so often, even after answering all questions honestly, a driver may be detained further as officials make a more thorough inspection of the vehicle or its contents. (Also see the following entries in this chapter: Alcoholic Beverages; Duty-free Shopping; Guns/Ammo; Pets; Plants.)

Campgrounds

Among those who love to camp, you'll find the spectrum of tastes and comfort zones. Some folks take their home with them on vacation in the form of a recreational vehicle—and their rolling accommodations include power, water, microwave, stove, refrigerator, toilet, shower, stereo, and VCR. At the other end of the scale are the tent campers, who sleep with a thin layer of waterproof material separating them from raw nature. No matter what the style, great numbers of mobile travelers have discovered the joys of camping.

As you travel throughout the north, you'll find plentiful options among campgrounds, and good signage to help direct you. In the chapters that follow, we've included directions and contact information for campgrounds along the way. Operated privately or by government agencies, campground offerings range from a simple opening in the forest with a picnic table and fire ring, to places equipped with extras such as a swimming pool, golf course, horseshoe pits, playgrounds, swimming beach, boat dock and, almost as important as hot showers to some campers, access to a computer modem.

RV travelers will be most interested in whether a campground offers full hookups, meaning power, water, and sewer service. In a partial hookup, power and water are usually available, but sewer service is not. In most cases, however, a dump station (or sani-station, as it's often called in Canada) is available for emptying gray water and sewerage. Also note that campgrounds in Canada will refer to sites as serviced or unserviced, indicating whether hookups are available.

In Alaska it is legal (but not much fun) to park for the night on a road wayside where the parking area is fully off the road. Nowhere in Alaska or Canada is it legal to dump sewerage or gray water anywhere except in designated dump stations.

For provincial parks, you'll usually need to pay in cash. Charge cards are accepted in most privately owned campgrounds. Checks are rarely accepted.

Canada-speak

Engaged in conversation with a Canadian, you could swear you were from the same country until an unusual treatment of a familiar word pops up: "I'm in the PRO-cess of moving," "Let's check the SHED-yule," or "Tell me a-BOOT your problem." Here are some tips to aid interpretation:

Eh? This non-word peppers the ends of many sentences. It is not a question, but rather a charming way to end a statement with an invitation for the other person to speak next ... or it's just a regional speech pattern that means nothing whatsoever.

Loonie. The $1 coin imprinted with the image of a loon

Toonie. The $2 coin, worth two Loonies

First Nations people. Descendants of the ancient Native groups who first made this region their home

YOOP. Yukon Order of the Pioneers

Mounties. Royal Canadian Mounted Police, or RCMP

Gold dredges. Floating gold PRO-cessing ships that sorted out nuggets from rock and soil before depositing the tailings back on the ground

Pumpjack. Slow-moving oil pumps that draw oil out of the ground and into a pipeline or storage tank; often seen in rolling fields

Stampede. The "rush" in gold rushes of a century ago, when men and women stampeded from one gold discovery to the next. Or the term for a regional rodeo event, as in the Calgary Stampede.

The Canadian government continues to widen and straighten sections of the Alaska Highway. The way to Alaska is shorter now than it was 50 years ago.

Children

Due to the increase in child abduction by noncustodial parents, travel agencies and airlines are suggesting that you always travel with paperwork that documents your right to travel with minor children. The same is true for border crossings between the United States and Canada. Carry birth certificates for the children and, if you're divorced, your proof-of-custody papers. For noncustodial parents or grandparents, ask the child's custodial parent to sign and notarize a permission slip for that child to travel with you, stating where you plan to go and the dates you will be traveling.

Daylight Hours

The farther north you travel in summer, the more daylight you will encounter, especially during the days surrounding June 20 or 21, the summer solstice. Fairbanks basks in 22 hours of daylight during its Solstice Celebration, which includes a Midnight Sun Baseball Game that begins at 10:30 P.M. without artificial lights. Farther south, in Anchorage, the longest day provides a mere 19.5 hours of daylight, enough to make bedtimes a challenge for adults and children alike.

Throughout the Yukon, northern British Columbia, northern Alberta, and Alaska, short growing seasons are supplemented by these long, long hours of sunlight, resulting in fabulous floral displays, grain crops, and certain vegetables that grow to gigantic proportions. Look for giant cabbages mixed in with border plants in many northern gardens.

On the other side of the calendar, December 20 or 21 is winter solstice, when darkness is at its peak after eating away at hours of daylight for months. In Fairbanks, the sun may rise and set before office workers get a chance to look out the window, rising at about 11 A.M. and setting just 3 hours later. In Dawson City, Yukon, daylight on winter solstice is 4.5 hours; in Whitehorse, the shortest day is 5.5 hours.

Duty-free Shopping

If the value of your purchases does not exceed $400, residents of the United States who travel in Canada for more than 48 hours and less than 30 days may bring home personal or household merchandise without paying U.S. duty and tax. The $400 figure applies for each member in your party. To avoid delays at the border crossing, keep receipts and purchases handy.

Fishing

A fishing license is required in all provinces and in Alaska, but it is easy to obtain one through most sporting goods stores or other businesses.

Alberta. Sportfishing licenses are available at Natural Resource Services offices, most tackle shops and sporting goods stores, and many department stores. No license is required for children 14 and younger. You may pick up the current *Alberta Guide to Sportfishing Regulations* when you purchase your license. For more information on licensing requirements and costs, contact Fish and Wildlife Services, 14515 122nd Avenue, Edmonton, Alberta T5K 2G6. Call 780-427-3574 or visit the website at www.env.gov.ab.ca.

British Columbia. You'll have to buy separate licenses for saltwater and freshwater fishing in British Columbia. You can pick them up at government agency offices, sporting goods stores, and many other retailers. Other specific licenses are required in all national parks and may be obtained at park headquarters. Call BC Fisheries in Victoria for general inquiries at 250-387-4573 or read the freshwater fishing regulations on the provincial Ministry of the Environment, Lands and Parks website at www.monday.com/fishing/index.htm. For saltwater regulations, the federal Department of Fisheries and Oceans website is at www.pac.dfo-mpo.gc.ca.

Yukon Territory. Salmon fishing is permitted throughout the Yukon, with restrictions. Pick up the Recreational Fishing Regulations Summary when you obtain your license, but be aware that short-notice closures can occur. Before you go fishing, check with the Department of Fisheries and Oceans at 867-393-6722. For salmon fishing, you must have both the Yukon Sport Fishing License and a Salmon Conservation Catch Card. As soon as you catch a salmon, record necessary details on your catch card. If you are fishing in Kluane National Park, Yukon, a separate National Park Fishing License is required. For a copy of *Anglers' Guide to Stocked Lakes in the Yukon Territory*, write Fisheries Section, Department of Renewable Resources, Box 2703, Whitehorse, Yukon, Canada Y1A 2C6.

Alaska. Sportfishing licenses are required for anyone 16 and older. A nonresident license costs $10 for a single day, up to $100 for a calendar year. Anglers fishing for king salmon can expect to double those fees to cover the cost of a "king stamp." Licenses are available at most sporting goods stores and grocery stores. To arrange a license in advance, or for more information, contact the Alaska Department of Revenue, Fish and Game License Section, 1111 West 8th Street, No. 108, Juneau, AK 99801. Call 907-465-4180 or visit the website at www.state.ak.us.local.akpages.fish. game/adfghome.htm.

Fuel

In Canada, gasoline is measured by the liter, which equals about a quarter of a U.S. gallon, so there are roughly 4 liters per gallon. To convert exactly, multiply the number of liters by 0.2642 to find the number of U.S. gallons. (See the section on Metric Conversion, in this chapter.)

You may see an unusual fuel pump at some stations: Propane-powered vehicles are becoming more common in western Canada.

Guns/Ammo

Canada has strict regulations regarding entry of firearms into the country. And below the federal level, individual provinces have varying regulations, so be sure to get all the facts before you pack.

At the border, you will be asked to declare any firearms. No joking on this matter. If your memory fails you, your firearms will be seized, and you may be fined. Sport or recreational-use firearms are admissible, and hunters may carry up to 200 rounds of ammunition. Before entry to any of Canada's national parks, rifles and shotguns must be broken down or in their cases. U.S. Customs suggests that U.S. residents register their guns at the border so that officials can match up the list on the return trip. Don't plan to add to your collection while you're on the trip, however. Only licensed gun dealers may import firearms. When you cross back into the United States, officials will want to ensure that the same guns are in your possession as when you entered Canada.

What is prohibited? The stuff of Rambo, James Bond, and Jackie Chan: fully automatic rifles and machine guns, silencers, excessive rounds of ammunition, sawed-off shotguns or rifles, automatic switchblades, tear gas, Mace, and some martial arts weapons. Revolvers and pistols also are prohibited. If you have questions, call the Canadian Firearms Center, 1-800-731-4000, or visit the center's website at www.canada.justice.gc.ca.

Headlights

Law officers suggest that you drive with your headlights on, day or night, and always when their use is posted, as on the Seward Highway in Alaska. Yukon law requires headlights at all times; in British Columbia and Alberta, watch for signs.

Hunting

Licenses and permits are required in individual provinces and in Alaska. No hunting is allowed in national parks.

Alberta. Licensing and permits are dependent upon the species, season, location, and other variables. For more information, contact Fish and Wildlife Services, 14515 122nd Avenue, Edmonton, Alberta, Canada T5K 2G6. Call 780-427-3574 or visit the website at www.env.gov.ab.ca.

British Columbia. For information, contact the Ministry of Environment, Lands and Parks Offices, 780 Blanshard Street, Victoria, B.C., Canada V8V 1X4. Call 250-387-9717.

Yukon Territory: To hunt for big game in the Yukon, you are required to arrange for a licensed guide. A waiting period is required for licensing, so plan ahead. Contact the Department of Renewable Resources, Field Services Branch, P.O. Box 2703, Whitehorse, Yukon, Canada Y1A 2C6. Call 867-667-5221 or fax 867-667-2691.

Alaska. U.S. citizens who are not residents of Alaska may obtain a nonresident hunting license for $85, or a combination hunting/sportfishing license for $135. Either is good for the calendar year in which it is purchased. Fees vary for nonresident aliens. An additional fee will be charged for a tag, with a fee amount that is dependent upon the animal that you're hunting. Licensed, nonresident hunters must hunt with a licensed guide or with a resident family member who is 19 or older. A federal migratory bird-hunting stamp must be obtained for duck hunting. For more details on fees, seasons, and management units, contact the Alaska Department of Fish and Game, Licensing Division, P.O. Box 25525, Juneau, AK 99802 or call 907-465-2376.

Insurance

Health insurance. U.S. citizens who need to see a doctor or visit a clinic while traveling in Canada should expect to pay for services up front. U.S. health insurance policies are not accepted. You'll have to file for reimbursement from your insurer later. Extra travel insurance is a good idea in case of an emergency that requires an ambulance or medevac services, which may not be covered on your regular policy.

Vehicle insurance. Check with your insurance agent before you leave home. You may need supplemental insurance for the trip. Make sure you understand how to file a claim if an accident occurs while you are driving in Canada. Carry proof of coverage with you at all times.

Lodging

Noncampers love the daily comfort of a clean, spacious bed, a hot shower, and cable television—and, if they're feeling especially wild, room service. In the following chapters, a list of hotels, motels, and lodges, along with contact information, follows each community profile. The amenities listed for each property will help you estimate the price range and whether the lodging is suitable for your party. As you travel north, fewer places advertise that they are air-conditioned, and more advertise their "winter plug-ins," parking places where winter travelers can plug in a vehicle that's equipped with an engine-block heater. Contact numbers for local bed-and-breakfast associations also are included in some listings.

Certain hotels in the United States and Canada display their Diamond Rating, awarded by the American Automobile Association or the Canadian Automobile Association. Ratings go from One Diamond for an establishment considered good, to Five Diamonds for a top-ranking luxury property with outstanding amenities.

Reservations are not always necessary, but it's best to call at least a day or two ahead anyway. Note that in some cases, toll-free numbers are operational only within the province or state, or only within Canada. If you hear that annoying message "Your call cannot be completed as dialed," it means you are outside the toll-free service area that was purchased by that business. Websites are included where available.

Metric Conversion

Canada uses the metric system of measurement, while the U.S. system prevails on the other side of the border. A Canadian speed limit of 90 kilometers per hour is roughly equivalent to 55 miles per hour. Most speedometers are equipped with a dual scale. After several days in Canada, U.S. residents usually become accustomed to the unfamiliar and make the conversion to kilometers easily.

Here's a tip: Use your speedometer as a scale to translate distances accurately. A kilometer is roughly six-tenths (0.6) of a mile; a mile is roughly 1.6 kilometers. Here are a few sample conversions, all approximate:

Kilometers		Miles
1	=	0.6
100	=	60
150	=	90
200	=	120
300	=	180

To convert precisely between U.S. and metric measurements, use the following chart:

U.S. / Metric Conversion

From	Multiply by	To get
miles	1.6093	kilometers
kilometers	0.6214	miles
feet	0.3048	meters
meters	3.2808	feet
U.S. gallons	3.7853	liters
liters	0.2642	U.S. gallons
imperial gallons	4.5460	liters
liters	0.2201	imperial gallons
pounds	0.4536	kilograms
kilograms	2.2046	pounds

Money

Visit your bank before you leave home to exchange pocket money into Canadian dollars. They'll inform you of the latest exchange rate, which fluctuates almost daily. Generally you'll get more bang for the U.S. buck in Canada. Also, Canadian businesses are savvy about calculating the exchange, and often will do so as a courtesy if you have only U.S. dollars. Vending machines and telephones will see U.S. quarters and Canadian quarters as the same denomination.

Traveler's checks (or *cheques* in Canada) are always a safe way to go, but you'll get the change in Canadian, and may end up with odd dollars and cents in your pocket when you re-enter the United States. If you don't want to carry around large quantities of Canadian cash, use your credit card for purchases and meals. Your bank will make the conversion to U.S. dollars on your billing statement. ATMs, or cash machines, may be found in most towns, and likewise your bank will make the conversion in your account. Be prepared to pay an ATM fee.

Also, get ready to carry your dollars in a coin purse or pocket. Canada's favorite nonpaper currency is the Loonie, a $1 coin imprinted with a loon. The $2 coin, worth two Loonies, is a Toonie. We found it easy to go through them faster than through paper bills, for some reason, and it was harder to keep track of how much change we were carrying, not unlike problems associated with the Susan B. Anthony dollar versus the 25-cent piece in the United States. Just a heads up!

In Alaska most businesses accept Canadian coins, except for the Loonie or Toonie. Visit the bank or currency exchange to trade the Canadian dollar coins and currency.

Mosquitoes

Alaskans like to joke that the mosquito is the Alaska state bird. After you see their unusually large size you may stop laughing and start running. Their cousins in Canada are just as big and persistent. They won't kill you, but they can make your outdoor experience an unhappy one.

Many a sourdough can recount stories of caribou herds incited to stampede because of mosquitoes, or backcountry hikers who jumped in a lake to escape. In fact, the term "gone caribou" often applies to people who, lacking spray-on repellent, begin hollering, waving their arms, and running to get away. Bring mosquito repellent and use it liberally. Anglers should not touch their fishing line with repellent on their hands, however. The chemicals will damage and weaken the line.

Sporting goods stores and catalogs offer hats equipped with mosquito netting to cover your face and neck. Hikers sometimes invest in a full suit of mosquito netting to wear over shorts and a T-shirt, rather than covering up and overheating in long sleeves and pants.

Here's a tip for those who jump in the car to escape a swarm of mosquitoes: No doubt many of them will follow you into the car. Rather than swat at them as you drive, open the windows and speed up to blow them out.

The gnat-size biting insects known as no-see-ums are a greater concern to backcountry travelers, as they can creep under cuffs and into tight places. Sometimes, swarms of no-see-ums can become so thick that, without a headnet, you cannot avoid breathing them in.

Pets

The most important piece of luggage for your dog or cat is a leash. Bring it along and use it. Campgrounds are pet friendly, as are some hotels and motels (call ahead), but all of them require pet owners to keep their "fur persons" on a leash when they are outdoors.

Nearly all rest stops have pet areas. Bring a rubber glove or plastic bags and pick up after your pet's daily constitutional. Plastic newspaper wrappers work great.

Take your dog or cat to a licensed veterinarian a week or less before you leave home, and obtain a signed health certificate with the declaration that the animal has received a rabies vaccination within the last 36 months. Keep its health certificate handy for international border crossings. The collar tag will not be enough proof. You may travel with a maximum of two puppies or kittens, along with a veterinarian's certificate stating that they are too young to vaccinate.

Make sure that your pet's prescription drugs are adequate for the number of days you'll be gone. Keep your hometown veterinarian's number close by in case an advisory call is needed.

Plants

If you're an RV traveler who likes the homey look of houseplants, fear not. They are excluded from your declaration at the U.S.–Canada border. Likewise, fresh fruits or vegetables that cannot be grown in Canada are not problematic, only those that can be grown there. Due to agriculture officials' concerns about native plant health, certain plants may not be allowed entry without an import permit. Check with an office of the U.S. Department of Agriculture for more information.

Postage

If you are traveling in Canada and sending mail to a U.S. address, expect to pay 52 cents (Canadian) for a stamp on mail weighing up to 30 grams (about 1 ounce). If your postcard or letter weighs up to 20 grams and is going to an international address, it will need a 90-cent stamp.

Restaurants

The restaurant listings in the chapters that follow include a mix of casual family dining establishments, take-out or fast-food restaurants, ethnic dining choices, and fine dining restaurants.

Because chefs of the northland pride themselves on their regional foods, we suggest you take advantage of northern specialties on the menu. In British Columbia, the Yukon, and Alaska, you may sample seafood entrees such as wild Pacific salmon (far superior in flavor and texture to farmed fish), king crab, shrimp, or scallops. Or try reindeer or buffalo for the first time. You're certain to discover new favorites or find a new spin on an old one.

In Canada, certain ethnic restaurants may also offer what they call a Western menu. You might think of it as an American menu—one for those who are in the mood for chicken or a hamburger.

Road Manners

Good manners know no international boundaries, so when you're driving the Alaska Highway, or any of the highways in this guide, give the other guy the benefit of the doubt, and don't drive like you're on the Beltway. Do not ride his bumper; do not pass in anger, or on a double yellow; and remember that RV drivers go only as fast as safety will allow. They know their vehicle limits.

Especially important for RV drivers: Alaska law states that if you are driving under the speed limit, and there are at least five vehicles behind you, you must pull over at the next available opportunity or you may be ticketed.

Should you pass by a wild animal on or near the road, flash your headlights to warn oncoming drivers to be on alert.

Keep your headlights on. Use your turn signals. Pass on the left. Smile and wave to the flagger. And have a good trip.

Royal Canadian Mounted Police

Originally established in 1873 as the North-West Mounted Police, the officers of the RCMP, or Mounties, bear the burden of the romantic image created in movies and books about their daring deeds. During the 1898 gold rush to the Canadian Klondike, the North-West Mounted Police brought order to Dawson City and to the border crossings at the Chilkoot and White Passes, demanding that stampeders carry a year's worth of supplies with them.

The Mounties are easily recognized in their dress uniforms of classic red tunics, sharply creased hats, and leather boots. Their daily work uniforms are much more mundane, as is the nature of most of their work. Like law enforcement everywhere, it's not all that romantic.

While few Mounties conduct their duties on horseback anymore, the image remains. In Whitehorse, you may catch sight of a red-uniformed Mountie and a horse named Chilkoot patrolling the streets and greeting visitors. In historic Fort Macleod, Alberta, you can view performances by RCMP horses and riders in a precision equestrian show called the "Musical Ride." In 1998 the RCMP celebrated its 125th anniversary.

Time Zones

Most of Alaska is in the Alaska Time Zone, one hour behind Yukon Territory and British Columbia (Pacific Time Zone), which is one hour behind Alberta (Mountain Time Zone). So if it is noon in Anchorage, Alaska, it is 1 P.M. in Whitehorse, Yukon; also

DAWSON
CREEK
FT. ST. JOHN   48
FT. NELSON   300
WHITEHORSE   916
FAIRBANKS   1523

MILE
'O'
A
L
A
S
K
A
H
I
—
W
A
Y

The Mile 0 Milepost in Dawson Creek, B.C., where it all begins.

1 P.M. in Prince George, British Columbia; and 2 P.M. in Calgary, Alberta. Daylight saving time applies to all of these time zones. They "spring ahead" one hour in April to daylight saving time, then "fall behind" one hour in October to standard time.

Weather

The following chart provides a range of temperature and precipitation information for Alaska, the Yukon, Alberta, and British Columbia. In Canada, temperature is measured on the Celsius scale, and precipitation is measured in millimeters. Values below have been converted to Fahrenheit and inches.

To convert between U.S. and Canadian measurements, use these formulas:

Fahrenheit to Celsius:
Subtract 32 from the Fahrenheit temperature. Multiply by 5 and divide by 9.

Celsius to Fahrenheit:
Multiply Celsius temperature by 9. Divide by 5. Add 32.

1 mm = .0394 inch   1 inch = 25.38 mm

Weather Chart

ALASKA	Temperatures °F		
Community	January Mean Low	July Mean High	Annual Precip./Inches
Anchorage	6	65	15
Denali Park	−8	43	15
Eagle	−13	73	11
Fairbanks	−21	72	10
Haines	18	67	47
Homer	15	61	24
Juneau	16	64	52
Ketchikan	29	65	156
Prudhoe Bay	−22	45	5
Seward	18	63	66
Skagway	19	67	28

YUKON TERRITORY	Temperatures °F		
Community	January Mean Low	July Mean High	Annual Precip./Inches
Burwash Landing	−9.2	54.5	11
Dawson City	−30.5	72	12
Watson Lake	−12.3	58.8	16
Whitehorse	−1.7	57.2	11

ALBERTA			
Calgary	14.7	61.5	16
Edmonton	6.4	60.8	18
Grande Prairie	4.3	60.8	18
Lethbridge	16.9	65.1	16

BRITISH COLUMBIA			
Abbotsford	36	62.8	62
Dawson Creek	5.2	59.2	19
Fort Nelson	−7.6	62.1	18
Lytton	27.9	70.5	17
Prince George	14.2	59.5	24

Wheelchair Access

Never before have so many travel opportunities opened for vacationers who rely on wheelchairs for mobility or for seniors who need a little extra help as they travel. Throughout Alaska and western Canada, you will find many hotels and motels equipped with access ramps, nonslip flooring, grab bars in the tub and shower, bath boards, and easy-open doors. Visitors with vision loss will be pleased to find large-print information cards, and phones with extra-large numbers; those with a hearing loss may reserve a room with a phone that amplifies sound.

Throughout western Canada, watch for the Access Canada logo in hotel and motel windows. These member businesses have geared a number of their rooms with physical access in mind. For more information on Access Canada and which hotels are participating, contact the following provincial tourism offices.

Alberta: Alberta Hotel Association, 5241 Calgary Trail South, Edmonton, Alberta T6H 5G8. Call 403-436-6112 or visit www.albertahotels.ab.ca.

British Columbia: Tourism British Columbia, Box 9830, 1803 Douglas Street, Victoria, B.C. V8W 9W5. Call 1-800-663-6000 or visit www.snbc-res.com.

Yukon: Tourism Yukon, P.O. Box 2703, Whitehorse, Yukon Y1A 2C6. Call 867-667-5340 or visit www.touryukon.com.

In Alaska, businesses are tuning in to the needs of visitors who require wheelchair access. State parks and recreation areas are often equipped with wheelchair-accessible rest rooms, plus wide, paved surfaces for trails into the woods. Even some of the best fishing holes have been reserved for anglers in wheelchairs. For details, check with the Alaska Division of Tourism, Box 110801, Juneau, AK 99811-0801. Contact the division at 907-465-2010 or at www.travelalaska.com or by visiting the state of Alaska's website at www.state.ak.us.

Wildlife

You cannot pretend that you are driving back in the Lower 48. Every so often, the path of a plodding moose intersects the highway, and the person in the navigator's seat scrambles to grab the camera as you slow the vehicle and pull over in haste. The panic stop will happen again for a band of Dall sheep, for a caribou, a fox, a ptarmigan. It's hard to think clearly when the adrenaline is rushing through your veins, but stay aware of traffic ahead and behind you, and pull completely onto the shoulder before you stop.

What a rare and thrilling opportunity to observe a world that remains so unchanged in the 21st century. But please be mindful of a few basic rules:

Please don't feed the wildlife. Keep a respectful distance, knowing that powerful creatures such as bison or moose may panic and harm you. In the far north, animal life is plentiful, and there are no protective bars between you and the wild things.

A few years ago, a Fairbanks woman driving on Chena Hot Springs Road came car hood to kneecaps with a bull moose standing in the middle of the road. She had slowed and stopped, but the moose didn't appear to be in a hurry. He stayed put. She honked her horn. He snorted. She honked again. He lowered his head and did significant damage to her car's front end before he shuffled off in a huff. The moral of the story is: Don't harass the animals. For roadside wildlife sightings—and you're likely to experience several—it's best to stay in the car. But don't creep closer, honk, or yell. From the comfort of your vehicle, enjoy the vision before you, up close and in focus, with your binoculars or camera equipped with a telephoto lens.

If you are involved in an accident with a big animal, immediately contact the local authorities. A charity will be contacted to field-dress the moose, caribou, or bison, and the meat will be donated to needy families.

Full-day or half-day cruises on the ocean afford the opportunity to see marine mammals in spectacular settings. They are well worth the cost, and often include lunch. Several day-cruise operators have ticket offices in downtown Anchorage, and some provide shuttle transportation to their vessels in a community south of the city, such as Seward, Whittier, or Homer. If you spend any time along the Inside Passage, you'll be treated to views of otters, eagles, plentiful bird life, and occasionally a whale.

Chapter 3

History of the Alcan: The Soldiers' Road

Protecting America's northernmost possession was a matter of national security in the early 1940s, and the task became especially critical after the Japanese bombed Pearl Harbor in December 1941. Alaska then became a potential enemy target. Without a land route between the Lower 48 states and Alaska, the U.S. military outposts in Fairbanks, Anchorage, and elsewhere in the territory were virtually stranded, dependent on supply deliveries by water and air, and vulnerable to attack.

In 1942, Ladd Air Field in Fairbanks became especially strategic to the Allies' defense plan. Ladd was the final U.S. destination for warplanes that were flown along the Northwest Staging Route from the continental United States to Fairbanks. Small airstrips along the way constituted a dot-to-dot route through the Canadian wilderness. Along this line, Lend-Lease Program pilots—many of them women, who

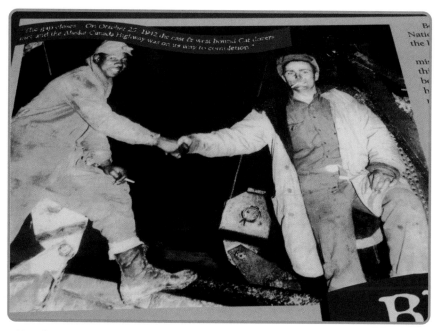

Soldiers from two engineering regiments worked from the north and south to meet at Beaver Creek in October 1942. This sign at Beaver Creek, Yukon Territory, honors that historic day.

A Lone Road Through the Wilderness

At Watson Lake, the Alaska Highway Interpretive Centre includes a mini-museum on the building of the highway.

Alaska Highway Facts

Length of historic route to
   Fairbanks: 1,523 miles (2,451 km)

U.S. troops used in construction: 11,000

Civilian workers: 16,000

Pieces of heavy equipment: 7,000

Bridges constructed: 133

Culverts installed: 8,000+

Highest mountain pass: Summit, 4,250 feet, at Historic Mile 392

Cost: $140 million

Began: March 1942

Completed: October 1942

Officially opened: November 20, 1942, at Soldiers Summit, Mile 1061

Time: 8 months, 12 days

Opened to the public: 1948

Beginning, Mile 0: Dawson Creek, British Columbia

Official end: Delta Junction, Alaska, Mile 1422

Unofficial end: Fairbanks, Alaska, Historic Mile 1523

After 50 years of road improvements, Fairbanks is now 1,488 miles
   (2,395 km) from Dawson Creek, B.C. •

were not allowed to fly in combat—ferried aircraft for delivery to Russian pilots waiting in Fairbanks. These pilots then continued the journey over the Bering Sea to Russia. All told, nearly 8,000 fighters, bombers, and cargo planes were flown along the Northwest Staging Route.

Clearly a road was needed, and in fact it had been considered as early as 1905, when Major Constantine of the North-West Mounted Police was charged to build a road to the Klondike but was later recalled from that effort. In the late 1920s and early 1930s, other proposed routes were examined and discarded. World War II was catalyst enough, and in March 1942, Canada and the United States came to terms on building the military road then known as the Alcan. Canada allowed rights-of-way and provided construction materials, while the U.S. military provided the manpower. It was agreed that the Canadian portion of the road would be turned over to Canada at the war's end.

When troop trains began pulling into Dawson Creek, B.C., a quiet hamlet boomed from a population of 600 to more than 10,000 by late March 1942.

Diaries recorded by the men who built the road portray an existence just as life-threatening as it might have been in battle. In the preliminary stage, workers felled trees to create a corduroy road, and the first bridges floated on pontoons. At Charlie Lake, three American soldiers drowned while crossing the lake on a pontoon barge.

That winter, the piercing cold was the enemy, along with the crude, temporary accommodations, bad food, and backbreaking, seven-days-a-week labor. Heavy equipment was sucked into the miry shoulders and sometimes abandoned. In below-zero temperatures, the big machines were kept running 24 hours a day, as they might not start again if allowed to cool. Trucks and bulldozers were pulled out of seemingly bottomless mud holes, and troop morale sagged with little contact from the outside world. In the summer, mosquitoes, no-see-ums, and black flies tortured the work crews.

Just as the American military had feared, Japan attacked and landed troops on U.S. soil in June 1942, briefly invading Alaska's Aleutian Islands at Kiska and Attu, and further heightening the sense of need for the road's completion. An ensuing battle at Kiska killed soldiers on both sides before Japanese troops retreated under cover of fog. Several Native Alaskans were taken from Attu to Japan as prisoners of war.

On September 25, 1942, the 35th Regiment of the U.S. Army Corps of Engineers, working from the south, met the soldiers of the 340th Regiment, working from the north, at a place named by the soldiers themselves: Contact Creek. The final link occurred a month later in Beaver Creek, Yukon Territory, when members of the 97th Engineers met the 18th Engineers and opened the road for military convoys to pass.

A photograph from that day shows two nose-to-nose bulldozers and two weary soldiers—one African-American, one white—shaking hands and smiling broadly for the camera. The official opening, along with a formal ribbon-cutting ceremony, came on a bitterly cold day—November 20, 1942—at Soldiers Summit at Kluane Lake, Mile 1061. Members of the Royal Canadian Mounted Police suffered in their dress uniforms at –35°F.

The Alcan would not be opened to civilian traffic until 1948, well after the war, and it remained a fearsome journey suitable only for jeeps and specially equipped vehicles for many years.

The Canadian Army took over jurisdiction of the Canadian portion of the road in 1946 and continued maintenance until 1964, when that responsibility was given to the Federal Department of Public Works. Since 1971 the Yukon Department of Highways and Public Works has been in charge of the portion that passes through the Yukon Territory.

With the 50th anniversary celebration of the Alaska Highway in 1992, commemorative license plates were issued for those who drove the route. In preparation for the anniversary year, paved but damaged sections of the highway were repaired, and unpaved stretches were widened and improved.

Tourism associations on both sides of the border joined forces to erect "historic mileposts"—which in most cases do not match current milepost or kilometer-post numbers. That's because the highway is now shorter than it used to be, thanks to all of the straightening and rerouting improvements of the last half-century.

Significant historic sites include construction camps, airstrips of the Northwest Staging Route, the memorably steep Suicide Hill, memorial sites for those who lost their lives, and boundary lines marking responsibility of various contractors. A free mile-by-mile guide is available at the Dawson Creek Visitor Information Centre, at Mile 0, or at the Alaska Highway Interpretive Centre at Watson Lake, Yukon Territory, at Mile 613. The interpretive center's exhibit on the building of the Alcan includes historic documents, photos, and displays of life in the work camps.

In 1996 the emergency wartime road that was built with remarkable speed received special recognition for the wonder that it is. The Alaska Highway was named an International Historical Engineering Landmark, joining the Eiffel Tower and the Panama Canal among the world's construction marvels.

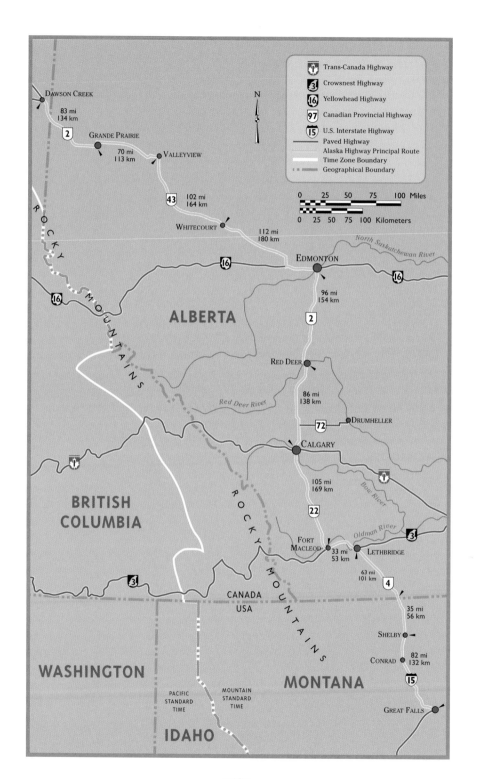

Chapter 4

The Eastern Route: Through Alberta to Dawson Creek, B.C., and Mile 0

Indefinable Alberta. If you find beauty in quiet landscapes and unbroken views, then you will cherish the drive north through Montana, across the border, and into Alberta. Far from boring, this is a landscape that is settling to the soul—farms and fields, horses and cattle, and well-used barns. Looking out the side window, your gaze may be met by a cow looking back. Fertile farmland rolls away in gentle, undulating waves beneath a bright sky. In late August, farmers may be seen baling hay, and huge, golden rolls are strewn about the fields in broad symmetry. In small towns, grain elevators are clustered next to the railroad tracks. The pace is nice and easy.

And yet this corridor into Alberta no more represents the entire province than the Chilkoot Pass represents all of Alaska. Depending on where you spend most of your time, your definition of Alberta may be drawn from the stark badlands surrounding Drumheller, from the stunning mountain vistas of Waterton Lakes National Park, from the cityscapes of Edmonton and Calgary, or from the raw, mountainous wilderness of the far north.

Within the past 200 years, across the desertlike landscape of southern Alberta, the Plains Indians once roamed freely and hunted wild game such as buffalo, pronghorn antelope,

North of Calgary, the divided road is straight and easy-going.

and coyotes. Here and farther north, these people of the First Nations lived an untrammeled existence until the arrival of explorers, traders, cowboys, law officers, and government representatives bearing treaties. The stories of the Natives—or at least a portion of them—are told today in culturally important places such as Head-Smashed-In Buffalo Jump, Fort Whoop-Up, Indian Battle Park, and Calgary's Heritage Park, and in smaller interpretive sites throughout the province. In western Canada, as in other regions of North America, Native groups are reawakening to some of their lost practices, and regaining tribal pride through dance, song, storytelling, and art.

More recent settlers of southern and central Alberta came to farm, work in the forests, or draw oil and natural gas from beneath the ground. Today farming is flourishing with the aid of modern irrigation practices, and oil, timber, and tourism also feed the province's healthy economy. As you motor through, you'll see livestock sharing some fields with working oil pumpjacks. In "fields" of their own, dense forests are grown for the purpose of cutting, just like wheat and hay—but harvest seasons are decades, not months, apart. Roadside signs show the date when a particular forest was last logged and replanted. In mill towns, visitors are invited in to see the latest manufacturing processes.

Tourism is a burgeoning industry as well, growing in leaps after the Alaska Highway was opened, when travelers were more apt to discover the attractions of Alberta during their long-distance journey. Its diverse wildlife, topography, and climate make this province more than just a place to pass through, but rather a place to count among your travel destinations.

For raw backcountry experiences, go northeast to the northern woods surrounding Lesser Slave Lake, or to the top of the province, where much of the wilderness remains untouched. To thrill to the province's prehistory, go east to Drumheller, where the onetime presence of dinosaurs is now a tourist attraction. If outdoor recreation is part of your vacation, throughout Alberta you'll find plenty of opportunity for camping, fishing, boating, swimming, and the like.

Private campground owners often advertise outdoor recreation as part of the appeal for their particular location. In addition, the province oversees numerous campgrounds, provincial parks, recreational areas, and other protected lands that fall under the jurisdiction of Alberta Environmental Protection. Fees vary among campgrounds, depending on how many services are offered, and reservations usually can be made between May 1 and Labour Day in early September. Firewood usually is provided, and officials remind you to refrain from bringing your own. Alberta is currently free of Dutch elm disease, and the province asks your help to keep their trees from becoming infested.

To learn more about what to see and do in Alberta, travel information is available at the following website: www.explorealberta.com. If you are interested in staying in bed-and-breakfast accommodations, visit the Alberta Bed & Breakfast Association website at www.bbalberta.com.

*M*ONTANA–ALBERTA BORDER

To Lethbridge, Alberta: 63 miles (101 km)
To Dawson Creek, B.C.: 750 miles (1,200 km)

Before you leave Montana, top off the fuel tank in Shelby. The price there will be lower than any other you'll encounter throughout western Canada. Driving north, the terrain will be familiar in Alberta. Like northern Montana, it is virtually treeless, with grainfields sweeping away from the roadsides. The road is generally straight and wide, with little changing except the occasional rise and fall. Oil pumpjacks are sometimes visible here, too, where a minor oil field lies beneath the farmland.

On the Montana side of the international border, the speed limit is 75 mph (110 kmh). Once you cross the border and start up Alberta Highway 4, no place will be higher than 110—more often it's 100. In construction sections just after the border crossing, the speed limit may drop to between 50 and 80 kmh (30 to 50 mph).

The border crossing is a cluster of buildings in the middle of nowhere. On the Montana side, the place-name is **Sweetgrass**, a name it shares with the Sweetgrass Hills, a low mountain range on the eastern horizon. **Coutts** is the Canadian border town. Northbound travelers will stop at U.S. Customs and Immigration to answer a few questions, then continue to Canadian Customs and Immigration. Between them, you'll see the **Altan Duty Free Shop**. The shop may be more attractive to southbound U.S. citizens as the place for "last chance" shopping. Here you can purchase Canadian goods with Canadian funds on Canadian soil, with savings on liquor, tobacco, perfume, souvenirs, toys, T-shirts, and caps. (See the section on Border Crossings in Chapter 2, What You Need to Know.)

Road Notes

Like northern Montana, southern Alberta enjoys a semiarid climate, with so much sunshine that farmers rely heavily on irrigation. Above the more level farms, the foothills are wrinkled and dimpled, treeless except for occasional clusters in the distance.

At **Milk River**, 13 miles (21 km) north of the border, you'll find a small, reasonably priced public campground with 34 sites. Full and partial hookup as well as dry camping is available.

Farther up the road in the heart of town, multiple grain elevators alongside the railroad tracks are cleverly painted to look like milk cartons. Expect to see little else but farm country on both sides of the road all the way to Lethbridge—irrigated fields and grain elevators, ranging from the classic wooden buildings to new shiny metal structures.

Just north of Milk River, you can take a tour of ancient petroglyphs by turning east for 26 miles (42 km) on Route 501 and following the signs to **Writing-on-Stone Provincial Park**. This archaeological preserve features huge sandstone outcrops with

Dinosaurs used to roam southern Alberta, and several entire skeletons were unearthed in the last century. The Dinosaur Trail near Drumheller offers more information on the subject.

petroglyphs and pictographs inscribed by the Shoshoni and Blackfoot Indians. No unguided tours are permitted; however, free guided tours are available weekdays at 2 P.M. or weekends at 10 A.M. throughout the summer. For more information, call 403-647-2364.

Devil's Coulee Dinosaur Egg Interpretive Centre is located in Warner, about 12 miles (19 km) north of Milk River. In the early 1990s, scientists discovered the world's largest dinosaur nesting site in this incredible land formation. A guided hike allows visitors to view the excavation site, including intact embryos. Work continues here as paleontologists search for more clues to this area's prehistory dating from 230 to 65 million years ago. For more information, call 403-642-2118.

$\mathcal{L}$ETHBRIDGE

From the border: 65 miles (105 km)
To Fort Macleod: 35 miles (56 km)

A lovely settlement along the Oldman River, Lethbridge offers the attractions of a big city in a little package. All services and facilities are available in this city of 66,000, from top-rated golfing to a natural history center, art galleries, a theater, beautifully landscaped gardens, and a university and archives. Shopping malls, vast retail outlets, and little shops provide plenty of shopping opportunities. Dine in style or eat on the run, choosing from among dozens of cafés, restaurants, and fast-food establishments.

The **Chinook Country Tourist Association** operates a visitor center near the junction of Highway 4 and Highway 5 (Mayor Magrath Drive). Call 1-800-661-1222 for information.

Among the premier attractions in Lethbridge is its beautiful **High Level Bridge,** the longest and highest steel viaduct railroad bridge in the world. It spans the Oldman River Valley and soars above the site of a historic trading post. Here at **Indian Battle Park**, the last of the intertribal battles of North America took place, between the Cree and Blackfoot Indians. Besides picnic areas and playgrounds, the park features walking trails.

Also beneath the High Level Bridge is **Fort Whoop-Up Interpretive Centre**, a great place to learn about the city's beginnings. With its log construction, old-time displays, and friendly gift shop, historic Fort Whoop-Up today seems like a tame tourism stop. Although this is a replica of the original, don't forget that log walls such as these have seen passion, fury, and acts of utter lawlessness.

Established in 1869 by two American fur traders, Fort Whoop-Up was once a critical post for whiskey runners. At that time, trade in buffalo

Fort Whoop-Up in Lethbridge flourished as a whiskey-running stop until the North-West Mounted Police arrived to stop the illegal activity.

robes flourished between Montana and Alberta. Payment with guns or illegal alcohol was commonplace, and powerful men took advantage of those who were addicted to the drink—trappers and pioneers, as well as members of local tribes.

With the arrival of the North-West Mounted Police in 1874, the lawlessness was contained, but the name stuck. A sign in northern Montana—the southern end of the whiskey trail—offered this explanation for the unusual name: "Origin of the name Whoop-Up is possibly from a conversation by a trader on the whiskey-for-furs trade route. Upon his return to Fort Benton, Johny LaMotte was asked 'How's business?' His reply, 'Aw, they're just whoopin' 'er up!'"

For outdoor enthusiasts, the **Helen Schuler Coulee Centre** is an urban nature retreat that includes interpretive programs and touchable displays, as well as self-guided trails through the coulees and cottonwood forests on a 200-acre reserve. Watch for great-horned owls, deer, and porcupines that make their homes in the reserve. The city offers numerous other hiking and biking opportunities, too, especially around **Henderson Lake Park**.

Check with the visitor center to see what's happening at the **Lethbridge &**

Nikka Yuko Japanese Garden

The walkway to the entrance of Nikka Yuko Japanese Garden offers a clue to the visual treasures on the other side of the gates. The garden is located off Mayor Magrath Drive in Henderson Lake Park. On either side of the entry path, pink and white impatiens have been planted to create a specific, rigid pattern. But that is the last of the brash color. Don't enter this garden expecting a rush of floral sights and scents. A true Japanese garden offers quietude and the opportunity for meditation, not overstimulation of the senses. In these 4 acres, you will appreciate the beauty in simplicity.

At the center, an authentically built Japanese house—shoes off at the door, please—is surrounded by carefully groomed walkways, pruned trees, and paths that have been meticulously landscaped. Nothing is out of place, not even the rocks in the pond, or the pebbles along its shore specially chosen for their size and shape, then laid in an overlapping design. Everything about this controlled landscape reflects the Japanese desire to express an understanding of humanity's place in the environment.

In the distance, you'll occasionally hear the low, muffled toll of a huge bell. You will find it at eye level near the end of a path, and you may move the clapper if you like. The weight of the bell hanging inside a unique gazebolike structure actually keeps the walls and beams together. Like the Japanese house, this perfectly engineered structure contains no manufactured nails.

Kimono-clad women of Japanese heritage guide the way and explain cultural practices, as well as relate how this lovely place came to be. Admission is charged. For more information, call 403-328-3511.

Other attractions within Henderson Lake Park include a picnic area, bowling green, golf course, swimming pool, and rose gardens. ●

District Exhibition grounds at 3401 Parkside Drive. Over the year, close to a million visitors will roam the 67-acre grounds during events such as horse races, agricultural fairs, and the popular **Whoop-Up Days**, held in early August, highlighting professional rodeo events.

Sir Alexander Galt Museum & Archives is located in what was once the Galt Hospital, overlooking the Oldman River Valley at the west end of 5th Avenue South. Galt was founder of North Western Coal and Navigation Co. Displays and interactive programs teach about the history of Lethbridge, the settling of southern Alberta, and the area's first people.

Golfers will be thrilled to play at **Paradise Canyon Golf Resort**, rated among Alberta's top seven golf courses by *Canada's Golf Course Ranking Magazine* and one of the best in North America by *Golf Digest*. Another option is a round at the **Henderson Lake Golf Course** in the heart of the city.

The **Alberta Airshow** is one of western Canada's best, according to *Canadian Aviation News*. Scheduled for mid-August at the Lethbridge Airport, the show features military and civilian aircraft in flying demonstrations, while ground displays invite visitors for a closer look. For details, call 403-380-4245.

For more information about Lethbridge, call the Chinook County Tourist Association at 1-800-661-1222 or visit its website: www.albertasouth.com.

Taber: Market Garden of Canada

One of the pleasures of road travel is stopping at a roadside stand and picking up fresh fruits or vegetables for the night's meal. Or you may choose to just eat a sweet, juicy peach right there over the grass and let the juice drip off your chin and fingers. I quickly became obsessed with finding the best sweet corn.

Driving through this part of western Alberta, or west in British Columbia, you'll see many fruit and vegetable stands with crudely made signs declaring **Taber Corn!** "What in the world is Taber corn," we wondered, "and what makes it better than any other?" We got our answers when we stopped where a woman was selling several corn varieties from the back of her truck—and was giving out corn recipes and information with each purchase. She knew a lot about flavor differences among varieties, and she solved for us the mystery of Taber corn.

It seems that the Taber area, east of Lethbridge on Highway 3, has become known far and wide for its sweet corn: delicate and white, or bulky yellow, or multicolored beauties. A flyer boasted of the success achieved by grower Gary Valgardson, who is regularly chosen Corn King at Taber's Corn Festival. With an average of more than 2,300 hours of sunshine a year and up to 120 frost-free days, the Taber area grows much more than just corn. It is known as the Market Garden of Canada, with crops that include beets, potatoes, grains, and many types of vegetables.

"The area has near-perfect growing conditions," Valgardson says in his flyer, "with sandy loam soil, long warm summers and irrigated fields." We picked up half a dozen ears and immediately learned why Taber is the corn capital. For me, a corn-loving Midwesterner living in Alaska for 20 years, eating Taber corn was like coming home again. The kernels fairly exploded with sweetness. If you appreciate a good ear of corn or other fresh vegetables and fruits, make road-stand shopping part of your drive.

If you're traveling through the area in late August, make a point of joining the end-of-season harvest celebration at the **Taber Corn Festival**. For more information, call 403-223-2265. ●

Lodging

Best Western Heidelberg Inn

1303 Mayor Magrath Drive

1-800-791-8488 or 403-329-0555

66 air-conditioned rooms with cable TV.
Fitness room. Three-Diamond rating,
AAA/CAA. Pub, liquor store, JB's
Restaurant.

Bridge Town House Motel

1026 Mayor Magrath Drive

1-800-597-1114 or 403-327-4576

37 units, cable TV, refrigerators, VCRs. Free
breakfast. Outdoor heated pool. Smitty's
Family Restaurant.

Chinook Motel

1303 Mayor Magrath Drive

1-800-791-8488 or 403-329-0555

20 air-conditioned rooms, telephones,
cable TV.

Days Inn Lethbridge

100 3rd Avenue South

1-800-DAYS INN or 403-327-6000

91 units including nonsmoking rooms.
Cable TV, movies, exercise room,
whirlpool. Free continental breakfast,
coffee. Winter plug-ins, coin laundry.
Senior discount.

Lethbridge Lodge Hotel

320 Scenic Drive

1-800-661-1232 or 403-328-1123

Full-service hotel with 191 rooms around
tropical courtyard, indoor pool, hot tub.
Anton's restaurant, Café Garden,
lounge. Kids 18 and younger stay with
parents free.

Parkside Inn

1009 Mayor Magrath Drive South

1-800-240-1471 or 403-328-2366

60 air-conditioned rooms. Cable TV, room
service, laundry service, whirlpool,
exercise room, sundeck. Lounge with
live entertainment. By Henderson Lake
and Nikka Yuko Japanese Garden. Kids
17 and younger are free with parents.

Pepper Tree Inn

1142 Mayor Magrath Drive

1-800-708-8638 or 403-328-4436

56 air-conditioned rooms, with
refrigerators, fax jacks, cable TV, and
movies. Nonsmoking and kitchenettes
available. Senior discount; no charge for
children under 17 in parents' room.

Quality Inn

1030 Mayor Magrath Drive

1-800-561-9815 or 403-328-6636

56 air-conditioned units, with cable TV and
movies. Nonsmoking and kitchenettes
available. Free continental breakfast;
laundry. Kids 11 and under stay free with
parents.

Sandman Hotel

421 Mayor Magrath Drive

1-800-726-3626 or 403-328-1111

139 air-conditioned rooms, with
nonsmoking available. Cable TV and
movies. 24-hour Denny's restaurant with
room service. Children 17 and younger
are free in parents' room.

Super 8 Lodge
2210 7th Avenue South
1-800-661-8091 or 403-329-0100
91 air-conditioned units, some nonsmoking.
Movies, laundry. Pets welcome. No
charge for children under 12 sharing
parents' room.

Campgrounds

Bridgeview RV Resort
1501 2nd Avenue West (access from north
side Highway 3; 0.3 miles west of
Oldman River)
403-381-2357
86 sites, new facility with pull-throughs,
full and partial hookups. Laundry,
heated pool.

Henderson Lake Campground
3419 Parkside Drive South (next to
Henderson Lake Park)
403-328-5452
100 sites with full or partial hookups.
Showers, laundry, rest rooms. Grocery
store, canoeing. Shopping and dining
nearby.

Restaurants

Also note in the Lodging list that most
major hotels include restaurants and
lounges.

Boston Pizza
904 1st Avenue South, No. 200
403-327-4548
Pizza, pasta, and more.

Coco Pazzo
1254 3rd Avenue South
403-329-8979
Italian specialties, wood-fired pizza oven.

JB's Restaurant
1303 Mayor Magrath Drive South
In Best Western Heidelberg Inn
403-329-0555
Three meals a day, plus special homemade
pies.

The Lethbridge No. 1 Fire Hall
402 2nd Avenue South
International cuisine, lounge, game room,
wines from around the world.

The Regent Restaurant
1255 3rd Avenue South
403-328-7800
Dim sum daily, lunch buffet, weekend
karaoke.

Sven Ericksen's Restaurant
1715 Mayor Magrath Drive South
403-328-7756
Breakfast, lunch, dinner, cocktails.

Road Notes

Driving west from Lethbridge on Highway 3, and then north from Fort Macleod on
Highway 2, you won't see a lot of rest stops. So plan your stops around these bigger
towns instead.

The prairies of southern Alberta are windy. The prevailing wind tousles the crops
on either side of the road, and it takes only a little imagination to see the surface of
the grainfields as sea waves or a living thing that ripples with movement. Lift your
eyes and enjoy this far-reaching, big-sky country.

About 18 miles (29 km) west of Lethbridge, you'll enter the Oldman River Valley. Note where the river has created coulees: treeless valleys beneath high ridges. To the west, the Canadian Rockies are visible.

The Fort Macleod Chamber of Commerce hosts a **Tourism Information Center** accessible from either side of the divided highway on the south end of town. In Fort Macleod, at the junction of Highways 3 and 2, you'll take Highway 2 north.

Go West to Canada's Crown Jewel

Consider a side trip to **Waterton Lakes National Park**, which lies about 75 miles (120 km) south and west of Lethbridge on Route 5, or the same distance traveling due west from Milk River on Highways 501 and 5. This area is rich with biological diversity and is extraordinarily beautiful, marked by vast lakes, waterfalls cascading from dramatic mountain peaks, and streams full of fish. The park's southern boundary lies adjacent to **Glacier National Park** in Montana. Like Waterton Lakes, Glacier National Park is a natural beauty worthy of exploration. Of course the two national parks are part of a single landscape onto which political boundaries have been applied—and that was only yesterday in geologic time. Indeed, billion-year-old rocks have been identified in this glacier-carved region.

In 1932 Waterton Lakes National Park and Glacier National Park were together designated as the first International Peace Park, commemorating the friendship between the countries and their commitment to shared resource management. The combined national parks are included on a list of modern-day wonders of the world as a UNESCO World Heritage Site. Both parks offer backcountry hiking, camping, horseback riding, rafting, biking, and other recreation. For more information on Waterton Lakes National Park, call 403-859-2224. For more on Glacier National Park: 406-888-7800 or www.nps.gov/glac.

Fort Macleod

From Lethbridge: 33 miles (53 km)
To Calgary: 105 miles (169 km)

This charming city of 3,200 people is centrally located on the crossroads of Highways 2 and 3. One of Alberta's oldest communities, Fort Macleod (muh-CLOUD) was founded in 1874 by the North-West Mounted Police when the patrol established a post on the Oldman River. Today the downtown historic district includes more than 30 historic and architecturally significant buildings dating from 1880 to 1920. Guided or self-guided walking tours are fun, and shopping is plentiful.

Among those buildings is the **Museum of the North-West Mounted Police**, at 219 25th Street, a replica of the original fort that depicts pioneer and Native life in the late 1800s. Summer visitors will enjoy the fort's Mounted Patrol Musical Ride, with red-uniformed riders executing parade dressage, four times a day in July and August. Admission is charged.

Other buildings include the **Fort Macleod Empress Theatre**, 235 Col. Macleod Boulevard, which was established in 1910 and is still in operation. Ask about the resident ghost. The theater is located on what is known as the Red Coat Trail, across from the mounted-police museum. Visit the theater's website at www.discoveralberta.com/empresstheatre.

The province government operates a campground on the Oldman River, north of town on Highway 2 near the bridge (see list of campgrounds), and a wildlife reserve adjacent to the Oldman River offers hiking, biking, birding, and fishing. The reserve habitat supports deer, many species of birds, and beavers. Spend a few hours berry picking for local varieties such as Saskatoon, chokecherry, and buffalo.

A side trip to the municipality of **Crowsnest Pass**—56 miles (91 km) west of Fort Macleod on Highway 3—brings you to several attractions. A nearby interpretive center provides a slide show, self-guided walks, and programs that recall the **Frank Slide**, the 1903 disaster that wiped out half the town of Frank as it dumped 90 million tons of rock. Exhibits also explore the early days of life in this coal-mining valley. An admission fee is charged. For more information: 403-562-7388 or www.frankslide.com.

Elsewhere in Crowsnest Pass, you may go underground for a tour of the **Bellevue Mine**. Throughout the guided tour, each visitor wears a hard hat equipped with a miner's lamp. You will descend through about 330 feet (100 m) of the main rock tunnel and into 660 feet (200 m) of the coal seam. Admission is charged. Call 403-564-4700.

At the **Peigan Reserve**, west of Fort Macleod off Highway 3, you can learn about early Native culture of this area. The reserve includes the **Oldman River Cultural Centre**, with artifacts, historical photos, and resources on the history and language of the Peigan people. Open weekdays. Call 403-965-3939.

The **Piikani Lodge Interpretive Centre** on the reserve invites visitors to join interpretive hikes and special events, such as the Peigan Nation Annual Celebration and Powwow held in August. Call 403-965-4000 for details.

Sundance Traditional Tours offers a live wild horse show and buffalo chase in reenactment of traditional hunting practices, plus saddle bronc and bareback riding competitions. Visitors learn about Blackfoot legends in trail rides and camping trips. Call 403-965-2156 for reservations.

Head-Smashed-In Buffalo Jump

For centuries, the buffalo hunters of the Plains Indians counted on this region's topography to help them kill their prey. Incited to stampede, a portion of the herd would follow the natural contours of the land along a route that gradually narrowed until the animals encountered an escarpment, 37 feet high and 1,000 feet long. The buffalo would fall headlong to their deaths, and the waiting party at the bottom of the cliff would immediately set to work on the meat and hides. Only the bones were left behind to disintegrate with time.

The Plains Indians hunted buffalo this way for more than 6,000 years. At the first arrival of Europeans, there were an estimated 16 million bison on the North American plains. By 1879 they were virtually extinct due to hunting by non-Natives.

Head-Smashed-In is the site of the largest and best-preserved buffalo jump on the continent. Most jumps were disturbed prior to World War II because they held centuries of bones, which are high in phosphorous, a necessary ingredient for munitions, explosives, and gunpowder. Through these hurried and haphazard excavations, most archaeological sites of the Plains Indians were destroyed.

To reach Head-Smashed-In, turn off from Highway 2 about 4.5 miles (7 km) north of Fort Macleod. Then take Route 785 west for 10 miles (16 km) to the RV parking area.

A seven-story interpretive center built into the cliffside is open year-round. Displays include a diorama with full-size mounted buffalo, films explaining the traditional hunt, a restaurant, and a gift store. Visitors can handle objects such as a stone club, an arrow, a buffalo robe, tools made from bone, a hide scraper, and a flint knife. Native interpreters are on duty to add to the store of information. A wheelchair-accessible trail leads to the buffalo jump along the edge of the escarpment.

In the museum, the treatment of Natives at the hands of non-Natives is presented without anger: The objects and documents are allowed to tell the tragic stories. Artifacts include a payment book from 1890 listing names of reservation residents and what they were paid annually. Men, women, boys, and girls were paid differently, amounts ranging from $1 to $7. Also on display is a book of passes to leave the reservation, which required the signature of a Department of Indian Affairs agent. Each person's name seems to hold a story: One Owl; Rises with the Sun; No Account Woman.

The name Head-Smashed-In comes from the story of a young man, many years ago, who hid beneath the escarpment during a buffalo hunt and died from a skull fracture.

Westerly winds are nearly constant at Head-Smashed-In, blowing 314 days of the year, sometimes with almost hurricane force. Wear a scarf or a secure hat and clothes that you can button up or zip shut. Bring your sunglasses, too. For more information, call 403-553-2731, or visit the center's website at www.head-smashed-in.com.

Lodging

Century II Motel
462 Main Street
1-888-497-7757 or 403-553-3331
14 air-conditioned units, some nonsmoking.
Telephones, cable TV, coffee.

D.J. Motel
416 Main Street
403-553-4011
15 air-conditioned units, some nonsmoking.
Cable TV and movies, data ports. No
charge for children 15 and younger in
parents' room.

Fort Motel
451 24th Street
403-553-3606
14 air-conditioned units, with cable and
satellite TV. Nonsmoking, kitchenettes,
rooms with data ports available. Free
coffee, tea, hot chocolate. RV and truck
parking.

Heritage House Motel
On Col. Macleod Trail West End
403-553-2777
12 units, most with air-conditioning. Cable
TV, coffee, family plan.

Kozy Motel
On Main Street
403-553-3115
13 air-conditioned units. Cable TV, movies,
phones, refrigerators, barbecue area.

Red Coat Inn
359 Main Street
403-553-4434
28 units, most air-conditioned. Cable TV,
movies, senior and family rates.

Sunset Motel
103 Highway 3 West
1-888-554-2784 or 403-553-4448
22 air-conditioned units. Refrigerators, free
coffee. Fax-ready telephones, cable TV
and movies, winter plug-ins. Adjacent
to self-service laundry. Two-Diamond
rating, AAA.

Campgrounds

Buffalo Plains RV Park & Campground
7.5 miles (12 km) west of Fort Macleod, via
Route 785
403-553-2592
23 sites with views of foothills and
mountains, full and partial hookups.
Tenting area, firewood, community fire
pit. Showers, laundry, rest rooms, dump
station. Playground.

Daisy May Campground
On Lyndon Road
403-553-2455
120 sites, with full and partial hookups.
Laundry, camp kitchen. Heated pool,
game room, mini-golf. Near golf course.
Open May—October.

Oldman River Provincial Recreation Area
0.3 miles (0.5 km) northwest of Fort
Macleod on Highway 2
403-627-3765
40 sites on Pincher Creek. Sheltered picnic
areas, dump station, fishing, canoe
access.

Restaurants

Aunty Lynda's Dining Room
One-half block from Fort Museum
403-553-2655
Family dining featuring steaks, seafood,
pasta, soups, salad.

Scarlet & Gold Inn
2373 7th Avenue
403-553-3337
Steaks, seafood, Sunday brunch
specialties.

Road Notes

This semiarid region seems like a Hollywood Western backlot. There is little shade from the sun, the soil is dry and rocky, and hot wind snaps your clothing when you step outside. It's easy to imagine that this place was once thick with buffalo, and you can picture nomadic Indian tribes setting up seasonal hunting camps as they traveled and hunted.

Just ahead is a UNESCO World Heritage Site called "Head-Smashed-In Buffalo Jump," where the hunting practices of the Plains Indians, as well as their cultural history, is presented in a beautiful interpretive center. (See sidebar.)

As you continue driving north, the road divides **Claresholm**, a town of about 3,500 people. The Claresholm Museum is housed in an elegant old sandstone railroad station at 5126 Railway Avenue; call 403-625-3131. You can also visit the town's original 1903 schoolhouse and a nearby log cabin dating from 1902. Other local offerings include bowling, billiards, motels, auto repair, a car dealer, and a grocery store. Call 403-625-3131.

About 25 miles (40 km) beyond Claresholm, you'll enter the historic village of **Nanton**, where antiques are taken seriously. Downtown Nanton shops hold uncountable treasures, crafts, and collectibles, plus the town's old blacksmith shop, the Willow Creek Forge. Also downtown: a tearoom, restaurants, and auto repair and gas services. Aircraft buffs will enjoy a stop at the Nanton Lancaster Society Air Museum on Highway 2 South.

As we drove north of Nanton, we encountered our first roadside wildlife: a buffalo herd grazing in the grass. Numbering about a dozen, they didn't seem to mind the traffic or the idea of having their picture taken by a woman leaning out of an RV window.

What this part of Alberta lacks in topographic beauty (as compared to more spectacular, mountainous regions), it makes up for in the openness of sky, in the phenomenal shades of blue from delicate to rich, velvety hues—and the natural artistry in the clouds, in their streaks, layers, balls, and fingers in tones from gray to bleach white. It's a pleasure to just gaze at the heavens.

About 163 miles (262 km) north of the Canadian border, you'll see the turn onto Highway 23 West for **High River**, population 8,300. Architects, geologists, and historians alike will enjoy touring High River's sandstone buildings. You can also take a guided tour of local murals. Each summer the city hosts championship chuckwagon racing and a favorite local event, the Little Britches Rodeo. For more information, call the Chamber of Commerce at 403-652-3336. This is the last stop before Calgary, 37 miles (59 km) to the north.

CALGARY

From Fort Macleod: 105 miles (169 km)
To Red Deer: 86 miles (138 km) (not on map)
To Edmonton: 181 miles (291 km)

At the confluence of the Bow and Elbow Rivers, with the purple Rocky Mountains to the west, Calgary is a marvelous place to work and play. And judging from the city's calendar of events, it seems that there's plenty of both here.

Populated by 820,000 people, this town is experiencing a growth spurt, but it hasn't forgotten its roots in the Wild West. It is that usual contrast of wilderness and metropolis, cowboys and businessmen, a rodeo among the skyscrapers, that makes Calgary such a popular destination. Throughout western Canada, this city has gained a winning reputation for its restaurants, shopping, museums, festivals, art, music, and flowers. And in the world of professional rodeo throughout North America, it is famed for its main event, the Calgary Stampede.

In the summer of 1875, when an expedition of North-West Mounted Police arrived to establish a fort here, the place very nearly was named Fort Brisebois. Inspector Ephraim Brisebois, an unpopular leader of the troop, intended to name the new fort for himself. Instead, Col. James Macleod, a Scotsman, suggested the name Fort Calgary in remembrance of his ancestral castle on the island of Skye. His choice prevailed.

Calgary is a city of parks and skyscrapers surrounded by farmlands.

The presence of white settlers was troubling and unwelcome to the local Niitsitapi, which means "real people" in the Blackfoot language. More than a century of resistance had already passed in bloody and destructive warfare. In 1877 the tribes of the Blackfoot Confederacy signed an important peace agreement, called Treaty 7, that designated boundaries for Native land reserves. Representing the North-West Mounted Police for the Queen of Great Britain and Ireland was James Macleod. Timing was important to the government, which planned to build a transcountry railway across aboriginal land by 1881.

Southern Alberta's Blackfoot Confederacy tribes—Blood, Peigan, Siksika, and Stoney—continue to practice traditions handed down from generation to generation. Learn more about the First Nations people at the **Tsuu T'ina Culture Museum**, 3700 Anderson Road. The museum features artifacts from Edmonton's Provincial Museum and from area residents whose ancestors traded with aboriginal people. For more information, call 403-238-2677.

The Calgary Exhibition and Stampede, held in mid-July each year, fills the town with rodeo fans, cowboys, and cowgirls who come for some of the hottest competition in North America. Events include saddle bronco-riding, bull-riding, chuckwagon races, bareback riding, wild cow milking events, and wild horse races. Rodeo clowns, parades, agriculture exhibitions, square dancing, a midway, and lots of food fill out the 10-day celebration. For more information, visit these websites: www.calgary stampede.com or www.visitor.calgary.ab.ca.

Calgary was the host city for the 1988 Winter Olympic Games, and the ski jump, bobsled run, and slopes became familiar sites to television viewers, who can now ski the same slopes at **Canada Olympic Park**. In fact, you may even meet one of tomorrow's Olympic champions among the many skiers who train here year-round. You can share the slopes, the 295-foot ski jump, and the bobsled run from November through March.

The **Olympic Hall of Fame and Museum** in the park honors the stars of Olympic history. Bobsled and ski jump simulators make the experience real, and exhibits teach about developments in snow sports through decades. Admission is charged. For more information, call 403-247-5452 or visit www.coda.ab.ca/cop.

Wondering where to take the kiddies? Cool off at **Village Square Leisure Centre**, an indoor water-slide park with a wave pool, hot tubs, a diving tank, and a pool for the little ones. Rain or shine, you can have fun in the water. Call 403-280-9714.

Fort Calgary Historical Park, at 950 9th Avenue SE, is a reconstruction of the original 1875 fort on a 40-acre site at the confluence of the Bow and Elbow Rivers. Reconstruction work is continuing, with volunteer carpenters using period tools. Interpreters share the stories of the early settlers and of this site. For information, call 403-290-1875.

Even if you were just an average student in science, you'll reawaken a sense of discovery during a visit to the **Calgary Science Centre**. Hands-on, discovery-oriented exhibits make science fun again. Enter a world of adventure in the Discovery Dome theater, a surround-your-senses journey. The center is located at 701 11th Street SW. Admission is charged. Call 403-221-3700 for more information.

Glenbow Museum, Art Gallery, Library and Archives, at 130 9th Avenue SE, has something of interest for everyone, from excellent displays on cultural and military history to a mineralogy exhibit that includes one of the oldest rocks on the planet. The art gallery shows off its collection of block prints, early watercolors, and Inuit sculpture. For information, call 403-268-4100 or visit www.glenbow.org.

Calgary Zoo Botanical Garden & Prehistoric Park is not just for the kids. This world-class zoo features more than 1,100 animals, including some rare and endangered species, and a tropical aviary. Walk among spectacular, life-size replicas of dinosaurs in a vast park that's a re-creation of their surroundings. It's all found on

Take a Walk Through History

Experience time travel as you stroll the grounds of **Heritage Park**, Canada's largest living-history village, set in a 66-acre park at 1900 Heritage Drive SW. One section features an 1860s fur trading post. Another is reminiscent of an 1880s pre-railway pioneer settlement; another is a street of businesses and residences set in about 1910. You are free to mill in and out of the buildings, relax in the grassy areas, or travel on a steam railway, a riverboat, or an antique carnival ride.

Antique machinery is well oiled and working at the old wooden oil rig. Elsewhere, the village blacksmith is hard at work, but willing to share his knowledge with visitors. A schoolmarm invites you into the old one-room school. Other costumed interpreters reenact a suffragette march, a wedding, a shootout. Children play on the antique carnival rides while parents read about how these attractions were the hit of their day.

Take a ride on the riverboat SS Moyie as it cruises the adjacent reservoir. Peek into every room in the circa-1904 Burnside Ranch House, and wander through the Hudson's Bay Company fort and Indian village across the way. Buy goodies at the bakery, see how a printing press worked, step inside the historic church, savor an ice cream cone in the heat of the day.

It's a lot of walking, but you can pick up a ride on the train or a horse-drawn buggy. Plan your time well and make a day of it. If you arrive between 9 A.M. and 10 A.M. and pay full admission price, you are entitled to the buffet-style breakfast served in the Wainwright Hotel.

The entire park is a simple pleasure. Follow suggested walking trails if you want to soak it all in. Parking may be some distance from the park entrance, but you can hop on an antique trolley to shorten the ride. For more information, contact 403-259-1900 or www.heritagepark.ab.ca.

St. George's Island in the middle of the Bow River. Call the zoo at 403-232-9300.

If you're up for outdoor adventure, call **Chinook River Sports**, a raft company with more than 15 years' experience. They'll supply all the gear, the guide, and the meals. Book a half-day to a full five days of adventure. Call 1-800-482-4899 in Canada or 403-263-7238, or visit the website at www.chinookraft.com.

Rainbow Riders Adventure Tours takes families or first-timers on rafting trips along the Kananaskis River. All gear is provided. Contact 403-850-3686 or www.rainbowriders.com.

If you haven't brought your mountain bike along, there's still hope for you. Contact **Canusa Cycle Tours**, which offers experienced guides for trips through some of the most scenic areas of the Canadian Rockies. Canusa will set up accommodations for

Breaking Bread with Strangers

Doug Carpenter of Deer River, Minnesota, stopped for lunch at the same wayside that we did, so we struck up a conversation. Judging from the looks of his big silver bus with the bicycle attached to the front, he was an advanced road warrior, so I figured he would be a good resource for advice.

Carpenter had been on this trip for only 10 days, traveling with his grandchildren and demonstrating his brand of "random acts of kindness" in campgrounds. He likes to set up his big outdoor cookstove and make huge meals, then invite over young campers who are traveling on a shoestring.

His advice for fellow travelers: "Don't overextend your vacation. It shouldn't be the challenge of making the trip. Enjoy it. Each day, I get after the kids to tell me a story, what they've seen, what was nice. They know that as soon as we're out of being nice, we're going home.

"This is their inheritance. This is my job. I'm in my sunset years. All I've got left is my ability to teach."

Doug Carpenter stopped to visit on Trans-Canada Highway 1, which connects Calgary, Alberta, and Cache Creek, B.C.

camping or hotel stays. Get more information at 1-800-938-7986 or visit the website at www.tcel.com/~canusa.

For information on Calgary attractions and events, call the **Calgary Convention and Visitors Bureau** at 1-800-661-1678 or 403-263-8510.

Dino-riffic Drumheller

If you have an extra day in your travel schedule, take a side trip to Alberta's Badlands and the city of **Drumheller***, 83 miles (134 km) east of Crossfield and Highway 2, via Highway 72. The town is named for American businessman Sam Drumheller, who in 1911 launched the area's first coal-mining operation. Now his name is synonymous not with coal, but with dinosaurs. Just outside town, follow the Dinosaur Trail on a 33-mile (53-km) loop from the north side of the river off Highway 9 into the Valley of the Dinosaurs.*

Along the way, in Midland Provincial Park, you'll find the **Royal Tyrrell Museum of Paleontology***. In 1884 Joseph Burr Tyrrell found a fossil of a dinosaur nearly as large as the famed tyrannosaur; he named the find Albertosaurus. His discovery launched even more digging as other paleontologists arrived to launch their own excavations. The museum features more than two dozen complete dinosaur skeletons, along with finds of other prehistoric creatures. Little is left to the imagination in walk-through, diorama-style exhibits. It's as if you were entering the days of the dinosaurs. Admission is charged. Call 403-823-7707.*

Lodging

Best Western Port O' Call Inn
1935 McKnight Boulevard NE
1-800-661-1161 or 403-291-4600
201 rooms, nonsmoking floors, movies, laundry service. Indoor pool, whirlpool, fitness center. Restaurant and two lounges. 15 minutes from downtown.

Best Western Suites Downtown
1330 8th Street SW
1-800-981-2555 or 403-228-6900
123 suites with kitchens, cable TV, laundry, fitness center, sauna. Three-Diamond rating, AAA. Close to downtown attractions and Stampede grounds.

Budget Host Motor Inn
4420 16th Avenue NW
1-800-661-3772 or 403-288-7115
72 air-conditioned rooms, some nonsmoking. Cable TV, free coffee. Kids 11 and younger free in parents' room.

Calgary Marriott Hotel
110 9th Avenue SE
1-800-228-9290 or 403-266-7331
384 air-conditioned rooms, nonsmoking floors, cable TV, valet parking, gift shop. No charge for children 17 and younger in parents' room.

Coast Plaza Hotel
1316 33rd Street NE
Off Highway 1 at 36th Street
1-800-661-1464 or 403-248-8888
148 rooms, cable TV, movies, voice mail, coffee. Indoor pool, sauna, whirlpool. Restaurant, lounge.

Delta Bow Valley Inn
209 4th Avenue SE
1-800-258-1133 or 403-266-0007
398 rooms, nonsmoking floors. Cable TV, exercise facilities, gift shop. Kids 11 and younger stay free with parents.

Econolodge
Off Highway 1 in Motel Village
1-800-4CHOICE or 403-289-2561
56 rooms and kitchenettes, laundry. Fitness center, pool, free movies. Restaurant. Kids 11 and younger stay free with parents.

Elbow River Inn & Casino
1919 Macleod Trail SE
1-800-661-1463 or 403-269-6771
75 rooms, cable TV. Restaurant with outdoor patio, cocktail lounge, casino. On the Elbow River, opposite Calgary Stampede grounds.

Greenwood Inn
3515 26th Street NE
1-888-233-6730 or 403-250-8855
150 rooms, new full-service hotel. Cable TV, nonsmoking floors, laundry and room service. Indoor pool, whirlpool, steam room. Restaurant, lounge. Rated 3 Diamond, AAA. Close to airport.

Highlander Hotel
1818 16th Avenue NW
1-800-661-9564 or 403-289-1961
130 air-conditioned rooms. Movies, gift shop, liquor store. Piper Coffee Shop, Black Angus Dining Room. 10 minutes to downtown.

Holiday Inn Downtown
119 12th Avenue SW
1-800-661-9378 or 403-266-4611
188 rooms, cable TV, movies, year-round outdoor pool. Restaurant, lounge, café. Downtown, close to attractions and shopping.

Lord Nelson Inn
1020 8th Avenue SW
1-800-661-6017 or 403-269-8262
56 air-conditioned rooms, some nonsmoking units. Refrigerators, cable TV, data ports, heated parking. Kids 17 and younger stay free with parents.

New Crossroads Hotel
2120 16th Avenue NE
1-800-661-8157 or 403-291-4666
185 deluxe rooms, executive suites, hospitality suites. Fitness room, pool, whirlpool, sauna. Nightclub, Dunn's Famous Delicatessen.

Quality Inn
2359 Banff Trail NW, off Highway 1
1-800-661-4667 or 403-289-1973
105 rooms. Indoor heated pool, whirlpool, sauna, steam room. Lounge, poolside restaurant.

Royal Wayne Motor Inn

2416 16th Avenue NW

1-800-834-8423 or 403-289-6651

53 rooms, cable and satellite TV,
refrigerators, microwaves. Outdoor pool,
whirlpool.

Sandman Hotel Downtown

888 7th Avenue SW

1-800-726-3626 or 403-237-8626

301 rooms, cable TV, movies, voice mail.
Indoor pool, whirlpool, sauna, fitness
center. 24-hour Denny's restaurant,
room service, sports pub.

Westgate Motor Inn

3440 Bow Trail SW

1-800-661-1660 or 403-249-3181

74 rooms, cable TV. Coffee shop, dining
room, liquor store. Nightclub with Top
40 music. Next to 27-hole golf course.

The Westin Calgary

320 4th Avenue SW

1-800-WESTIN-1 or 403-266-1611

525 air-conditioned rooms, nonsmoking
available. Cable TV, gift shop. Senior
discount; no charge for children 17 and
younger who stay with parents.

Campgrounds

Calaway RV Park and Campground

6 miles (10 km) west of Calgary on Highway
403-249-7372

109 sites in country setting. Showers,
laundry, dump station. Grocery store.
Walking distance to amusement park.
Shuttle service to Calgary Stampede
grounds.

Calgary West KOA

On western city limits, Highway 1 southside
near Olympic Park

1-800-562-0842 or 403-288-0411

More than 300 sites, with and without
hookup. Showers, laundry, flush toilets,
dump station. Picnic grounds, outdoor
pool, mini-golf. Bus service to
downtown and, in season, to Calgary
Stampede. Open April 15–October 15.

Mountain View Farm Camping

2 miles (3 km) east of Calgary on Highway 1

403-293-6640 or 403-285-0326

200 sites, with and without hookup.
Showers, rest room, campfire pits,
shelter. Mini-mart. Playground, petting
zoo, fish pond, mini-golf. Tours
available by coach or van. Open year-
round.

Symons Valley RV Park

Northern city limits, corner of 144th Avenue
and Symons Valley Road NW

403-274-4574

139 sites with power. Tent camping
available. Showers, laundry, dump
station. Store, dining lounge. Shuttle
available during Calgary Stampede.

Whispering Spruce Campground

8 miles (12 km) north of Calgary off
Highway 2

403-226-0097

85 sites with power; 100 without. Shower,
rest room, dump station. Mini-mart. TV
room, playground, picnic area.
Reservations accepted.

Restaurants

The Calgary Tower
101 9th Avenue
403-266-7171
Above downtown Calgary, a revolving
restaurant with a 360-degree view of
city and mountains; breakfast, lunch,
and dinner.

The Inn on Lake Bonavista
747 Lake Bonavista Drive SE
403-271-6711
Elegant dining, Sunday brunch, lake views.

Kyoto 17
908 17th Avenue SW
403-245-3188
Japanese cuisine.

La Brezza
990 1st Avenue NE
403-262-6230
Italian dishes including pasta, fish, veal
specialties.

La Dolce Vita Ristorante Italiano
& Enoteca da Franco
916 1st Avenue NE
403-263-3445
Pasta, veal, seafood in a Little Italy-area
restaurant.

Maurya
1204 Kensington Road NW
403-270-3133
East Indian cuisine; many vegetarian menu
items.

Rose Café
3802 Brentwood Road NW
403-220-9888
Family dining with a play area.

Santorini Greek Taverna
1502 Centre Street North
403-276-8363
Authentic Greek-style dishes.

Sultan's Tent
909 17th Avenue SW
403-244-2333
North African; lamb, couscous, tagines.

*Calgary's Heritage Park
reflects upon the city's roots,
from the days of the
Hudson's Bay Company forts
to farming and oil.*

Road Notes

Highway 2 between Calgary and Edmonton follows the route of a century-old trail. In the mid-1880s, entrepreneur John Dickson established several "stopping houses" along this rude trail. When he abandoned the southernmost stopping house, a neighboring homesteader, Johnston Stevenson, claimed the site and building and reopened it. Their names were merged as "Dickson-Stevenson Stopping House" for the roadhouse that served travelers during the decades that followed.

Although that building no longer stands, motorists can still pull over near its original site for rest and refreshment at the modern **Dickson-Stevenson Stopping House**, located about 24 miles (38 km) north of Calgary on Highway 2. The rest stop offers snacks, fast food, visitor information, and historical plaques about the Old Calgary Trail. The first automobile journey over the decaying trail between Calgary and Edmonton took place in 1906.

If you've been missing the nostalgic flavor of **A&W root beer** in your hometown, you'll be pleased to see that the restaurant chain is flourishing in western Canada. Northbound travelers on Highway 2 will find a quick burger and root beer at exits for Airdrie, Olds, Red Deer, and Lacombe.

A distinct line exists between city and farmland as you travel north out of Calgary. Clearly, controlled growth is under way as subdivision homes are tightly clustered in the middle distance, while cows graze alongside the road. The speed limit is 110 kmh on this six-lane highway. It's easy driving on a flat landscape. You can see a rain shower coming for miles before the first drop hits the windshield.

About an hour north of town, we discovered **Bowden**, population 936. Calgary has its Stampede, yes, but smaller versions play out in many of Alberta's midsize and small communities. In tiny towns like Bowden, kids grow up with a western legacy of competitive horsemanship. On the day we drove out of Calgary, we spotted a rodeo under way at the high school in Bowden. The town itself was nearly deserted because everyone was at the rodeo. If you see a small-town happening like that, be spontaneous. These are great opportunities to set the itinerary on the dashboard, meet some down-to-earth folks, and contribute a few bucks toward developing local talent. Who knows? Maybe you'll be helping a future star of the Calgary Stampede.

As you continue north, dairy cattle become more and more a part of the landscape, and the road is no longer a superhighway. The land begins to roll in low hills, and more sections are wooded. Here and there, you'll see evidence of the oil industry with solitary pumpjacks at work in fields and pastures.

As we entered **Red Deer**, we spied a hawk perched on the sign that gave the name of the town. We laughed because he looked like a stuffed bird in a museum exhibit that was grossly mislabeled. He just glared into space as we drove by, obviously not getting the joke.

Red Deer

From Calgary: 86 miles (139 km)
To Ponoka: 35 miles (56 km)
To Edmonton: 96 miles (154 km)

Roughly halfway between Calgary and Edmonton, Red Deer is the government seat for a county of the same name. A city of 60,000, it offers full services for travelers, from automotive repair to major shopping areas, entertainment, lodging, campgrounds, and an abundance of restaurants.

Red Deer takes pride in its area parklands, which range from swimming beaches and wooded trails, to an equestrian facility, golf courses, and (surprisingly) a ski area amid these low, rolling hills. The Red Deer River cuts a canyon through the fertile farms and parklands, and flows through the center of town.

Heritage Ranch on Highway 2 north of 32nd Street is a gateway to the Waskasoo Park system, which lies at the heart of Red Deer. A visitor center at the ranch includes knowledgeable staff, a gift shop, and a café. From here, you can walk, skate, or cycle the vast corridor of river valley nature trails. Within the park you'll find picnic areas, playgrounds, and fishing ponds. There are pony rides for the kids, too. Admission is free. Call 1-800-215-8946 or 403-346-0180

The **Kerry Wood Nature Center** hosts nature walks and canoe tours, as well as presentations for children. An exhibit gallery, theater, and bookstore are on site at 6300 45th Avenue. Admission is free. Call 403-346-2010.

You can wander through the original James Bower homestead on a lovely 10-acre site bordering Piper Creek. The homestead is at the **Sunnybrook Farm Museum and Agriculture Interpretive Centre**, which offers a relaxing as well as informative tour and a look back at the pioneering ways of running a farm. Donations are welcome. Call 403-340-3511.

Another county jewel is **Sylvan Lake**, 10 miles (16 km) west of Red Deer on Highway 11, which has been developed for holiday fun since 1901. Each summer the lake is dotted with fishermen and water-skiers, boaters, and windsurfers. Even parasailers can be seen flying overhead. Its sandy beaches are perfect for family fun, and playing on the Wild Rapids water slides will consume a whole day before you know it. Nearby are several private campgrounds and the Sylvan Lake Provincial Park.

For more information about Red Deer events and attractions, call 1-800-215-8946 or 403-346-0180, or visit the city's website at www.visitor.red-deer.ab.ca.

Lodging

Black Night Inn
2929 Gaetz Avenue
1-800-661-8793 or 403-343-6666
98 deluxe rooms, suites, cable TV.
   Whirlpool, indoor/outdoor pool, spa.
   Restaurant, lounge.

Capri Centre
3310 Gaetz Avenue
1-800-662-7197 or 403-346-2091
154 air-conditioned rooms, cable TV,
   movies, coffee. Winter plug-ins.

Courthouse Inn
4707 Ross Street
403-347-5551
58 air-conditioned rooms, cable TV, bar
   and grill. Downtown location.

Holiday Inn Express
2803 Gaetz Avenue
1-800-223-1993 or 403-343-2112
92 air-conditioned rooms, family suites.
   Cable TV, laundry, coffee. Indoor atrium
   with saltwater pool.

Red Deer Lodge
4311 49th Avenue
1-800-661-1657 or 403-346-8841
233 deluxe rooms, air-conditioning,
   phones, coffee. Indoor pool, whirlpool,
   restaurants.

Thunderbird Motel
37549 Highway 2
1-800-268-7132 or 403-343-8933
40 air-conditioned units, kitchenettes.
   Small pets welcome. Winter plug-ins.
   Adjacent to 24-hour restaurants.

Travelodge
2807 Gaetz Avenue
1-800-578-7878 or 403-346-2011
136 air-conditioned rooms, kitchenettes and
   nonsmoking available. Modem access,
   self-service laundry. Indoor pool,
   whirlpool. Restaurant.

Waskasoo Inn
4124 Gaetz Avenue
1-888-822-9696 or 403-342-6969
48 air-conditioned rooms, kitchenettes and
   nonsmoking available. Cable TV.
   Restaurants nearby.

Area Campgrounds

Red Deer:

Lions Campground
Riverside Drive, east of 49th Avenue
403-342-8183
89 sites with full hookups, 38 with partial.
   Dump station. Playground, bike trails to
   Waskasoo Park.

Sylvan Lake:

A-Soo-Wuh-Um Campground
West off Highway 2 on Route 592 for 6.5
   miles (10.5 km)
403-886-2001
Campsites, free showers and firewood. Boat
   launch, fishing, playground.

Lakeside Family RV Park
5040 53rd Street
403-887-4234
61 sites with full hookup, 18 dry campsites.
   Showers, rest rooms, picnic tables, fire
   pits. Next to golf; across from water
   park and marina.

Lakewood Golf Course & RV Park
North of Sylvan Lake on Highway 20, then
 east
60 RV sites with full or partial hookups.
 Showers, laundry, whirlpool,
 playground. Next to golf course.

Sunny Siesta RV Park
Corner of Highway 11 and Route 781
1-888-888-1187 or 403-887-2173
77 large sites with full or partial hookups,
 some pull-throughs, tent camping.
 Showers, rest rooms, picnic tables,
 playground.

Sylvan Southland Golf & Resort
Corner of Highway 11 and Route 781
403-887-5100
39 sites with full or partial hookup, some
 pull-throughs. Picnic tables, fire pits.
 Nine-hole golf course and driving
 range.

Restaurants

City Roast Coffee House
4940 50th Street
403-347-0893
Specialty coffees, lunches, desserts.
 Downtown.

Dino's Family Restaurant
4617 50th Avenue
403-347-5585
Italian and western cuisine, pizza, pasta.

The Donut Mill
On Highway 2, south end of town
403-347-8904
Windmill-style donut shop; also
 sandwiches, soups. Open 24 hours.

Earl's Place
2222 50th Avenue
403-342-4055
Burgers, pasta, steak, and more.

Glenn's Family Restaurant
On Highway 2, south end of town
403-346-5448
Pastries, daily specials.

Humpty's Family Restaurant
Two locations:
7110 Gaetz Avenue: 403-340-3288
2325 Gaetz Avenue: 403-346-9590
Breakfast specialty; burgers, soups,
 sandwiches, pizza.

The Keg Steakhouse & Bar
6365 50th Avenue
403-309-5499
Steak, prime rib, seafood, pasta.

Molly B's Family Restaurant & Lounge
2810 Bremner Avenue
403-342-0035
Breakfast, lunch, dinner; patio seating.

Rosie's Restaurant
2085 Gaetz Avenue
403-343-3833
Family dining; kids' menu.

Wildflower Bistro
1927 Gaetz Avenue
403-341-5400
Seafood, steak, chicken, ribs.

Road Notes

A clever farmer just beyond Red Deer has an interesting combination of livestock in his pasture: Arabian horses, llamas, and alpacas can be seen grazing together in harmony.

Farther along, a display well-rig stands on the left amid more fields. During late summer, farmers bale the hay into huge, golden rolls that remain in the fields.

As you travel, you'll decide where to spend your nights—in the dazzling excitement of the big city, off the highway in a provincial park, or maybe in a private campground.

During our trip, the day was winding down as we approached Edmonton. Rather than push hard and navigate a strange city in the dark (in an RV), we chose to spend the night in Ponoka, 35 miles (56 km) north of Red Deer.

$\mathcal{P}$ONOKA

From Calgary: 121 miles (195 km)
To Edmonton: 60 miles (97 km)

This sleepy little western town of 6,147 people explodes into life each summer when the **Ponoka Stampede** picks up speed. In late June and early July, the city hosts a six-day rodeo extravaganza—second only to the Calgary event in all of Canada. Highlights include professional rodeo, chuckwagon races, midway rides, entertainment, fireworks, a beer garden, and a dance. RV parking on site is free during the Stampede, but it's a first-come, first-served opportunity. For tickets or information, call 403-783-0100.

Ponoka ("elk" in the Blackfoot language) lies on the Battle River, site of a major clash in the early 1880s between two local Native peoples, the Blackfoot and the Cree.

Just south of town, you'll find a first-class, 18-hole golf course at **Wolf Creek Golf Resort**. History buffs will want to visit **Fort Ostell Museum** in Centennial Park, at 5320 54th Street. For information, call 403-783-5224.

An interesting slice of history can be seen at the **Rodeo Museum**, next to the Stampede grounds. We camped at the RV park adjacent to the grounds (see list of campgrounds). I remember hearing the comforting moo of cattle as I dozed off. (Magpies woke us up the next morning.) Later, I learned that Ponoka is known as the Cattle Capital of Canada. As we drove back to the highway, I spotted the expansive stockyards near the RV park.

To restock your RV refrigerator or cooler, you'll find an **IGA grocery store** on the main drag, at 4502 50th Street. The store has a spacious parking lot for RVs and offers fresh-baked goods, produce, meat, grocery, deli, and a post office. A 24-hour cash machine is located at Ponoka Savings & Credit Union, at 4802 50th Street.

For more on accommodations or other visitor information, contact 403-783-4431 or www.ponoka.org.

Lodging

Oasis Motel

5641 48th Avenue (corner of Highway 2A
and Highway 53)
1-888-506-2747 or 403-783-3452
12 air-conditioned rooms, some
kitchenettes. Cable TV, in-room coffee,
refrigerator.

Ponoka Stampeder Inn

4215 63rd Street (on Highway 2A south)
403-783-5535
58 air-conditioned units, some kitchenettes.
Cable TV, wheelchair-accessible room.
Adjacent to restaurant.

Riverside Motor Inn

3825 45th Street (on Highway 53 east)
403-783-4444
40 rooms, cable TV. No charge for children
under 12 sharing parents' room. Adjoins
park.

Wolf Creek Inn

West side of Highway 2, just south of
Highway 2A turnoff to Lacombe
403-782-4716
20 rooms, satellite TV, continental
breakfast. Golf packages available.

Campgrounds

Ponoka Stampede Trailer Park

On Highway 53, east of Highways 53 and 2A
junction

403-783-5611
RV and tent camping next door to the
Ponoka Stampede grounds. Full hookups
available, or sites with or without
electric; drive-through sites. Showers,
dump station. Open May–September.

Poplar Grove Mobile & RV Park

6025 54th Street
403-783-6504
9 full-service RV sites, dump station, no
public washrooms. Playground, trees,
quiet.

Restaurants

Boston Pizza

Corner of Highway 2A and 60th Street
403-783-6600
Pizza, steaks, pasta, salads. Satellite TV in
the lounge.

Hamilton's IGA Deli

4502 50th Street
Near Stampede grounds
403-783-3001
Deli sandwiches and baked goods to go.

Super Food Drive-In Restaurant

5413 48th Avenue
403-783-3434
Big burgers, chicken, ice cream, shakes.

Road Notes

Back on the road to Edmonton, just north of Ponoka you'll find a roadside turnout
with a litter barrel and pay phone. Along here the trees have thinned out again. It's
mostly farms and fields, and many local drivers sport cowboy hats. Fifteen miles
(24 km) from Ponoka is a major rest stop for northbound travelers, with a diner, fuel,
store, and picnic area.

We recommend a side trip through Devon on your way to Edmonton. Just before the town of Luduc, turn west on Highway 39, then north on Highway 60 to visit the **Leduc No. 1 Historic Site**, birthplace of Alberta's oil industry. Here the first major oil find was made on February 13, 1947. A 174-foot (53-m) replica of the original oil derrick stands beside an information center. Other tools of the trade and interpretive signs may be viewed in outdoor and indoor exhibits.

From May to mid-October, you can visit the **Devonian Botanic Garden**, operated by the University of Alberta, on Highway 60 about 3 miles (5 km) north of Devon. Various gardens roll over its 80 acres, including the popular Kurimoto Japanese Garden. You can walk among the butterflies in the Butterfly House and on trails through forest and wetlands. Orchid lovers will find their own house of orchids. There's a gift shop and picnic area, too, and plenty of parking for RV travelers.

$\mathcal{E}$DMONTON

From Calgary: 181 miles (291 km)
To Whitecourt: 112 miles (180 km)

Edmonton is an old city by western standards. It dates back to 1795, when the Hudson's Bay Company established Edmonton House, a trading post along the mighty North Saskatchewan River. Here, local Cree and Blackfoot Indians traded furs for goods. After a century of growth, it was an incorporated city of 700 people. Another century passed to find Edmonton a city of polish and sophistication sprouting in the midst of fields, reminiscent of the Emerald City in *The Wizard of Oz*. The area population today: 628,000.

This is Alberta's capital city, Canada's second-largest metropolitan area west of

The Edmonton Space & Science Centre is an architectural beauty.

Toronto, and the fifth-largest city in Canada. Edmonton also is home to West Edmonton Mall, the largest shopping mall in the world (see accompanying sidebar).

Edmonton is known as the **Oil Capital of Canada**. Edmonton Tourism cites this amazing statistic: The amount of crude oil processed in metropolitan Edmonton each day is enough to change the oil of every car in Canada.

The dollars from oil have been poured into the culture and comfort of the citizenry. The city has 22 art and history museums and 13 theater companies (more per capita than any other city in Canada). Rain or shine, downtown pedestrians can freely move about in elevated, enclosed walkways or through underground and street-level "pedways."

There are 24 golf courses within the city limits, hundreds of shops, dozens of hotels, and more than 2,000 dining establishments. If you want to spend money and feel like you're getting something for it, this is the place to visit. And by the way, Alberta has no provincial sales tax.

Edmonton is a city that loves to play—every month, it seems, the city hosts a festival, rodeo, carnival, anniversary, or other celebration, earning it yet another title: Festival City. Here's a flavor of the year-round celebrations of music, theater, history, horsemanship, and home:

Spring. The Edmonton Boat & Sportsmen's Show (early March); LaBatt Brier Curling (mid-March); Edmonton Home and Garden Show (late March); Northlands Farm & Ranch Show (late March); Cody Snyder's Bullbustin' (early April); Edmonton Kiwanis Music Festival (late April); Kinsmen Rainmaker Rodeo (late May).

Summer. Northern Alberta International Children's Festival (early June); Medieval Days (early June); Jazz City International Music Festival (late June, early July); The Works: A Visual Arts Celebration (late June, early July); Edmonton Canada Day—Celebrate Canada (early July); Edmonton International Street Performers Festival (early to mid-July); Edmonton's Klondike Days (late July); RCMP's March West (late July); Edmonton Heritage Days Festival (early August); Edmonton Folk Music Festival (early to mid-August); Cariwest: Edmonton Caribbean Carnival (mid-August); Fringe Theatre Festival (mid- to late August).

Fall/Winter. The Edmonton Symphony Orchestra Festival (early September); World Championships of Musical Whistling (early September); Edmonton Fall Women's Show (mid-October); Fairfarm International (mid-November); Canadian Finals Rodeo (mid-November); Festival of Trees (late November); Edmonton's First Night Festival (December 31).

For stunning beauty, albeit manmade, visit the **Great Divide Waterfall** on the High Level Bridge. Built to honor Alberta's 75th anniversary, the waterfall is 24 feet higher than Niagara Falls.

The **Provincial Museum of Alberta** is one of Canada's most popular museums, featuring exhibits on a broad range of subjects, from the province's aboriginal people to dinosaurs, geology, insects, Ice Age mammals, and more. Admission is charged. Call 780-453-9100 or visit www.pma.edmonton.ab.ca.

Fort Edmonton Park, at Fox and Whitemud Drives, is a 158-acre living-history park, the country's largest, with 60 period buildings to explore. Walk through time at the 1846 fort, or down streets from 1885, 1905, and 1920. Watch a blacksmith or an old-fashioned rope-maker at work. Catch a ride on a stagecoach or the steam train. This is a great place to teach kids about history while they're having fun. You'll find plenty of gift shops and restaurants. For more information: 780-496-8787 or visit the website www.gov.edmonton.ab.ca/fort.

A futuristic building at 142nd and 112th Avenues houses the **Edmonton Space & Science Centre**. Inside, kids and adults alike will enjoy observation and hands-on science—from helping to solve a crime with forensic science, to learning more about wildfires, the weather, and other natural phenomena. Features include a planetarium, laser shows, mock Challenger missions, and an IMAX theater. Call 780-451-3344 or visit www.edmontonscience.com.

Shopping with a Map

The **West Edmonton Mall** sprawls over a 110-acre site, featuring 800 stores and services, an ice arena, thrill rides, kiddie rides, a water park, and aquariums. Located at 87th Avenue and 170th Street, it's not hard to find. Roadside signs will lead the way. And once you're inside, you'll pick up a map to figure your way from there. Wear your walking shoes, and be sure to bring your swimsuit, ice skates, and maybe your bowling ball.

This remarkable indoor megamall—billed as the largest shopping and entertainment center in the world—includes more than 110 restaurants, plus a host of attractions that could serve as parks all by themselves. Kids in Edmonton have no excuse for saying, "There's nothing to do." More likely it's, "There's too much to do!"

The mall includes Galaxyland Amusement Park, with 24 rides and attractions; World Waterpark, with slides, a wave pool, and kiddie water play; the Deep Sea Adventure, with submarine rides, performing dolphins, and a full-size replica of the Columbus ship Santa Maria; Professor Wem's Adventure Golf, a miniature course; and the Ice Palace, an ice rink that's occasionally used by the Edmonton Oilers hockey team. Dining and entertainment options include Planet Hollywood, Red's, Hard Rock Café, and Jubilations Live Dinner Theatre.

For more information, call 780-444-5200 or visit www.westedmonton mall.com. ●

Church Street (officially 96th Street) is listed in *Ripley's Believe It or Not* for the 16 churches you'll find in one small section. Another local "oddity," although it's not listed in *Ripley's*, is Edmonton's prized four-story-high cowboy boot at **Western Boot Factory**, 10007 167th Street. This city also claims the distinction of having the longest stretch of urban park in Canada: the North Saskatchewan River Valley park system.

The **Alberta Legislature Building**, at 10800 97th Avenue, is an architectural wonder built in 1912 on the site of Fort Edmonton. An interpretive center follows the building's history and provincial politics. Guided tours are available daily. Call for scheduled times at 780-427-7362 or visit the website at www.assembly.ab.ca.

If the one-armed bandit or cards are your game, visit **Casino Edmonton** in two locations: 7055 Argyll Road or downtown at 10549 102nd Street. Call 780-424-9467. These establishments offer poker, blackjack, slots, roulette, fine dining, and entertainment. Another gaming option is **Baccarat Casino** at 10128 104th Avenue. Call 780-413-3178.

For more information on local events and attractions, call **Edmonton Tourism** at 1-800-463-4667 or 780-496-8400 or visit their website: www.tourism.ede.org.

Lodging

Argyle Plaza Hotel
9933 63rd Avenue
1-800-661-6454 or 780-438-5876
48 rooms, kitchenettes, suites, cable TV, movies. Whirlpool, sauna, lounge, restaurant.

Best Western City Centre
11310 109th Street
1-800-666-5026 or 780-479-2042
110 air-conditioned rooms, indoor pool, whirlpool. Restaurant, lounge. Close to shopping.

Best Western Westwood Inn
1-800-557-4767 or 780-483-7770
18035 Stony Plain Road
169 air-conditioned rooms, cable TV, movies, laundry service. Indoor pool, sauna, whirlpool, steam room, squash court. Restaurant, lounge.

Chateau Louis Hotel
11727 Kingsway
1-800-661-9843 or 780-452-7770
146 rooms, suites, family rooms. 24-hour room service, restaurant, lounge.

Coast Edmonton Plaza Hotel
10155 105th Street
1-800-HOTELS1 or 780-423-4811
295 deluxe rooms, suites, cable TV, laundry service. Exercise room, indoor pool. Lounge, family restaurant. Downtown, close to business and government.

Coast Terrace Inn
4440 Calgary Trail North
1-888-837-7223 or 780-437-6010
234 air-conditioned rooms. Fitness and racquet club, indoor pool, sauna, steam rooms. Restaurant, lounge, pub. Located between airport and downtown.

Comfort Inn—Journey's End
17610 100th Avenue West
1-800-228-5150 or 780-484-4415
100 rooms, cable TV, movies, restaurant.
Close to West Edmonton Mall.

Crowne Plaza Chateau Lacombe
10111 Bellamy Hill
1-800-661-8801 or 780-428-6611
307 deluxe rooms, suites, in 24-story hotel.
Gift shop, revolving restaurant, café,
two lounges. Close to shopping,
entertainment. Airport shuttle.

Delta Edmonton Centre Suite Hotel
10222 102nd Street
1-800-661-6655 or 780-429-3900
169 deluxe suites and rooms. Whirlpool,
sauna, restaurant, lounge. Downtown,
in Eaton Centre Shopping Complex.

Edmonton House Suite Hotel
10205 100th Avenue
1-800-661-6562 or 780-420-4000
300 four-room suites with kitchens,
balconies. Indoor pool, exercise and
game rooms. Store, restaurant, lounge.
Airport shuttle.

Greenwood Inn
4485 Calgary Trail NB
1-888-233-6730 or 780-431-1100
224 rooms in new southside hotel. Cable TV,
movies, laundry service. Indoor pool,
whirlpool, steam room, exercise room.
Gift shop, restaurant.

Howard Johnson Plaza Hotel
1001 104th Street
1-800-446-4656 or 780-2450
138 air-conditioned rooms, cable TV,
balconies. Laundry facilities, room
service. Indoor pool, whirlpool, sauna.
Restaurant, lounge.

Ramada Inn & Waterpark
5359 Calgary Trail
1-800-661-9030 or 780-434-3431
122 rooms, nonsmoking floor, cable TV,
movies, laundry service. City's first
water-park hotel, with two water slides,
pool, exercise room, hot tub.
Restaurant, lounge.

Rodeway Inn
10425 100th Avenue
1-888-384-6835 or 780-423-5611
108 air-conditioned rooms. Indoor pool,
sauna, whirlpool. Restaurant, lounge.
Downtown.

Trailway Motel
3815 Calgary Trail North
780-435-3863
50 air-conditioned rooms and kitchenettes.
Laundry service, winter plug-ins. Close
to West Edmonton Mall and airport.

Travelodge Beverly Crest
13414 118th Avenue
1-800-665-0456 or 780-474-0456
86 rooms, cable TV, adjoining units. Barber
shop, restaurant, lounge. Cold-weather
hookups. Easy access to Yellowhead
Highway.

Travelodge Edmonton South
10320 45th Avenue South
1-800-578-7878 or 780-436-9770
223 rooms with cable TV, movies, room
service. Indoor pool, whirlpool.
Restaurant. Close to shopping, dining,
nightclubs.

Area Campgrounds

Leduc:

Lions Campground
20 miles (32 km) south of Edmonton
50th Street South, then east on Rollyview
   Road
780-986-1882
55 sites with full hookups, tent area.
   Washroom, phone, dump station.
   Heated picnic shelter. Reservations
   accepted.

Devon:

River Valley Lions Campground
20 miles (32 km) southwest of Edmonton
520 Haven Avenue
780-987-4777
125 sites with and without full hookups; tent
   camping. Rest rooms, fire pits. Playgrounds, baseball diamond, horseshoe
   pits. On the North Saskatchewan River.
   Open May 1—October 15.

Sherwood Park:

Half Moon Lake Resort
16 miles (25.5 km) east of Edmonton via
   23rd Avenue
780-922-3045
196 sites, with and without power. Hayrides,
   ponies, horseback rides, petting zoo,
   wading pool, lake, playground, trout
   pond, mini-golf, boat rentals.
   Reservations accepted.

Edmonton:

Glowing Embers Travel Centre RV Park
2 miles (3.2 km) west of Edmonton on
   Highways 16A and 60
780-962-8100
273 full-service sites. Washrooms, laundry,
   store. Close to West Edmonton Mall.
   Reservations accepted.

Klondike Valley Campground
1660 Calgary Trail SW (Highway 2 and
   Ellerslie Road)
780-988-5067
160 sites, full hookups and pull-throughs
   available, tent camping, group
   camping available. Showers, laundry,
   toilets, washrooms. Grocery store. Close
   to West Edmonton Mall. Open May 1—
   September 30.

Rainbow Valley Campground
Whitemud Park off 122nd Street, south of
   Whitemud Freeway
1-888-434-3991 or 780-434-5531
85 sites, with and without power; tent
   camping. Showers, washrooms, laundry,
   dump station. Store, playground. Open
   mid-April—September 30. Reservations
   accepted.

Shakers Acres
21530 103rd Avenue (off Highway 16A)
780-447-3564
170 sites with full or partial hookups,
   showers, laundry, public phone.

Restaurants

Avenue Pizza & Lounge
8519 112th Street
780-431-0091
Pizza, pasta, hamburgers.

Chili's Texas Grill
Three locations:
17020 100th Avenue: 780-489-6060
9315 137th Avenue: 780-478-0606
10333 34th Avenue: 780-430-0606
Southwest cooking.

The Crêperie
10220 103rd Street
780-420-6656
French country, crêpes.

Edmonton Queen
Rafter's Landing, south side of the river
403-424-2628
Authentic paddlewheeler, with lunch and
    dinner cruises. Buffet-style dining with
    Dixieland entertainment.

Hardware Grill
9698 Jasper Avenue
780-423-0609
Canadian fare with seasonal specialties.

Hy's Steak Loft
10013 101A Avenue
780-424-4444
Specializing in Alberta beef.

Louisiana Purchase Restaurant
10320 111th Street
780-420-6779
Cajun specialties for lunch or dinner.

Sorrentino's
Six locations:
10844 95th Street: 780-425-0960
10162 100th Street: 780-424-7500
6867 170th Street: 780-444-0524
10612 82nd Avenue: 780-434-7607
595 St. Albert Road, St. Albert: 780-
    459-1411
1020 Sherwood Drive, Sherwood Park: 780-
    449-1384
Italian ambience and cuisine. Winner of
    Birk's Silver Spoon Award as voted by
    Edmonton's hotel concierges.

Syrtaki Greek Island Restaurant
16313 111th Avenue
780-484-2473
Authentic Greek dining.

Road Notes

To leave Edmonton, take Highway 43 west toward Spruce Grove and Stony Plain.
You'll stay on Route 43 all the way across northern Alberta as it wends north and west.

A series of small towns along Route 43 forms a dot-to-dot line between Edmonton
and Whitecourt. Services and facilities such as gas stations, self-service laundries,
restaurants, motels, and campgrounds are available all along this stretch.

(A few miles past Stony Plain is the junction for the westbound Yellowhead
Highway 16. For more information, see the section on the Yellowhead-Cassiar
Highways in Chapter 7, Western Canada's Northbound Byways.)

WHITECOURT

From Edmonton: 91 miles (147 km)
To Valleyview: 102 miles (164 km)
To Grande Prairie: 175 miles (282 km)

The confluence of the Athabasca and McLeod Rivers, two major transportation
routes, seemed a natural place for a settlement to spring up in rich, forested land. A

family-operated sawmill was established here in 1922 and has since grown into a major employer, along with two other timber-related companies. Forestry, oil and gas, sand and gravel, and tourism keep Whitecourt's people happy and hard at work. The proof lies in the statistics: Less than 3 percent of the population of 8,200 is unemployed, and nearly half of all adults are involved in some form of volunteerism.

The **Whitecourt Tourist Information Centre** is open 7 days a week in summer, and offers directions and advice as well as plenty of printed material. Choices for local recreation include horseback riding, boating, fishing, shopping, or visiting a guest ranch. Watch for moose, deer, and elk in this area. Less visible are black and brown bears.

Golfers are invited to try their hand at the par-72 **Graham Acre Golf and Country Club**. There's something to satisfy every level of expertise, from practice on the putting green and driving range to the challenging 18-hole course itself. Refreshments and snacks are available in the clubhouse.

To prepare for a fishing adventure, call the Fish and Wildlife office in downtown Whitecourt at 780-778-7112 for license and season information. Go after walleye,

Just Local Folks on Holiday

Labor Day is spelled Labour Day in Canada, and it's just as good a reason to go on holiday in early September with the family. At Williamson Provincial Park in Alberta, we found a young family enjoying a long weekend on the lake.

Lloyd McKinney, wife Carla, and their children Ashley and Kyle had driven more than 100 miles north to get to this picturesque campground on Sturgeon Lake. For travelers headed to Alaska, that's a blip along a long, long road. But for the McKinneys, who live in Whitecourt, that's a road trip. Although they live along the Alaska Highway, they've never been to Alaska, Lloyd said, but they're thinking about heading up the highway soon. ●

The McKinney family enjoys a four-day weekend at a provincial campground along Sturgeon Lake.

northern pike, rainbows, and grayling. Another option is to hire a guide at operations such as **Eagle River Outfitting**, at 780-778-3251, which offers half-day and full-day services or drop-off fishing, wilderness camping, and float fishing trips over several days. With a guide, you can expect to pay close to $100 for half a day or about $170 for a full day per person.

The forest products industry has a standing invitation for visitors to tour local state-of-the-art sawmills and fiberboard and pulp plants. For a program of industrial tours, stop by the Chamber of Commerce office on Highway 43 by the traffic lights.

Just northwest of town on Highway 32, you'll find the **Eric S. Heustis Demonstration Forest**, with 4 miles (6.5 km) of self-guided trails and interpretive sites about forest management and the forest industry. Near the entrance, a variety of trees are identified on interpretive plaques.

For more information on Whitecourt, visit the city's website at www.town. whitecourt.ab.ca.

Lodging

Glenview Motel
Just off Highway 43 Southwest
780-778-2276
31 air-conditioned rooms, nonsmoking available. Cable TV, café.

Green Gables Inn
3527 Highway Street
780-778-4537
49 units, kitchenettes, some nonsmoking. Cable TV with movie channel, free coffee.

Quality Inn
5420 47th Avenue, just off Highway 43 North
1-800-228-5151
80 air-conditioned rooms, suites. Executive rooms with fax/modem outlets. Cable TV, sauna, hot tub, exercise facility. 24-hour café, restaurant; dining overlooks McLeod River.

Renford Inn - Whitecourt
Just off Highway 43 Southwest
780-778-3133
Newly renovated air-conditioned rooms and kitchenettes. Laundry facilities, free coffee.

The Ritz Café & Motor Inn
Highway 43 North, between Athabascan and McLeod Rivers
780-778-5055
62 air-conditioned rooms, executive and honeymoon suites available. Refrigerators, fax service, free coffee. Pets welcome.

Royal Oak Inn
3305 Highway Street
780-778-4004
28 rooms, some nonsmoking. Complimentary newspaper, entertainment on Friday and Saturday nights. Children under 12 free in parents' room.

Super 8 Motel Whitecourt
4121 Kepler Street
780-778-8908
61 air-conditioned rooms, king and queen
suites with whirlpool. Continental
breakfast, voice mail, modem outlets,
laundry service.

Travelodge Hotel Whitecourt
5003 50th Street
1-888-778-2216 or 780-778-2216
74 air-conditioned rooms, suites,
nonsmoking available. Cable TV and
movie channel, fax/modem outlets,
pool, sauna. Lounge, family restaurant,
country nightclub.

Campgrounds

Alaska Highway Motel & RV Park
3511 Highway Street
780-778-4156
22 campsites. Showers, rest rooms, dump
station. Sheltered picnic sites.

Carson-Pegasus Provincial Park
16 miles (25 km) north of Whitecourt on
Highway 43; follow signs
780-778-2664
182 sites with partial hookup; group
camping, firewood. Showers, laundry,
tap water, dump station. Store. Beach,
swimming, fishing, wheelchair-
accessible fishing area, horseshoe pits.
Reservations accepted.

McLeod River Campground & Cabins
6 miles (10 km) on Highway 32 south of
Whitecourt, then about a mile and a
quarter (2 km) east on McLeod River
780-778-3251
RV and tent campsites, some along the
river; full hookup available. Guest
cabins, kitchenettes. Swimming, fishing,
boat rentals, guide service. Reservations
accepted.

Sagitawah Tourist Park
780-778-3734
Full hookups, pull-throughs. Free showers;
laundry, fire pits. Store, propane sales,
RV parts and service. Playground, mini-
golf, movie rentals. Senior discount.

Whitecourt Lions Club Campground
1 mile (1.5 km) east of Whitecourt on
Highway 43
780-778-6782
Pull-throughs, water, firewood, showers,
laundry facility, dump station. Lots of
trees, playground, horseshoe pits.
Senior discount.

White-Kaps Motel & RV Park
Next to tourist information center on
Highway 43
780-778-6782
70 sites with power and tap water. Free
showers; laundry, washrooms.

Restaurants

A & W
Hilltop on Highway 43
780-778-6611
Burgers, fries, shakes, root beer specialties.

Boston Pizza

3836 Kepler Street, Highway 43 SW

780-778-2500

Family dining, pizza, pasta, sandwiches.

Ernie O's Restaurant & Pub

Next to the Guest House Inn

780-778-8600

Steaks, seafood.

Green Gables Inn Restaurant

Highway 43

780-778-3142

Lunch and dinner, steaks, seafood, ribs,
prime rib, salad bar.

KG's Sandwich Bar

4912 50th Avenue

780-778-5286

Fresh-baked cinnamon buns, homemade
soups.

Mountain Pizza & Steakhouse

3823 Highway Street

780-778-3600

Pizza, steaks, Italian food, ribs, chicken,
soups, salad.

Road Notes

Between Whitecourt and Grande Prairie are 172 miles (277 km) of increasingly striking vistas as the route leads toward the foothills of the Canadian Rockies and away from populated areas. The Athabasca River, then the Little Smoky River, may be seen along the road as you continue north and west on Highway 43.

Fifty miles (80.5 km) past Whitecourt is **Fox Creek**, the seat of the area's oil-and-gas exploration efforts. Lodging, meals, laundry facilities, and gas stations may be found in this community. A few miles farther still is the tiny town of Little Smoky.

Just before you enter **Valleyview**, a roadside visitor information center and rest stop offers picnic tables, water, and a dump station for RV travelers. You can make a phone call, mail a letter, and buy souvenirs here, too.

Valleyview calls itself the Portal to the Peace Country, a region through which the mighty Peace River flows. Originally a transportation route for trappers, explorers, and traders, the river today is famed for its outdoor recreation opportunities. When you reach Valleyview, you have traveled 214 miles (344.5 km) from Edmonton. Grande Prairie, the next large community on the Alaska Highway, lies 70 miles (112.5 km) ahead, via Highway 43.

Eleven miles (17.5 km) past Valleyview, we followed the signs to **Williamson Provincial Park** for our next overnight stay. Located on Sturgeon Lake, Williamson Park is a forested campground, which lends a sense of privacy to each campsite. The park offers 60 sites, with full or partial hookups, or tent camping. There are showers, a dump station, and a public phone. The nearby lake is an easy place to launch a boat to fish for perch, pickerel, northern pike, or whitefish.

Other camping also is available on this stretch of Highway 43 that leads to Grande Prairie. Watch for private and provincial campground signs.

$\mathcal{G}$RANDE PRAIRIE

From Whitecourt: 175 miles (282 km)
To Dawson Creek: 75 miles (121 km)

Grande Prairie, at the junction of Highways 43 and 40, is the regional center for northwest Alberta and northeast British Columbia, with an economy that's based on agriculture, forestry, oil, and gas. The city symbol is the trumpeter swan, and these elegant white birds are frequently seen on local lakes. As you enter the city, stay on the Highway 43 bypass and watch for the blue-and-white question-mark signs that lead the way to the **Visitor Information Centre**, with rest rooms and tourism literature. Right next door is a Rotary Club campground along the reservoir (see list of campgrounds). The fraternal organization offers a free city tour every Monday.

This region was home to First Nations people for centuries. The first white arrivals were fur traders, who came on the scene in 1771. The town's name is credited to Father Emile Grouard, who first viewed this vast, treeless around Lake Saskatoon in the mid-1800s and called it *la grande prairie*. The first settlement here was established in 1911. Today more than 34,000 people live in a city that has prospered since its founding.

At the information center, ask for directions to **Kleskun Hills**, east of town, where you can view fossilized marine life and dinosaur remains in an area that was once a river delta. Or visit the **Crystal Lake Waterfowl Refuge** for birding, walking along nature trails, or just soaking up the sunshine. Call 780-538-0451 for details.

Another local natural treasure is **Muskoseepi Park**, which covers about 1,000 acres in Bear Creek Valley. The park pavilion is the stage for outdoor concerts and festivals. Recreation includes camping, golf, hiking, wildlife-watching, and lawn bowling. The park also invites swimming, boating, fishing, and other water sports.

In this wonderful park you'll find the **Grande Prairie Museum**, which features exhibits on dinosaurs, aboriginal tribes, explorers, trappers, traders, missionaries, and pioneer families. Early-day buildings, churches, and bridges moved here from their original sites tell the story of the city's beginnings. The museum is wheelchair accessible and open year-round. Call 780-532-5482.

To learn more about northern Alberta's forestry industry, visit the pulp mill, sawmill, and forests of **Weyerhaeuser Canada**, which offers public tours every weekday. Call 780-539-8687 for a reservation.

Lodging

Canadian Motor Inn
10901 100th Avenue
1-800-291-7893 or 780-532-1680
63 air-conditioned rooms, kitchenettes and
    nonsmoking available. Cable TV, in-room
coffee, laundry, whirlpools, winter
plug-ins. Restaurant, pub.

Golden Inn

11201 100th Avenue

1-800-661-7954 or 780-539-6000

102 air-conditioned rooms, executive suites, kitchenettes, nonsmoking rooms available. Cable TV, gift shop, liquor store, shuttle.

The Grande Prairie

11633 Clairmont Road

1-800-661-6529 or 780-532-5221

Deluxe air-conditioned rooms. Whirlpool, sauna, indoor pool. Gift shop, restaurant, piano bar lounge, nightclub. Three-Diamond rating, AAA. Next to major shopping mall.

Igloo Inn

11724 100th Street

1-800-665-0769 or 780-539-5314

80 air-conditioned rooms. Indoor pool, water slide, hot tub, sauna.

The Lodge Motor Inn

10909 100th Avenue (Highway 2 West)

1-800-661-7874 or 780-539-4700

Air-conditioned rooms with cable TV. Heated outdoor pool in summer. Restaurant.

Sandman Hotel Grande Prairie

9805 100th Street

1-800-726-3626 or 780-513-5555

137 air-conditioned rooms, executive suites, nonsmoking available. Cable TV, fax/modem outlets, in-room movies and games. Fitness facilities, swimming pool, hot tub, whirlpools. 24-hour Denny's restaurant adjacent.

Service Plus Inns & Suites

10810 107A Avenue

780-538-3900

99 deluxe air-conditioned rooms. Cable TV, movies, laundry service, continental breakfast. Indoor pool. Restaurant, lounge/casino.

Silver Crest Lodge

11902 100th Street

1-800-422-7791 or 780-532-1040

95 rooms, 40 with air-conditioning; nonsmoking available, kitchenettes. Cable and satellite TV, free coffee and donuts. Winter plug-ins. No charge for children under 12.

Stanford Inn

11401 100th Avenue

1-800-661-8160 or 780-539-5678

209 newly renovated rooms, nonsmoking available. In-room movies and coffee, computer jacks. Restaurant, pub, liquor store. Children under 12 free in parents' room.

Super 8 Motel

10050 116th Avenue

1-888-888-9488 or 780-532-8288

103 air-conditioned rooms, suites, kitchenettes; nonsmoking floors available. Laundry, free continental breakfast and newspaper. Indoor heated pool with water slide, exercise room, barbecue area with playground.

Travelodge Trumpeter Motor Inn

12102 100th Avenue

1-800-661-9435 or 780-539-5561

116 air-conditioned rooms, suites, nonsmoking available. In-room coffee and newspaper. Liquor store.

Campgrounds

Camp Tamarack RV Park

5 miles (8.5 km) south of Grande Prairie on
Highway 40
1-877-532-9998 or 780-532-9998
87 sites with power and water, most with
pull-throughs. Private showers, laundry,
rest rooms, dump station. Satellite and
cable hookups, fax machine, Internet
access. Store, RV supplies, RV pressure-
wash, recreation room. Newly opened
park, lots of trees.

Country Road RV Park

2.5 miles (4 km) west of Highways 43 and 2
junction
780-532-6323
19 sites with full hookups, some pull-
throughs; tent sites. Showers, laundry,
washrooms, fire pits, lots of trees. Open
year-round.

Grande Prairie Rotary Park

On Highway 43 bypass
780-532-1137
59 sites with full and partial hookups.
Firewood, shelter, laundry, phone. No
reservations.

Saskatoon Island Provincial Park

13 miles (21 km) west of Grande Prairie and
2.5 miles (4 km) north of Highway 43
780-766-2636
96 sites with partial hookups; group
camping and day-use area. Dump
station, store. Beach, swimming,
playground, wheelchair access.

Restaurants

Boston Pizza

12117 100th Street
780-532-0310
Ribs, sandwiches, pizza, salads, lounge.

Dragon Palace Restaurant & Lounge

10512 100th Avenue
780-539-5540
Chinese cuisine, prime rib, steak, seafood.

The Golden Star

10112 101st Avenue
403-532-7549
Chinese and western dishes.

Moxie's Classic Grill

11801 100th Street, No. 212
780-532-4401
Family dining, pasta, desserts.

Paolo's Ristorante

9728 Montrose Avenue
780-814-7400
Authentic Italian cuisine, seafood, steaks.

Shell's

1000 101st Avenue
780-539-5002
Seafood specialties and more.

Road Notes

Eighty-three miles (133.5 km) ahead is Dawson Creek. Don't let a finish-line mentality stop you from enjoying the hospitality offered by small towns between Grande Prairie and Dawson Creek, however. **Wembley, Beaverlodge, Tupper,** and **Pouce Coupe** are towns of varying size and distinct personalities. This region is steeped in pioneering history, so be sure to take in small-town attractions such as the **South Peace Centennial Museum**, just east of Beaverlodge, where antique farm equipment has been restored to working order. Also, Pouce Coupe is proud of its museum in the old railroad station, which houses artifacts tracing this community's beginnings as a trading post in 1908.

These roadside communities also offer fuel, meals, and lodging. Multiple camping opportunities lie along this stretch of the road, from small municipal campgrounds to provincial parks. Watch for the signs.

As you near Dawson Creek and enter British Columbia, be sure to set your clocks back one hour to reflect the **Pacific Time Zone.** If you follow the Alaska Highway through British Columbia and the Yukon Territory, you won't have to change the time again until you cross the Alaska–Yukon border.

$\mathcal{D}$AWSON CREEK, British Columbia

From Grande Prairie: 83 miles (134 km)
From the Montana border: 750 miles (1,200 km)
To the Alaska border: 1,190 miles (1,915 km)
To Fairbanks: 1,488 miles (2,395 km)

Symbolically, Dawson Creek is the end of this road, and the beginning of another. You have arrived at Mile 0 of the famed Alaska Highway, and a new leg of your adventure is about to begin. For a complete description of Dawson Creek and its services, facilities, and attractions, see Chapter 6, The Alaska Highway.

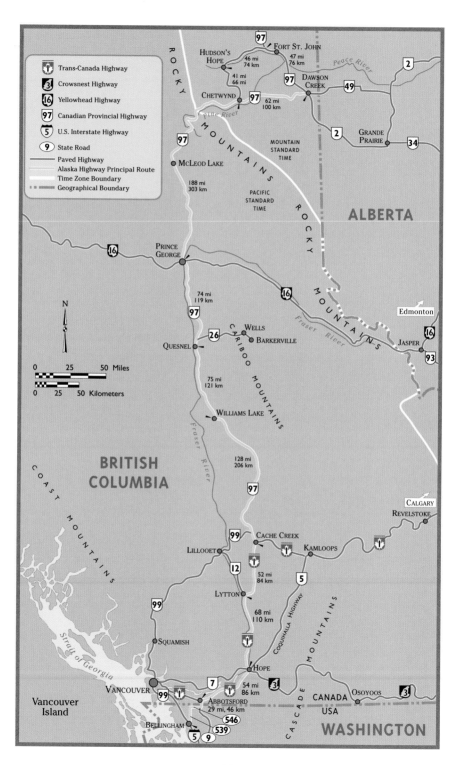

Trans-Canada Highway
Crowsnest Highway
Yellowhead Highway
Canadian Provincial Highway
U.S. Interstate Highway
State Road
Paved Highway
Alaska Highway Principal Route
Time Zone Boundary
Geographical Boundary

ROCKY MOUNTAINS

97 FORT ST. JOHN
HUDSON'S HOPE
46 mi 74 km
47 mi 76 km
Peace River
2
41 mi 66 mi
97 DAWSON CREEK
49
CHETWYND
97
62 mi 100 km
2
GRANDE PRAIRIE
34

97

MOUNTAIN STANDARD TIME

ROCKY MOUNTAINS

ALBERTA

McLEOD LAKE

188 mi 303 km

PACIFIC STANDARD TIME

16 PRINCE GEORGE

16

74 mi 119 km
97

Edmonton

26 WELLS
BARKERVILLE
QUESNEL

CARIBOO MOUNTAINS

Fraser River

JASPER
16
93

N

75 mi 121 km

0   25   50 Miles
0   25   50 Kilometers

WILLIAMS LAKE

Fraser River

128 mi 206 km

97

BRITISH COLUMBIA

COAST MOUNTAINS

CALGARY
REVELSTOKE

99 CACHE CREEK
LILLOOET
KAMLOOPS

12
52 mi 84 km
5

LYTTON
68 mi 110 km

Coquihalla Highway

MOUNTAINS

99
SQUAMISH

Strait of Georgia

HOPE
7
54 mi 86 km
3

VANCOUVER
99
ABBOTSFORD
29 mi, 46 km
CANADA
USA
OSOYOOS
3

CASCADE MOUNTAINS

Vancouver Island

BELLINGHAM
546
5 9 539

WASHINGTON

Chapter 5

The Western Route: Through British Columbia to Dawson Creek, B.C., and Mile 0

Beautiful British Columbia. If natural beauty were measured on a scale of 1 to 10, British Columbia would easily break out the top, like an overheated thermometer. This is an exceptionally beautiful province, from south to north, west to east.

Motoring along the northbound highways that lead to Dawson Creek, you will see for yourself the fascinating juxtaposition of the cultivated and uncivilized: orderly farms and untamed rivers, formal street grids beneath a tumble of mountains, logging trucks rumbling by tearooms.

In British Columbia, evidence of British, French, and American influence is present. This region also is rich in ancient culture that should not be overlooked in your travels. In museum exhibits and in daily practice, the First Nations people demonstrate the continuation of centuries-old traditions.

Be sure to stop at the wonderful culture-based attractions offered by members of various Native American groups. Learn about life in this country before contact with Europeans, along with customs and traditions in dance, art, and storytelling that continue today.

This traditional homeland of Canada's first people remains rich in resources such as big game, fish, birds, and small furbearers. As you drive, take care to watch for wildlife-viewing opportunities. We saw caribou, stone sheep, bison, eagles, hawks and other birds, plus numerous species of fish during our trip. In the case of big game on the road, keep your eyes open for safety's sake, as well as for photographic opportunities.

Canada's southwestern province also can boast of its magnificent coastline, the Fraser and other wild rivers, fruitful farmlands, mountain lakes, glaciers and ice fields, and the longest stretch of the Canadian Rockies. Victoria and Vancouver, its major cities in the southwestern part of the province, rival many in Europe for cultural attraction and architectural wonder. Fertile farms in the south feed British Columbia and contribute to the province's export economy. Farther north, the historic Cariboo Country holds stories of a gold rush that lingered well past that of the Klondike.

As you travel toward Cache Creek, the landscape turns drier and rockier, and the scent of sagebrush and juniper lingers in the air, bringing with it a sense of the Old West. Indeed, Canada's Old West holds as much wonderful and bizarre history as that of the United States, with ranchers, cowboys, miners, outlaws, and the women who loved them. You can visit historic Hat Creek Ranch or Barkerville to learn more about the Cariboo Wagon Road and the stagecoach line that once connected the western towns.

Like elsewhere in western Canada, the northernmost reaches are the rough-and-ready regions, where timber, oil, and natural gas take economic precedence over farming. This is not surprising, considering that the number of frost-free days shrinks with every northbound step in latitude, and the soil tends toward spotty sections of permafrost. As you drive, you'll also see incredible evidence of mankind's ability to harness energy through building dams and extracting oil and gas.

*W*ASHINGTON–BRITISH COLUMBIA BORDER

To Chilliwack, B.C.: 27 miles (43 km)
To Dawson Creek, B.C.: 705 miles (1,128 km)

To begin your northward journey through British Columbia, you will likely be starting out on north-south U.S. **Interstate 5** in western Washington. Take I-5 north from Seattle to Bellingham, the southernmost port city on the Alaska Marine Highway System. (See Appendix 1 for more information on ferry routes.)

At Bellingham, I-5 connects with northbound Route 539. Take Exit 256 and stay on this road for 25 miles (40 km) to the international border. (See the section on Border Crossings in Chapter 2, What You Need to Know.)

On the U.S. side, the border town is Sumas, Washington; on the Canada side, it's Huntington, B.C.

Road Notes

Heading north from the border, stay on Highway 11 for a few miles to **Abbotsford**, a community famous for its abundant raspberry, blueberry, and strawberry crops. Pick your own at area farms, and join the Berry Blitz festival in June and July for a taste of desserts and berry entrees.

The mechanically oriented member of the family will enjoy a tour of the **Barrowtown Pump Station**, 10 miles (16 km) east of Abbotsford off Trans-Canada Highway 1, where since 1923, pumps have drained what once was Sumas Lake, helping to create 16,000 acres of farmland and 5,000 acres of wooded hillside. Call in advance for a tour: 604-823-4678.

To learn more about Abbotsford-area attractions, visit the Chamber of Commerce at 2462 McCallum Road or call 604-869-9651.

From Abbotsford, follow Highway 1 east for 17 miles (27 km) to Chilliwack.

CHILLIWACK

From the border: 27 miles (43 km)
To Hope: 27 miles (43 km)

The **Fraser River Valley** is a suitable setting for a painting, with snowcapped peaks as a backdrop to widespread farms and a pretty city. This is a place for folks who appreciate life in a rural setting with the convenience of a nearby metropolis. Vancouver is just an hour's travel to the west.

Home to 60,186 people, Chilliwack prides itself on its recreational opportunities as well as its agriculture-based economy. Water is the tie that binds—the Fraser River, Chilliwack River, and Cultus, Chilliwack, and Harrison Lakes are playgrounds for locals and visitors.

Generous water sources, along with southern B.C.'s temperate climate and good soil, have made agriculture king here. In local fields, you'll find flowers, grain, corn and other vegetables, herbs, pumpkins and, like the northwest United States, apples. Among growers with an open-door policy is **The Apple Farm**, which produces

Fabulous Minter Gardens

For a flower hound like me, Minter Gardens was a 27-acre wonderland. Each flower bed or hanging planter or groomed shrub was an individual work of art within the greater whole, like the perfection found in just one corner of a Dutch masterpiece. Allow at least 2 hours to walk the various paths among the gardens, aviary, and bonsai display.

With 7,000-foot Mount Cheam as a backdrop, skilled gardeners show off their skills in theme gardens and a fragrance garden, in artfully pruned shrubbery, or in an archway of trained boughs.

Among my favorites were the topiary sculptures, like the shrub-woman whose Southern belle hoopskirt was a blaze of flowers, or the peacock whose body was a piece of topiary art and whose tail feathers swept across a downward slope in a rush of color.

One of the most photographed gardens is a tidy hillside with the words "Minter Gardens" snipped with sharp-edged precision in letters so large, you have to stand a half a football field away just to get your picture.

This place is a treasure, and it's easy to find. Just east of Chilliwack on Highway 1, take Exit 135 and follow the signs to 52892 Bunker Road. On the grounds, you'll also find a gift shop and snack and coffee bar. For more information, call 1-888-646-8377 or 604-794-7191. ●

25 varieties of apples. A guided tour of the orchards and apple tastings are available by reservation. For a farm guide, visit the **Chilliwack Visitor Information Centre,** 44150 Luckakuck Way, or call 1-800-567-9535 or 604-858-8121.

If golf is your game, you'll find more than 10 courses within a half-hour from downtown Chilliwack. Among them is a full range of challenge up to world-championship level, and in southern B.C.'s mild temperatures, you can easily golf into late autumn.

Grab a taste of cultural history at any of several museums in the area. At the **Sto:lo Native Interpretive Centre and Longhouse,** you can learn about the aboriginal people who lived in this region long before Chilliwack's 1908 incorporation. At the **Chilliwack Museum,** objects and artifacts help tell the story of this community's beginnings and the diverse people who have lived in this valley. Rated one of the top 10 museums in British Columbia by *Westworld Magazine,* the Chilliwack Museum is located at 45820 Spadina Avenue, in a 1912 structure that was the former city hall. Call 604-795-5210.

In mid-May, Chilliwack hosts the **Country Living Festival,** a celebration of its agricultural roots. The three-week event includes agricultural exhibitions, horse races, a parade, arts and crafts displays, and concerts.

For family fun, look just east of Chillwack, where **Bridal Falls** offers a dinosaur theme park, golfing, water slides, and bumper boats. Campsites for tents or RVs are nearby. Take Exit 138 to Popkum Road and follow the signs.

Or check out the **Cultus Lake** area, where either the provincial park or resort accommodations offer more fun for all members of the family. On the water: canoeing, kayaking, and fishing. On land: hiking, biking, and walking trails. Or in the resort park, enjoy the water slides and go-carts. Access to Cultus Lake is via Exit 119 south.

For more information, contact Tourism Chilliwack at 1-800-567-9535, 604-858-8121, or www.tourismchilliwack.com.

Lodging

Best Western Rainbow Country Inn
43971 Industrial Way
604-795-3828
74 air-conditioned rooms. Laundry, coffee, sauna, whirlpool. Restaurant, coffee shop.

Comfort Inn
45405 Luckakuck Way
1-800-228-5150 or 604-858-0636
Air-conditioned rooms, nonsmoking available. Restaurants, shopping nearby. Kids 18 and younger stay with parents or grandparents free.

Econo Lodge
8600 Young Street
1-877-793-1234 or 604-795-9155
39 deluxe air-conditioned rooms, cable TV, coffee. Heated outdoor swimming pool, playground. Close to restaurants.

Holiday Inn Chilliwack
45920 1st Avenue
604-795-4788
110 air-conditioned rooms. Coffee, sauna, whirlpool, restaurant, lounge. Downtown location.

Rainbow Motor Inn
45620 Yale Road
604-792-6412
40 air-conditioned rooms, efficiencies,
movies. Senior discount. Pets allowed.

Traders Inn
45944 Yale Road
1-888-792-9829 or 604-792-0061
Air-conditioned rooms, cable TV, movies.
Internet access. Whirlpool, sauna,
exercise room.

Campgrounds
Bridal Falls Camperland
53730 Bridal Falls Road, Exits 135 or 138 off
Highway 1
604-794-7361
High-quality resort camping with
amenities: pool, hot tubs, clubhouse,
restaurant. Near dining, attractions,
golf, entertainment.

Chilliwack RV Park & Campground
7 miles (11 km) east of Chilliwack on
Highway 1
604-794-7800
48 sites with full hookups, some pull-
throughs. Showers, laundry, store. Near
golf course.

Cottonwood Meadows RV Country Club
44280 Luckakuck Way
604-824-7275
Level sites with full hookups, pull-throughs,
cable hookup. Showers, clubhouse,
steam room. Close to services.

Cultus Lake Provincial Park
Sunnyside Campground
3405 Columbia Valley Highway
604-858-5253
www.cultuslake.bc.ca
300 campsites. Showers, rest rooms,
firewood. Boat launch, fishing,
canoeing, hiking.

Wild Rose RV Park
Highway 1, Exit 165 or 168
1-800-463-7999
www.wildrosecamp.com
Full hookups, pull-throughs, free cable
hookup. Tent camping. Near restaurant.

Restaurants
C-Lovers Fish & Chips
7670 Vedder Road
604-824-7959
Dine in or take out.

The Gardenia House
9254 Nowell Street South
604-792-0767
Seafood, steak, chicken specialties.

Grand West Family Restaurant
8559 Young Road
604-792-8383
Greek, seafood, pasta, pizza, steaks.

The Greek Islands Restaurant
46095 Yale Road
604-702-1881
Steaks, seafood, schnitzel, pasta, and more.

Humpty's Family Restaurant
45609 Luckakuck Way
In Cottonwood Mall
604-824-4810
Full menu, open 24 hours.

La Mansione Ristorante
46290 Yale Road East
604-792-8910
Steak and seafood; historic setting.

The Pantry
45610 Yale Road West
604-792-2110
Family dining, breakfast all day. Seniors'
and children's menus.

Road Notes

Wouldn't a nice soak in a mineral hot springs do the trick right now? If you're willing to follow that urge, just past Chilliwack take Exit 135 to Highway 9 and east to Highway 7.

Harrison Hot Springs is a gorgeous resort village in the mountains, and only about a half-hour away from Chilliwack. Fewer than 1,000 people live here on the shores of Harrison Lake, but water enthusiasts come from miles around for boating, windsurfing, swimming, or camping. Each September, sand sculptors and their fans arrive for the World Championship Sand Sculpture Competition on the beaches of the lake. Their amazing creations remain on display for a full month. The hot springs itself is a rare treat, with water coming out of the ground so hot that it must be cooled to 105°F. The public pool is open year-round. For more information, call 604-796-3425.

If you go, retrace your route back to Highway 1 for the best, fastest access to Hope.

Hope

From Chilliwack: 27 miles (43 km)
To Lytton: 68 miles (110 km)

This charming community at the confluence of the Fraser and Coquihalla Rivers is home to 6,247 people. Hope seems surrounded by mountains as well as by rivers, and its beautiful natural setting has made it a vacation destination as well as the site for two major motion picture productions: *First Blood*, starring Sylvester Stallone as John Rambo, and *Shoot to Kill*, starring Sidney Poitier and Kirstie Alley. The area and its temperate climate attract a unique variety of coastal and interior birds, so birders often arrive hoping to add to their life lists.

For all the possibilities of how Hope was named, there is no agreement. One of our favorites was attributed to old-time gold miners who wintered here between lousy mining seasons: "They lived in Hope and finally died in despair."

This little city vies with Chetwynd, B.C., as Chainsaw Sculpture Capital of British Columbia. Hope's grassy, treed downtown park features the chainsaw artistry of a local sculptor named Pete Ryan. In 1991, when a few of the giant old trees in **Memorial Park** began to die, Ryan made a proposal. Rather than raze the trees, he asked the city to leave 12-foot stumps. From them he has carved detailed works of art depicting miners, burros, rams, and, best of all, bears. Today you can see two dozen or more of his works in the park and in other venues around town.

In 1981 Hollywood transformed Hope into a movie set for its filming of *First Blood* at sites all over town. A hundred locals were cast as extras, and for a while, actors Sylvester Stallone and Brian Dennehy were small-town regulars. Just outside the visitor center, a full-size wooden cutout of Stallone (minus the face), in warfare gear and muscles, allows visitors to photograph each other in good humor.

East of town, in the **Coquihalla Canyon Provincial Recreation Area**, five tunnels were cut through solid granite for the now-abandoned Kettle Valley Railway, built from 1911 to 1916. Because the chief engineer was a Shakespeare fan, he used Shakespearean names on railroad bridges, waysides, and this grouping of five tunnels: the Othello-Quintette Tunnels.

Hiking trails for all levels of fitness can be found throughout the area, and the **Hope Visitor Information Centre** has detailed maps of local trails, plus maps of nearby Manning and Skagit Valley Provincial Parks. Members of the Hope Volunteer Search & Rescue have prepared trip itineraries for you to fill out and leave at the visitor center, in case of an emergency. Visitor center maps include walking tours to Pete Ryan's sculptures and to locations where *First Blood* was filmed.

The helpful people at the center will tell you about local activities and attractions and answer questions about highway conditions and weather, as well as direct you to lodging and restaurants. The center is at 919 Water Avenue, along Highway 1. Call 604-869-2021. The Chamber of Commerce has a website at www.hopechamber.bc.ca.

Lodging

Best Western Heritage Inn
570 Old Hope–Princeton Way
1-800-528-1234 or 604-869-7166
Air-conditioned rooms, family units. Cable
   TV, refrigerators, coffeemakers. Spa,
   whirlpool. Three-Diamond rating, AAA.

City Centre Motel
455 Wallace Street
604-869-5411
Air-conditioned rooms, in-room coffee/tea,
   movies. Senior discount.

Inn Towne Motel
510 Highway 1
1-800-663-2612 or 604-896-7276
Air-conditioned rooms, deluxe suites,
   kitchenettes, nonsmoking available.
   Laundry, indoor pool, whirlpool, sauna.

The Maple Leaf Motor Inn
377 Old Hope–Princeton Way
604-869-7107
Air-conditioned rooms, kitchenettes, cable
   TV, movies. Indoor pool, whirlpool, sauna.

Park Motel
832 4th Avenue
604-869-5891
Air-conditioned rooms, family units,
   nonsmoking available. Movies and
   sports channels. Senior rates.

Quality Inn
350 Old Hope–Princeton Way
1-800-899-5996 or 604-869-9951
Air-conditioned rooms, 24-hour movies,
   sports, news. Free continental breakfast.
   Indoor hot tub, pool, sauna. Three-
   Diamond rating, AAA. Walk to downtown.

Red Roof Inn

Fraser Avenue and Highway 1

604-869-2446

27 air-conditioned units, some
nonsmoking. Cable TV, indoor spa,
whirlpool. Mountain views, near
restaurants.

Skagit Motor Inn

655 3rd Avenue

604-869-5220

30 air-conditioned rooms at ground floor.
Continental breakfast, pool, whirlpool,
spa. Mountain views, close to
downtown.

*Chainsaw artist Pete Ryan has created wonderful works of art from the stumps of dead trees in Hope's
Memorial Park.*

Slumber Lodge

250 Fort Street

1-800-757-7766 or 604-869-5666

34 air-conditioned rooms, suites. Indoor
swimming pool, sauna, restaurant.

Swiss Chalets Motel

456 Highway 1

1-800-663-4673

Air-conditioned rooms, family chalets,
kitchenettes, fireplaces. Cable TV, in-
room coffee.

Every summer 2 million salmon migrate up Fraser River to spawn.

Windsor Motel

778 3rd Avenue

1-888-588-9944

Air-conditioned rooms, family units,
kitchenettes, nonsmoking available.
Cable TV, in-room coffee, senior
discount.

Campgrounds

Coquihalla Campsite

800 Kawkawa Lake Road

1-888-869-7118 or 604-869-7119

Partial hookups, riverfront sites, 24-hour
security. Laundry, dump station, store.
Recreation area, playground.

Holiday Motel RV & Campsite

Exit 168 off Highway 1

604-869-5352

Full hookups, cable hookup, heated outdoor
pool.

KOA Campground

3 miles (5 km) west on Flood Hope Road,
Exit 168 off Highway 1

604-869-9857

Full or partial hookups, pull-throughs, tent
sites. Showers, laundry, rest rooms.
Store, ice, gift shop. Game room,
swimming pool, playground.

Telte Yet Campsite

600 Water Avenue

604-869-9481

29 full hookup sites, tent camping.
Showers, laundry, dump station. Group
rates. Acres of trees along Fraser River.
Walking distance to Hope.

Whistlestop RV–Tent Park

59440 St. Elmo Road, Exit 160 off Highway 1

1-877-869-5132 or 604-869-5132

Full hookups, tent sites, fire pits. Wheelchair
access. Free showers; laundry, dump
station. Store, playground, grass and
shade.

Wild Rose Campground & RV Park

3 miles (5 km) west on Flood Hope Road,
Exit 165 or 168 off Highway 1

604-869-9842

www.wildrosecamp.com

Full hook-ups. Cable TV, showers, laundry,
dump station.

Restaurants

Alpenhaus Restaurant

273 Wallace Street

604-869-5714

Greek, pasta, seafood, steak, schnitzel.

Darrell's Place

241 Wallace Street

604-869-3708

Quality family dining.

Dee's Riverview Café

Green roof on Water Avenue

604-869-5534

Breakfast all day, hamburgers, soup,
sandwiches, sweets.

Gilligan's

823 6th Avenue

604-869-2121

Specializes in pizza (opens 4 P.M.).

Home Restaurant Too

250 Fort Street

604-869-5241

Home-cooked food, family dining.

Kan-yon Restaurant
800 3rd Avenue
604-869-2212
Chinese and Canadian fare.

Kibo Japanese & Canadian Grill
267 King Street
604-869-7317
Teriyaki, ribs, California roll, and more.

Rolly's Restaurant
888 Fraser Avenue
604-869-7448
Breakfast all day, casual dining.

Silver Creek Pancake House
2 miles (3 km) west on Silver Hope Creek
Road, Exit 168 off Highway 1
604-869-5713
Breakfast all day, full-course meals.

Susie Q Buffet Restaurant
259 Wallace Street
604-869-5515
Western and Japanese fare.

Road Notes

Fourteen miles (23 km) north of Hope, you'll come upon **Yale**, a historic village site along the gold rush trail. In its advantageous position at the southern entrance of the Fraser Canyon, Yale was the site for paddlewheelers to unload cargo that would continue its journey on the Cariboo Wagon Road, more commonly known as the Cariboo Trail. The Cariboo gold rush was still going strong by 1863, when the **Church of St. John the Divine** was constructed. As you take a tour of the town, peek inside the church and get an eyeful of its magnificently carved pump organ. Visit the pioneer cemetery with its unique grave markers. Arrange a rafting trip or try gold panning by calling 604-863-2324.

The Fraser Canyon is postcard beautiful from one end to the other. Just past the first of several tunnels in this section of road, note the historical marker at a pullout to the east. This explains more about the Cariboo Trail and the difficulty of transportation during that mid-1800s gold rush.

Farther north, about 33 miles (53 km) from Hope on Highway 1, you will encounter the natural wonder called **Hells Gate**, a tight narrowing in the canyon through which the Fraser River pours at great speed. From the edge, looking down, the water is fast and fearful, and it's no wonder the name stuck. **Hells Gate Airtram** offers a scary look at the river from above. For a fee, you can ride the tram across the canyon while descending 502 feet. On the opposite side, a pleasant, tourist-oriented boardwalk village has been built into the cliff. And for the intrepid, a suspension bridge lets you walk back over the river and enjoy an unadulterated view of the swirling current beneath your feet. Enjoy a meal at the **Salmon House Restaurant**, or buy some food and eat at a picnic table in the sun. Watch an interpretive film, spend some cash in the gift shop, and load up on fudge at the candy store. Informative signs add to the enjoyment. We were amazed to learn that nearly 2 million salmon swim up the Fraser River each summer. For more information, call 604-867-9277.

Between April 15 and October 15, camping is available about 10 miles (16 km) north of Hells Gate at **Canyon Alpine RV Park & Campground**, just off Highway 1. The campground offers 31 sites, with full hookups and pull-throughs, which work well for big rigs. On the grounds are fire pits, washrooms, and showers. The facility is close to a restaurant, store, phone, and self-service laundry. For information, call 1-800-644-PARK.

For a fee, you can ride the Hell's Gate Airtram over Fraser Canyon.

ℒYTTON

From Hope: 68 miles (110 km)
To Cache Creek: 52 miles (84 km)

Situated at the confluence of the **Thompson River** and the mighty **Fraser River** (Canada's third largest), Lytton is the place to park and play—a river-rafter's dream. Looking down at the rivers' confluence from above, you can see a distinct edge where the clear, blue Thompson blends into the cloudy gray of the Fraser. A third, the **Nahatlatch River**, is smaller and steeper, offering dramatic class 4 and class 5 rafting.

As the whitewater rafting capital of British Columbia, Lytton offers plentiful choices for outfitters. You can go with a group, hire a guide for your own group, or rent what you need to go on your own. You can't miss rafting company signs all along this stretch of road. Among them is **Kumsheen Raft Adventures**, which has been leading power and paddle rafting trips on area rivers for more than 25 years. Call 250-455-2296 or visit the website at www.kumsheen.bc.ca/raft.

This meeting place of the rivers has been a gathering spot for centuries, as evidenced in ancient pictographs and rock paintings. First Nations people chose the spot for its abundance of wildlife, water, and trees for food and building material. You can visit a reconstruction of a traditional pit house in **Lion's Heritage Park**. These semi-underground homes were used for winter quarters by local Natives up to about a century ago. During the annual Lytton Days, you can learn more about First Nations culture through art, dance, and storytelling. Native arts and crafts, including soapstone carvings, baskets, and beaded leather, can be purchased in Lytton. Call 250-455-2146 for more information.

After prospector Billy Barker discovered gold in 1862, more than 100,000 people joined the ensuing rush and swarmed into British Columbia to mine for gold, traveling the famed Cariboo Wagon Road to reach the goldfields. As a stop along the way, Lytton thrived as a place for the stampeders to outfit themselves.

In 1881 intrepid railway builders arrived to cut a rail bed into the sides of this canyon. The Canadian Pacific

Laying rail through Fraser Canyon proved a challenge for railroad builders of the last century.

Railway and the Canadian National Railway continue to move freight and passengers on this route that parallels the river and the road through Fraser Canyon.

This area is still rich with wildlife. Along the backroads and hiking trails, you may see elk, bighorn sheep, deer, eagles, and ospreys. Hidden from sight are the more human-shy animals: coyotes, bears, cougars, bobcats, and lynx.

The city was named for Sir Edward Bulwer-Lytton, whose writing is familiar to almost everybody. Drawing a blank? He's the one who penned the famous introductory phrase "It was a dark and stormy night."

Lytton is also Canada's "hot spot" with a recorded high of 111°F.

For more information on the area, contact the Lytton & District Chamber of Commerce at 250-455-2523 or the Village of Lytton at 250-455-2355.

Road Notes

In the 52 scenic miles (83.5 km) between Lytton and Cache Creek, you'll find two provincial parks and several private campgrounds.

Just 5 miles (8 km) beyond Lytton is **Skihist Provincial Park**, with 58 campsites, a picnic area, rest rooms, and an RV dump station. Another 12 miles (19 km) later, the less-developed **Goldpan Provincial Park** lies to the west, with 14 sites along the river. You can go fishing or put your canoe in the water here.

Along the way, pay attention to the historic buildings and opportunities to stop for coffee, pie, or a meal, and learn more about the area's gold rush history. Less than 10 miles (16 km) south of Cache Creek, the oldest roadhouse in British Columbia is still

---

You Want Coffee with That Jellyroll?

*Sedimentary geologists and other earth scientists will appreciate an unusual attraction in the heart of downtown Lytton. Across from Lytton's **Visitor Information Centre**, at 400 Fraser Avenue, is the tiny **Caboose Park**, where a retired Canadian National Railway caboose is parked alongside a picnic table and grassy area. But it's the thing on the exterior wall of an adjacent building that makes scientists and curiosity seekers walk closer and squint. The "thing" is called the **Lytton Jellyroll**, a cast of a geological formation that was discovered south of the village. The unusual structure is a rolled layer of silt encased in coarse sands and gravel. Scientists believe it was created from 11,000 to 25,000 years ago during an event in the last glaciation period. That makes it very young, by geological standards. But it is the size of the formation that makes it special. Normally a find such as this would be measured in inches, not feet. Erected by the Lytton and District Chamber of Commerce, this detailed replication of the real thing could fool an amateur.* •

in business, as it has been since 1862. The **Ashcroft Manor & Tea House** offers rooms, meals, jade gifts, and an invitation to walk the grounds and visit the historic outbuildings. For more information, call 250-453-9983.

Seven miles (11 km) south of Cache Creek is the **Eagle Motorplex**, a drag racing facility sanctioned by the National Hot Rod Association. Racers come from around the world to race and show their cars.

During Cache Creek's mid-June **Graffiti Days**, restored vehicles are paraded and parked for a show-and-shine celebration. Festivities include a dance, barbecue, and racing at the motorplex.

CACHE CREEK

From Lytton: 52 miles (84 km)
From Hope: 120 miles (193 km)
To Williams Lake: 128 miles (206 km)

Set in a semiarid region of low, rolling hills, Cache Creek is home to a scant 1,125 people who live at the confluence of the Bonaparte River and Cache Creek. Here, too, is the junction of Trans-Canada Highway 1 with Highway 97.

The scent of sage wafts through the air on hot, summer days, and at the town's main intersection, a wooden gold miner stands, arms extended, to welcome you to this frontier town that was built on the backs of gold miners.

These days there's less gold mining than there is cattle ranching and ginseng growing. That's the crop beneath the acres and acres of elevated black cloth that protects the delicate plants. Farmers also grow wheat in irrigated fields.

Cache Creek services include lodging, restaurants, grocery stores, a post office, and a golf course. Most visitors are passing through on their vacations. But 150 years ago, this town was overrun with miners and people who wanted to trade gold for goods and services.

As a major point on the Cariboo Wagon Road, Cache Creek grew quickly. After the rush, some mining continued, along with farming, logging, and cattle ranching. Tourism helps keep Cache Creek cooking, too.

Just north of town, an 1860 landmark along the Cariboo Wagon Road is the historic **Hat Creek Ranch**, at the intersection of Highways 97 and 99. This 320-acre ranch was once an important roadhouse stop for horse-drawn wagons along the B.C. Express Stage line (also known as the BX) that led to Barkerville and beyond. More than 20 buildings dating from 1863 to 1915 may be found on the grounds. Step back in time and explore the Victorian-style rooms of the main house, visit the BX Barn, watch the blacksmith at work, and view a First Nations pit house. You can also take a horse-drawn ride on the famous Cariboo Wagon Road and follow the footsteps of the gold miners. For more information, call 250-457-9722.

A sculpture of a miner and his tools welcomes visitors to Cache Creek, B.C., at the junction of Highway 97 and the Trans-Canada Highway 1.

Lodging

Bear's Claw Lodge
On Highway 97
1-888-552-CLAW
Air-conditioned rooms in new log lodge.
Cable TV, restaurant.

Bonaparte Motel
On Highway 97 North
1-888-922-1333 or 250-457-9693
Air-conditioned rooms and kitchenettes
with refrigerators, TVs, fax service.
Outdoor pool, whirlpool. Close to
restaurants and golf.

Desert Motel
South of Highway 1, center of Cache Creek
1-800-663-0212 or 250-452-6226
45 air-conditioned units, kitchenettes.
Cable TV and in-room coffee. Grass
courtyard with seasonal pool. Winter
plug-ins. Close to shops and restaurants.

The Good Knight Inn
1-800-736-5588
827 South Trans-Canada Highway
Rooms with cable TV and movies, data
phones, e-mail. Whirlpools, continental
breakfast.

Tumbleweed Motel
On Highway 1 East
1-800-667-1501 or 250-457-6522
Deluxe air-conditioned rooms, nonsmoking
rooms, cable TV.

Campgrounds

Brookside Campsite
0.6 miles (1 km) east of Cache Creek on
Highway 1
250-457-6633
Pull-through sites, free showers, heated
pool. Adjacent to golf course.

Cache Creek Campground

2.5 miles (4 km) north of town on
  Highway 97
250-457-6414
Pull-throughs, power available. Restaurant,
  pool, hot tub, 18-hole mini golf course.

Restaurants

A&W
Highway 97 North, at Copper Canyon
  Chevron
250-457-9668
Burgers, root beer, chicken, and more.

Green and Gold

Outside **Cariboo Jade & Gifts** in Cache Creek, B.C., at 1093 Todd Road, you'll see a massive boulder made of jade, an obviously valuable piece of inventory that just sits out on the sidewalk. Managers Ben Roy and Bill Elliott don't worry too much about shoplifting. It would take a D-9 Caterpillar to walk away with that boulder.

Inside, these two brothers-in-law manage the business traffic that the boulder generates, like a billboard that says, "Come inside." While we were there, a busload of French-speaking travelers from eastern Canada arrived and filled every aisle of the modest shop.

In the back of the shop, behind a glass partition, Ben cuts British Columbia jade on special rock saws to accommodate its extreme hardness. Bill's specialty is working in gold. Together they create jewelry and other specialty pieces. British Columbia jade is nearly as prized as gold. Four times harder than marble, this jade is difficult to cut and finish into sculpture and jewelry. For more information on B.C. jade, call 250-457-9566. ⬤

Ben Roy is manager of Cariboo Jade & Gifts in Cache Creek, B.C.

Dairy Queen
Junction of Highways 1 and 97
250-457-9924
Burgers, shakes, fries, ice cream delights.

North End Petro Can Restaurant &
  Convenience Store
On Highway 97, just north of Highways 1
  and 97 junction
250-457-6432
Breakfast and lunch specials, pastries.

Wander-Inn Restaurant
Junction of Highways 1 and 97
250-457-6511
Steaks, Chinese food, coffee shop, dining
  room, cocktail lounge.

Road Notes

From Cache Creek to the towns of 100 Mile House and 150 Mile House, the highway continues to follow the historic route of the Cariboo Wagon Road. The numbers used in the names of these towns and of other sites along this way are a measurement of their distance from Lillooet, which was Mile 0 on the mid-1880s Cariboo route.

100 Mile House today is a lumber town that also claims the title of International Nordic Ski Capital. It hosts the Cariboo Marathon each February, attracting skiers from around the world. Outside the town's information center, you can see the world's longest cross-country skis, 39-foot-long Karhu racers.

WILLIAMS LAKE

From Cache Creek: 128 miles (206 km)
To Quesnel: 75 miles (121 km)
To Prince George: 149 miles (240 km)

During construction of the Cariboo Wagon Road, a Williams Lake landowner would not lend money to road builders, so the trail bypassed the town, instead routing through 150 Mile House. That decision nearly killed the town's economy, putting it off the major transportation route for the thousands of people moving in and out of the goldfields.

Williams Lake was nearly abandoned, except for two business partners, William Pinchbeck and William Lyne, who built a lumber mill, grist mill, and a farm. But their real income earner was the sale of home-brewed whiskey. You might assume that this town took its name from the two Williams, but it is attributed to the local Shuswap Chief William.

By the 1940s, twenty years after the railway arrived, this was a ranching town that had grown into the largest cattle-shipping center in British Columbia. Today nearly 36,000 people live in the area, and ranching remains an important part of the economy.

Williams Lake is the Old West in action, and at no time of the year is there more action than during the **Williams Lake Stampede**, the first week of July. This family event includes chuckwagon races, barn dances, a rodeo, and mountain horse races. A parade and midway are part of the fun, too. Camping is available right next to the Stampede grounds. For more information, call 1-800-71RODEO or 250-392-6585. The **Museum of the Cariboo Chilcotin** is a full-fledged rodeo museum that is entrusted with the story of the Williams Lake Stampede, which dates back to 1919, and the history of this region, the Cariboo Chilcotin.

Williams Lake—the actual lake itself—lies along a major flyway for migrating waterfowl. **Scout Island Nature Centre**, at the west end of the lake, offers bird-watching opportunities along a corridor of trails. Between the Fraser River and the lake, you can see sandstone hoodoos—mushroom-shaped formations still standing after the forces of erosion removed the rock all around them.

The **Williams Lake Visitor Information Centre** can help you with such things as lining up a stay at a guest ranch or arranging for some horseback riding. Golfers can choose between two courses, and there's mini-golf for the kids. For more information on Williams Lake and the surrounding district, call 250-392-5025.

Lodging

Caesar Inn
55 6th Avenue South
250-392-7747
100 air-conditioned units, executive suites, kitchenettes. Cable TV, laundry, sauna, pub. Small pets welcome. Near shopping and Stampede grounds.

Drummond Lodge Motel
1405 Highway 98 South
250-392-5334
23 air-conditioned units, kitchenettes, nonsmoking units available. Movie and sports channels, in-room coffee, continental breakfast, laundry facilities. Overlooking lake.

Fraser Inn
285 Donald Road
1-800-452-6789 or 250-398-7055
www.fraserinn.com

75 air-conditioned units, cable TV, movies, room service. Gift shop, whirlpool, sauna, weight room. Restaurant, lounge, patio.

Jamboree Motel
845 Carson Drive
250-398-8208
33 units, kitchenettes, cable TV. Outdoor heated pool in summer. Winter plug-ins; pets allowed. Close to restaurants, bus depot.

Overlander Hotel
1118 Lakeview Crescent
1-800-663-6898 or 250-392-3321
www.overlanderhotel.com
60 units in full-service hotel. Fitness facilities, tour packages. Restaurant, lounge. Downtown location.

Sandman Inn
664 Oliver Street
1-800-726-3626 or 250-392-6557
www.sandman.ca
59 air-conditioned units, kitchenettes,
nonsmoking available. Coffee and tea,
laundry, indoor pool, 24-hour Denny's
restaurant. Small pets welcome. Two
blocks from city center.

Slumber Lodge Inn
27 7th Avenue South
1-800-577-2244 or 250-392-7116
58 rooms, kitchenettes, nonsmoking
available. Coffee, indoor pool,
restaurant. Close to shopping.

Springhouse Trails Summer Ranch
Dog Creek Road
250-392-4780
www.skybridge.bc.ca/springhouse
20 units; kitchenettes, some with fireplaces.
Meals, lounge. 12 RV full-hookup sites,
showers, washrooms. Horseback riding.

Stampeder Hotel
2 Lakeview Avenue
1-800-667-3911 or 250-392-4496
24 units, kitchenettes available.

Super 8
1712 Broadway Avenue South
250-398-8884
53 air-conditioned units, nonsmoking
available. Cable TV, whirlpool,
complimentary breakfast. Pets allowed.

Valleyview Motel
1523 Cariboo Highway 97
250-392-4655
20 air-conditioned sleeping and
housekeeping units. Cable TV, free
coffee. Near restaurant. Senior discount.
Pets allowed. Facing private lake
frontage.

Campgrounds
Big Bar Provincial Park
281 1st Avenue
250-398-4414
www.elp.gov.bc.ca/bcparks
Full and partial hookups, pull-throughs.

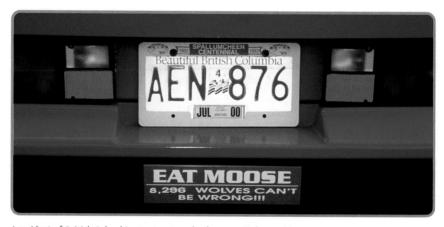

A resident of British Columbia sports a popular bumper sticker on his car.

Locked in a Time Warp

The buildings in Barkerville, B.C., each hold a story of the gold rush occupant. Actors in costume make the past come alive again.

For a worthwhile side trip, take the Highway 26 turnoff just beyond Quesnel and follow it for 51 miles (82 km) east to Barkerville, where the gold-rush past comes alive again.

Founded in 1862, **Barkerville** first sprang to life when Billy Barker discovered gold in Williams Creek. Now more than 125 heritage buildings and displays on the original town site celebrate the past. Costumed interpreters remain in character as they answer questions and carry on conversation, moving about the streets of the mining town.

Museum displays about mining and about Barkerville and its namesake are in the main building through which you access Barkerville—which is kind of like a Hollywood back-lot, except that these buildings are real. And at each one, you learn about its former resident or business owner. Street performances add to the feeling that this was once a busy town of miners, Chinese immigrants, churchmen, and partygoers. Two cemeteries hold the remains of former residents. A stagecoach driver invites passengers to ride to the other end of the town. Guided tours begin at regular intervals.

We were pelted by a hailstorm while visiting Barkerville, and people rushed into the saloon, candy store, general store, or museum building. Others huddled beneath building overhangs until the storm passed. This was in August—an indicator of this place's elevation of about 4,200 feet (1,280 m) above sea level. Museum docents explained that snow comes early in these mountains. The mining was hard work; the living was just as hard.

For more information, call BC Heritage at 250-994-3332 or visit the agency's website at www.heritage.gov.bc.ca.

Springhouse Trails Summer Ranch
Dog Creek Road
250-392-4780
12 RV full-hookup sites.

Williams Lake Stampede Campground
850 South Mackenzie Street
250-398-6718
www.imagehouse.com/rodeo
69 sites with full or partial hookups, phone,
cable hookup. Tent sites, free firewood.
Showers, rest rooms.

Restaurants

Fraser Inn
285 Donald Road
1-800-452-6789 or 250-398-7055
Outdoor seating available, lounge.

The Hearth Restaurant
99 South 3rd Avenue
250-398-6831
Sandwiches, soups, salads.

The Overlander
1118 Lakeview Crescent
1-800-663-6898 or 250-392-3321
Downtown restaurant, adjacent to hotel.

Rendezvous Restaurant
240B Oliver Street
250-398-8312
Family dining, full menu.

Savala's Steakhouse
36 North 3rd Avenue
250-398-8246
Steaks, seafood, pasta.

Road Notes

Seventy-five miles (116 km) north of Williams Lake is Quesnel, which, like many area towns, boomed during the Cariboo gold rush of the early 1860s. Today this town of 8,500 people is supported by lumber, pulp and plywood manufacturing, cattle ranching, mining, and, of course, tourism. All travelers' services may be found here, from shopping, lodging, and dining to assistance in planning your trip. Learn more about Quesnel's history, which really began long before the gold rush, at the Quesnel & District Museum and Archives, 705 Carson Avenue, which is rated among the top 10 museums in British Columbia

In mid-July, Quesnel celebrates Billy Barker's discovery of gold with Barker Days, four days of river races, dances, games, concerts, and contests for pie eaters and watermelon-seed spitters. A midway multiplies the family fun.

West of Quesnel the Blackwater River flows almost 200 miles (322 km) from the Coast Mountains to the Fraser River. Its pristine waters attract fly fishers, canoeists, and kayakers. The Alexander Mackenzie Heritage Trail parallels the river; in 1793, Mackenzie followed this Native trading trail to the Pacific Ocean.

Heading north toward Prince George, you will be within range of some excellent lake fishing for rainbow and brook trout, char, burbot, and more. There are about 1,600 lakes within a 100-mile radius of Prince George. Contact Tourism Prince George at 1-800-668-7646 or 250-562-3700 for a free fishing guide. Remember, you need two separate fishing licenses in British Columbia—one for freshwater and one for saltwater.

Ten Mile Lake Provincial Park, 7 miles (11 km) north of Quesnel, offers

142 campsites with water, showers, rest rooms, and an RV dump station. For recreation there's a playground, a swimming beach on the lake, and a boat launch, as well as nature trails for walking and wildlife viewing. Watch for several private campgrounds just south of Prince George, too.

$\mathcal{P}$RINCE GEORGE

From Quesnel: 74 miles (119 km)
To Chetwynd: 188 miles (303 km)
To Dawson Creek: 250 miles (402 km)

Here in what is known as the Lakes and Rivers District, Prince George is looked on as the capital of northern British Columbia. It is home to 76,500 people who understand and enjoy the natural treasure that's around them and the city they helped to create.

Just minutes from downtown in any direction, you'll find some form of outdoor recreation: walking, fishing, swimming, boating, backpacking. The local lakes and streams are thick with trout, salmon, burbot, Dolly Varden, char—for a fly fisher, this is world-class water. And there's no shortage of campgrounds, provincial and private. Hunkering in the distance is **Mount Robson**, highest peak in the Canadian Rockies, inviting those who prefer a lot of challenge in their outdoor adventure.

In winter, visitors and residents head out for downhill skiing, cross-country skiing, hockey, ice skating, even dogsledding. Snow typically begins in November and stays on the ground into late March.

The driving force behind the Prince George economy is the pulp and forest industry. **Northwood Inc.** offers scheduled tours of its pulp mill, sawmill, and plywood mills. Call Tourism Prince George to arrange a tour: 250-562-3700.

This is a frontier city at its roots, yet it "cleans up real nice" with its own brand of polish. Just as you finish a half-day trail ride, Prince George's nightlife offerings will revitalize you with concerts, art galleries, theater openings, or an evening of jazz. The city claims several resident theater groups, a symphony orchestra, and many dance troupes. The **Prince George Art Gallery** recently moved into its new digs at the downtown Civic Complex. And the **Prince George Playhouse** was recently renovated and expanded for an ever-growing audience.

Also downtown, the **Centennial Fountain** at 7th Avenue and Dominion Street depicts the early history of Prince George in mosaic tile, from life among the First Nations people to the arrival of explorers, settlers, the railway, and forward into 20th-century life.

Along the banks of the Fraser River, at the end of 20th Avenue, **Fort George Park** is a favorite among more than 120 parks in the city limits. Come down to the river to picnic, and follow the Heritage Trail that links this park with several others. Inside the park, you'll find the **Fraser-Fort George Regional Museum**, with natural and cultural

The Prince George Railway and Forestry Museum features retired vehicles, railway cars, cabooses, and track.

history exhibits and a small-gauge steam engine that offers rides for children. A hands-on science gallery accelerates learning by touching.

Nearby, stop by the **Prince George Railway and Forestry Museum**, an outdoor repository for antique or merely retired railcars, engines, and more. There's even a full-size train depot here, faithfully moved piece by piece from a spot along the British Columbia Railway between Quesnel and Prince George. Steam locomotives, cranes, sleeping cars, cabooses, even logging and agricultural machinery are part of the walk-about display. This is a great place to bring your favorite motorhead.

Summer visitors are welcome to attend a **First Nations powwow** at Cottonwood Park, at the confluence of the Fraser and Nechako Rivers, where you can watch the dancing and shop for Native-made crafts. Each July the work of Native artists is featured at the **Northern British Columbia Native Arts & Crafts Trade Show**, held in the Convention Center. For more information, call 250-567-5795.

A **Prince George visitor center** lies at the junction of Yellowhead Highway 16 and Highway 97. Just outside is an unmistakable greeting from a three-story "log man" whose friendly wave welcomes you to town. A second visitor center, the office of Tourism Prince George, is centrally located downtown at the corner of Victoria Street and Patricia Boulevard.

(For more on Yellowhead Highway 16, see Chapter 7, Western Canada's Northbound Byways. If you're heading to Dawson Creek, however, you will continue your journey north on Highway 97.)

For more information on the city's attractions and events, contact Tourism Prince George at 1-800-668-7646 or 250-562-3700 or www.tourismpg.bc.ca.

Lodging

Anco Motel
1630 Central Street (on Highway 97)
250-563-3671
65 rooms and kitchenettes. Cable TV, laundry, heated pool in season, restaurant.

Downtown Motel
650 Dominion Street
250-563-9241
45 air-conditioned rooms, cable TV, movies. Winter plug-ins.

Econo Lodge
1915 3rd Avenue
1-888-566-6333 or 250-563-7106
30 air-conditioned rooms, kitchenettes, nonsmoking available. Cable TV, in-room coffee, data ports. Whirlpool, exercise room. Winter plug-ins. Near restaurants, shopping.

Esther's Inn
1151 Commercial Drive
1-800-663-6844 or 250-562-4131
132 air-conditioned rooms. Whirlpools, sauna, exercise club, pool with water slides. Dining room, lounge.

Goldcap Motor Inn
1458 7th Avenue
1-800-663-8239 or 250-563-0666
77 air-conditioned efficiency units. Cable TV and movie channel. Laundry, beauty salon, sauna. Dining, lounge. Pets allowed.

Grama's Inn Ltd.
901 Central Street
1-877-563-7174 or 250-563-7174
62 air-conditioned rooms, hospitality room.

PG Hi-Way Motel
1737 20th Avenue
1-888-557-4557
45 budget and deluxe rooms, kitchenettes. Winter plug-ins. Near restaurants, laundry, shopping.

Prince George is proud of its economy base in timber—even the phone booths are made from log.

Campgrounds

Bee Lazee RV Park, Campground & Honey Farm

15910 Highway 97, 9 miles (15 km) south of Prince George

250-963-7263

Full hookups, pull-throughs, tent camping. Free showers; laundry, washrooms, car and RV wash. Playground, heated pool.

Blue Spruce RV Park and Campground

3 miles (5 km) west on Highway 16 from intersection with Highway 97

250-964-7272

128 sites with full hookups, pull-throughs, tent camping, cabins. Showers, laundry, store. Heated pool, mini-golf, playground.

Fraser River RV Park

On the Fraser River

250-330-4453

Forested lots, riverside spaces, spacious turnaround, power. Tent camping. Showers, rest rooms.

Hartway RV Park

7729 Kelly Road South, 6 miles (9 km) north of Prince George on Highway 97

250-962-9724

Full hookups, pull-throughs, cable TV. Free showers, self-service laundry, gift shop, near store.

Lakeside RV Park

11075 Hedlund Road, 7 miles (11 km) east of downtown Prince George

250-963-9515

Camping with partial hookups, tepees available. Pets welcome. Fishing, boat launch.

Sintich Trailer & RV Park

3 miles (5 km) south of Prince George on Highway 97

250-963-9862

Spacious lots for adult campers, pull-throughs, power, cable TV. Free showers; laundry. Near store and gas station.

Southpark RV Park

9180 Cariboo Highway South

Full and partial hookups, pull-throughs, showers, laundry. Near store, gas station, golf course.

Restaurants

Denny's

1650 Central Street

Adjoins Sandman Suites Hotel

1-800-254-8380

Family dining, open 24 hours.

Esther's

1151 Commercial Drive

250-562-4131

Restaurant, coffee garden in hotel.

Grama's Restaurant

910 Central Street

250-563-7174

Home cooking, pies and pastries.

The Log House Restaurant

11075 Hedlund Road, 7 miles (11 km) east of downtown

250-963-9515

Fine dining on the shores of Tabor Lake.

Ricky's Pancake & Family Restaurant

1515 Victoria Street

250-564-8114

Home-style meals.

Shogun Japanese Restaurant   250-563-0121
770 Brunswick Street   Japanese cuisine.

Road Notes

In the 188 miles (303 km) between Prince George and Chetwynd, you'll follow the John Hart Highway, which is Highway 97. The Rocky Mountain Trench, 95 miles (153 km) north of Prince George, marks the western boundary of the Rocky Mountains. This land of lakes, rivers, and fertile valleys beneath snowcapped peaks will have you shooting pictures in every direction.

$\mathcal{C}$HETWYND

From Prince George: 188 miles (303 km)
To Dawson Creek: 62 miles (100 km)

Whereas the town of Hope seems content with claiming the title of Chainsaw Sculpture Capital of British Columbia, Chetwynd is more ambitious—seeing itself as the Chainsaw Sculpture Capital of the World. Chetwynd is proud of the 35 sculptures you'll see around town, beginning with the welcome sign that features a family of curious bears. Stop at the **Chetwynd Visitor Information Centre** along Highway 97 to pick up a driving map that shows where the sculptures are on display: at the **Chainsaw Sculpture Park** and at businesses around town.

Chetwynd lies in coal and timber country in Little Prairie Valley. In fact, the early-day fur traders originally called it Little Prairie. The name Chetwynd honors Ralph Chetwynd, a government minister who helped bring the Pacific Great Eastern Railway to town. Many of Chetwynd's 3,200 people are employed at the sawmill, the coal mine, or the two dams up Hudson's Hope Loop. If you want to learn more about mining and forestry, industrial tours are available. Check at the visitor center for reservations.

Take a walk along any of the extensive trails in the Chetwynd Greenspace Trail System. They range from a 5-minute walk to an hour or more on trails varying from rustic to improved. A popular route is the **Old Baldy Hiking Trail**, which offers excellent views of the valley, along with plenty of places to rest. The **Community Forest** features interpretive walking and hiking trails, a tree registry, and a demonstration forest, along with picnic areas in forested settings.

Take the kids for a few hours of water fun at the **Chetwynd Leisure Wave Pool**, one of the best in the area, located at 46th Street and the North Access Road off Highway 97. Other local recreation includes your choice of two nine-hole golf courses, mountain biking, and terrific fishing. You can obtain your mandatory fishing license and all the tackle you need at **Lonestar Sporting Goods**. Call 250-788-1250.

For more information on any Chetwynd activities and events, call the Chetwynd Visitor Information Centre at 250-788-3345 or www.sun.pris.bc.ca/chetwynd.

Dam Drive

On the map, the **Hudson's Hope Loop** road—Highway 29 running north from Chetwynd—looks like a great way to shave off time and miles from your Alaska Highway trip. Don't be fooled by the two-dimensional aspects of the map. The 87-mile route will lead you through some beautiful country, but it is a narrow, winding affair that's best left to the sports-car set. And besides, if you take this cutoff, you'll miss Dawson Creek completely, along with the fun of seeing your way around the Mile 0 city.

Parts of British Columbia are suitable for shooting a Hollywood Western.

But do make a side trip along Hudson's Hope Loop to enjoy the countryside and visit two massive dams across the Peace River: the Peace River Dam and the W.A.C. Bennett Dam. See the dams, and then come back to Chetwynd so you can launch your Alaska Highway adventure at Dawson Creek.

Along Hudson's Hope Loop, the landscape changes from pasture to aspen forest to wheat fields in a broad river valley. The narrow road is patchy at times, and elevation changes can be rather steep, so you may just decide to pass on this side trip if you're driving a big rig.

Dinosaur footprints are part of an outside display at **W.A.C. Bennett Dam**. The dam itself is 600 feet (183 m) tall and 1.25 miles (2 km) long, creating Williston Lake, a 230-mile-long (370-km) reservoir that's the 10th largest in the world. In the modern visitor center theater, a film shows historical footage of the river before the dam's construction, and explains why it was built here and how it all came together. Hands-on science experiments demonstrate how much energy is needed to light a bulb. Take a tour of the underground powerhouse. Parking is plentiful, and there are excellent views and photo opportunities.

Farther along the loop road is **Peace Canyon Dam**. While this is the more modest of the two dams, the visitor center here includes museum dioramas that depict early life for settlers in this area. Just inside the front door are full-size replicas of dinosaurs that once roamed the region. An upper deck allows a generous view of the dam and the valley.

Chetwynd, B.C., has so many chainsaw sculptures around town that it claims the title of "Chainsaw Sculpture Capital of the World."

Lodging

Chetwynd Court Motel
5104 North Access Road
250-788-2271
Rooms, kitchenettes, cable TV, laundry
  facilities. Restaurant, liquor store.

Country Squire Motor Inn
5317 South Access Road
1-800-668-3101 or 250-788-2276
51 air-conditioned units, some kitchenettes
  and nonsmoking. Movie channel,
  laundry, sauna, fitness room. Winter
  plug-ins. Pets allowed. Restaurant.

Pine Cone Motor Inn
5224 53rd Avenue
1-800-663-8082 or 250-788-3311
54 air-conditioned units, including
  kitchenettes. Cable TV. Pets allowed.
  Coffee shop, dining room.

Stagecoach Inn
5413 South Access Road
250-788-9666
55 air-conditioned rooms, kitchenettes,
  nonsmoking available. Cable TV, sauna,
  whirlpool, laundry. Winter plug-ins.
  Pets on approval. Restaurant.

Campgrounds

Caron Creek RV Park
On Highway 97, west of Chetwynd
250-788-2522
Full and partial hookups, pull-throughs on
gravel and grass. Free showers;
washrooms.

Westwind RV Park
On 53rd Avenue, 2 miles (3 km) north past
junction of Highways 97 and 29.
250-788-2190
50 pull-through sites with full hookups.
Showers, laundry, rest rooms, dump
station. Fire pits, picnic area,
playground.

Restaurants

High Country Inn
5000 North Access Road
Adjacent to Chetwynd Court Motel
250-788-2271
Dining, cocktails.

Kentucky Fried Chicken
4800 North Access Road
250-788-9866
The fast-food favorite in chicken.

Murray's Pub
4613 47th Avenue
250-788-9594
Appetizers, meals, cocktails.

Stagecoach Inn
5413 South Access Road
250-788-9665
Dining with views of Sunkunka Valley.

Subway
5300 North Access Road
250-788-7824
Hot and cold subs, salads.

The Swiss Inn Restaurant
4812 North Access Road
250-788-2566
Steaks, European cuisine.

$\mathcal{D}$AWSON CREEK, British Columbia

From Chetwynd: 62 miles (100 km)
From the Washington border: 705 miles (1,128 km)
To the Alaska border: 1,190 miles (1,915 km)
To Fairbanks: 1,488 miles (2,395 km)

Symbolically, Dawson Creek is the end of this road, and the beginning of another. You have arrived at Mile 0 of the famed Alaska Highway, and a new leg of your adventure is about to begin.

For a complete description of Dawson Creek and its services, facilities, and attractions, see Chapter 6, The Alaska Highway.

A Dream Come True

Hugo and Helen Smith of Sterling, Colorado, were on their way home when we met them in Dawson Creek. They had been on the road for two months, and had come north through Alberta, British Columbia, the Yukon, and Alaska. They had put 7,000-plus miles (11,265 km) on their 1994 Bronco that towed a 24-foot travel trailer.

"Alaska was the only state in the 50 that I hadn't been in," Hugo said. "We were two years planning this. One of my big dreams was to see the glaciers. We took an 8-hour boat trip to the Kenai Fjords.

"The road is considerably above what I expected. Of course, construction in a few places got on my nerves.

"I do the driving; she's the navigator," he said, thumbing to his wife, who just smiled slightly.

"The people have been outstanding, friendly, helpful, courteous to a point that it was absolutely noticeable," Hugo continued. "And, by the way, we have a laptop with us, and I've been sending e-mail to about 18 people. We have a cell phone, too.

"You know, it was fascinating to see American and Canadian flags flying together. It was impressive to me and it was a beautiful thing. Almost brought a tear to my eye." Hugo really was choking up a bit, and the warmth of his patriotism overflowed onto me.

Finally, just about the time I figured Hugo was going to do all the talking for both of them, Helen shyly added: "The one I really liked was the trip to the Arctic Circle, on the tour bus." And I knew she meant it.

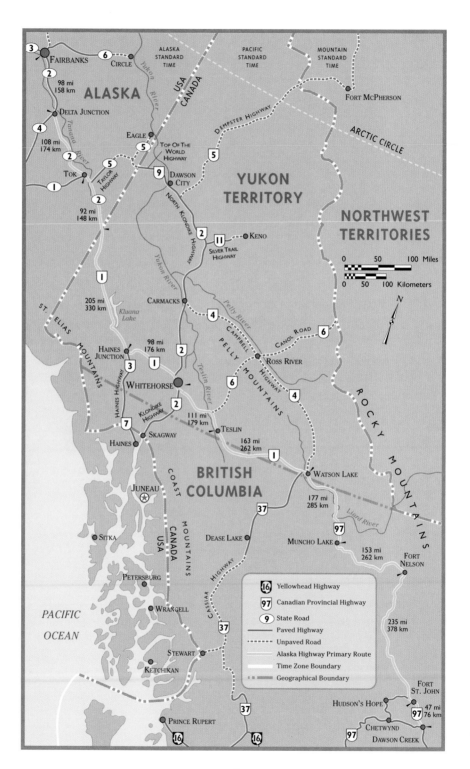

Chapter 6

The Alaska Highway

Whether you arrive in Dawson Creek, B.C., via the Alberta route or the British Columbia route, you are now about to begin a driving experience of a lifetime. After traveling hundreds of miles to get to this starting line, most people about to embark on the Alaska Highway shed any lingering road weariness in Dawson Creek. Instead, they are revived by a sense of excitement and anticipation.

However, don't expect the adventure part to begin immediately, for the road really doesn't change for many more miles. It's still paved and easy to navigate and is basically a continuation of what you've been seeing for a long distance already.

The starting line for the Alaska Highway lies in Dawson Creek.

Until you sense the wonder of place that gradually unfolds as you travel north, the start of this adventure is more of a mind-set. It's the knowledge that you are following in the footsteps of those intrepid workers who laid the groundwork for this highway more than five decades ago—and in the winter, no less—pushing a route through forests and along mountains, skirting jewel-colored lakes, battling the quagmire of newly exposed permafrost, to complete one of the world's great road-building projects. Carry those images with you as you travel, and be sure to stop at the historic mileposts to learn more about this incredible road north.

$\mathcal{D}$AWSON CREEK, British Columbia

Mile 0 of the Alaska Highway
To Fort St. John: 47 miles (76 km)
To the Alaska border: 1,190 miles (1,915 km)
To Fairbanks: 1,488 miles (2,395 km)

Tucked into the far northeast corner of British Columbia, little Dawson Creek gained international attention in March 1942 when thousands of U.S. troops "invaded" to begin construction of the Alaska Highway from the south end of the route. For a brief time, Dawson Creek was overpopulated, straining its transportation grid, local accommodations, and food services, and filling its streets with GIs. The boom was short-lived, however.

Dawson Creek, B.C., and Dawson City, Yukon, farther north, were both named for **George Mercer Dawson**, a geologist who surveyed these parts of Canada in 1879. His work paved the way for settlement and development in both Dawsons. Incorporated as a city in 1958, Dawson Creek remains a small town with fewer than 12,000 residents.

At the city limits, near Dawson Creek Airport, stands a welcome sign declaring **Mile Zero City, Where the Adventure Begins!** And at the traffic circle in Dawson Creek that connects Highway 2 to Highway 97, you'll spot the oft-photographed sign proclaiming: **You Are Now Entering the World Famous Alaska Highway.**

Another not-to-be-missed landmark, the **Mile 0 Milepost**, is in an unfortunate place—dead center in the busy intersection of 10th Street and 102nd Avenue—making posed photos a dangerous proposition. I asked my husband to let me out on a street corner; then I had him swing back around so I could take a picture of the RV as he drove by the milepost monument. But scampering out into traffic yourself is ill-advised. Perhaps a postcard will best suit that place in your scrapbook.

Atop the monument, sign-makers have painted the number of miles from Dawson Creek to Fort St. John (48), Fort Nelson (300), Whitehorse (918), and Fairbanks (1,523). The numbers no longer match the actual driving distance, because the road has been straightened (and shortened) since it was first constructed. At that time, Canada used miles to measure distance. The country has since switched to the metric system, and kilometerposts have replaced mileposts along the highway.

Just beyond the traffic circle connecting Highways 2 and 97 stands another landmark, a huge, wooden grain elevator that was relocated to this place in the **Northern Alberta Railway Park.** Today it houses an art gallery and features a spiral ramp, making access to the exhibits easy for persons of any age or physical ability. On Saturdays, come down to the **Farmers Market** on the park grounds for the freshest vegetables and fruits and for crafts and sweets.

Also in the park, a former railway station has been renovated to serve a new purpose. Each year between 35,000 and 40,000 people visit the **Station Museum and**

Dawson Creek Visitor Information Centre, at 900 Alaska Avenue. Enjoy the local and natural history exhibits, along with photographic displays of the highway's beginnings, its construction, and memories of early-day travel. A well-stocked gift shop offers books, T-shirts and sweatshirts, pencils, postcards, posters, rulers, ashtrays, you name it. You'll find a souvenir for every member of the family. For more information, call 250-782-9595.

This town supports a wide-ranging community of farming families. Agriculture and tourism are the leading economic drivers. If you're visiting during early August, be sure to make it to the Dawson Creek Exhibition & Stampede, which includes farming exhibits, horse shows, handicrafts, a food fair, and a rodeo. And for the fright of your life, watch the professional chuckwagon drivers' race.

There is no shortage of restaurants, hotels, campgrounds, bakeries, car and RV washes—anything you need for resting up or stocking up before beginning your journey up the Alaska Highway. For more information on the area's attractions, call the Visitor Information Bureau, 250-782-9595.

Lodging

Alaska Hotel
10213 10th Street
250-782-7998
www.alaskahotel.com
12 units, old-world decor. Restaurant, entertainment.

Cedar Lodge Motel
801 110th Avenue
250-782-8531
42 units, with kitchenettes, refrigerators, cable TV, laundry. Across from Dawson Mall.

The George Dawson Inn
11705 8th Street
1-800-663-2745 or 250-782-9151
80 well-appointed, air-conditioned rooms, executive suites, cable TV. Coffee shop, lounge, dining room.

Inn on the Creek
10600 8th Avenue South
1-888-782-8136 or 250-782-8136
Air-conditioned rooms, family restaurant.

The Lodge Motor Inn & Café
1317 Alaska Avenue
1-800-935-3336
40 air-conditioned rooms, cable TV, free local calls. Centrally located.

Northwinds Lodge
632 103rd Avenue
1-800-665-1759 or 250-782-9181
20 air-conditioned rooms, kitchenettes, movies. RV and truck parking. Near Co-Op Mall.

Peace Villa Motel
1641 Alaska Avenue
1-877-782-8175 or 250-782-8175
46 air-conditioned rooms, movies, laundry, office services, sauna. Senior discount. Near golf course and restaurants.

Trail Inn Dawson Creek
Junction of Highway 97 and Alaska Highway
1-800-663-2749 or 250-782-8595
www.neonet.bc.ca/trailinn
38 air-conditioned rooms, cable TV, free
continental breakfast. Four pet rooms.
Three-Diamond rating, AAA.

Campgrounds

Alahart RV Park
Junction of Highway 97 and Alaska Highway
250-782-4702
www.pris.bc.ca/alahart
Full hookups, pull-throughs, tent camping.
Free showers, self-service laundry,
dump station. Close to downtown.

Central RV Park
1301 Alaska Avenue
250-782-8525
10 sites with full hookup, close to shopping.

Mile 0 RV Park & Campground
Mile 1.5, next to Rotary Lake
250-782-2590
Partial hookups, shady sites. Free showers;
laundry, dump station. Free phone for
e-mail.

Northern Lights RV Park
On Highway 97 South, just west of junction
with Highway 97 North
250-782-9433
Spacious pull-throughs with full and partial
hookups. Free showers, self-service
laundry, washrooms. RV wash; full
service for Alaska Highway preparation.
Gift shop, trout-fishing pond.

Tubby's RV Park
1913 Hart Highway (Highway 97 South)
250-782-2584
97 full-hookup sites, pull-throughs,
tenting. Free showers, self-service
laundry, rest rooms, dump station. Car
and RV wash, auto services. Near
swimming pool and Pioneer Village.

Restaurants

The Alaska Café & Pub
Near Mile 0 milepost
250-782-7040
Private dining and meeting rooms.
Caravans welcome.

Lilly's Dining Room
11705 8th Street
In the George Dawson Inn
250-782-9151
Fine dining.

Ma's Stopping Place
11705 8th Street
In the George Dawson Inn
250-782-9151
Coffee shop featuring down-home
breakfasts, lunches, dinners.

Pizzarama Pizzeria
11300 8th Street
Next to Smitty's Family Restaurant
250-782-2441
Pizza and pasta.

Smitty's Family Restaurant
11300 8th Street
250-782-5442
Family dining, seniors' and children's
menus.

Road Notes

The price of gas in Dawson Creek is usually higher than in the smaller towns to the south. And after Dawson Creek, the pump prices only go up. The farther north you go, the more you pay.

As you drive north toward Fort St. John, notice the pumpjacks in the fields. These mechanisms draw the oil out of the ground and into a pipeline or a storage tank. Most of the oil and gas is sold to markets in Canada and the United States.

Get sweeter than honey just south of Fort St. John at **The Honey Place**, which features the world's largest glass beehive. You can learn about bee behavior and what makes quality honey. Get your honey here, or pollen, or other souvenirs. It's on the west side of the road, about 5 miles (8 km) before Fort St. John. Call 250-785-4808.

𝒥ORT ST. JOHN

From Dawson Creek: 47 miles (76 km)
To Fort Nelson: 235 miles (378 km)

Fort St. John calls itself The Energetic City, with a nod to the industries that power the city's economy: natural gas and oil extraction, hydroelectric power, forestry, agriculture, and tourism. This city of 15,000 people is the oldest non-Native settlement on the British Columbia mainland. Another 30,000 people live throughout the North Peace region, where the Peace River snakes through a broad, green valley. These rural residents and First Nations communities look to Fort St. John as a regional hub for business and services. The city offers shopping, dining, and cultural attractions such

This is "big sky" country too.

International Flavor

We had stopped at the Mile 80 wayside, north of Fort St. John, to use the rest rooms. On my return to the camper, I noticed that two couples were setting up a midmorning snack at a nearby picnic table. As they pulled goodies from the trunk of a rental car, I grew curious about how they were traveling. Were they staying in hotels as they went? I grew brave enough to ask.

The two couples, from Capetown, South Africa, were M. Viljoen and Rina Viljoen, and Professor D. deVilliers and Julia deVilliers. They were stopping for tea. They had traveled from Prince George, taking the Yellowhead Highway to the Cassiar Highway, which connected with the Alaska Highway just west of Watson Lake.

Mr. Viljoen served as spokesperson:

"We discussed it: Was it the right thing to do, this thing by car? All in all, it's been beautiful. Before we came here, we heard the road was awful. The guides said to bring a spare tire, spare fan belt, this, that, and a thousand other things. I said, 'Why don't we leave the clothes behind and take a spare car?'

"Usually we stay in motels or bed-and-breakfasts. The Cassiar Highway was very nice, especially if you take the turnoff to Stewart, and just over the river you get to Hyder, Alaska. We really enjoyed the bears there. Of course, the rangers were nearby.

"Driving the Alcan, and all the way from Vancouver, we've enjoyed every minute!"

At this point, Rina Viljoen paused from setting up their wilderness tea to say, "It's a wonderful experience to do this by car—we'll never forget it. The people are so friendly!"

as live theater, dance, and music at the **North Peace Culture Centre**, 10015 100th Avenue. Call 250-785-1992.

As the main town of the North Peace region, Fort St. John lies within a diverse landscape, from rolling farmlands and valleys to canyons carved by rivers. The staff at the **Visitor Information Centre**, 9923 96th Avenue, will help you plan an outdoor adventure. Call 250-785-6037. The center offers a list of local guides and outfitters and their specialties. Think about a day of hiking on **Fish Creek Community Forest** trails, golfing on one of the three nearby courses, swimming, horseback riding, or fishing for walleye or northern pike in **Charlie Lake**.

Check in with **Adventure Sporting Goods**, at 11116 100th Avenue, for mandatory fishing licensing as well as outdoor clothing and gear. The folks there can book a guide for you, too. Call 250-785-4500. Another local leader in outdoor adventure is **Muskwa Safaris**, which will set up your wilderness vacation, whether it's on horseback, in a raft, or in an airplane. Call 250-785-4681. Several private campgrounds and provincial parks are within an easy drive of town.

The **North Peace Leisure Pool** complex, at 9505 100th Street, is the newest addition to the recreational possibilities in Fort St. John. The facility includes a lap pool, wave pool, rapids channel, water slide, and a kiddie pool. Relax in the steam room or sauna and the road-miles will melt away. Call 250-785-POOL.

The annual **Fort St. John air show**, held in late July, includes flying by the Canadian Forces Snowbirds, Skyhawks, Warbirds, and Air Combat Canada. This flying spectacle attracts thousands each year.

Exhibits at the **Fort St. John–North Peace Museum** reflect on the region's First Nations roots, its settlement by fur traders, and its development into the regional power that it is today. Back in 1942, Fort St. John was the unofficial starting line for the builders of the Alaska Highway. A gravel road already existed between Dawson Creek and this outlying community, and that road was incorporated into the route. Six thousand troops descended on what was then a town of 200 people. You'll find the museum at the foot of the landmark oil derrick at 9323 100th Street. Call 250-787-0430.

Just north of town, you can turn west to access Highway 29, **Hudson's Hope Loop**, from the north end. This road leads to some beautiful driving country, but the road does get narrow and patchy in places. Steep grades and switchbacks are not advisable for oversize RVs. Two dams along this loop road are major area attractions, as is Hudson's Hope Museum. For more information, see the section on the town of Chetwynd in Chapter 5, The Western Route.

Lodging

Best Western Coachman Inn
8540 Alaska Road
1-888-388-9408 or 250-787-0651
70 deluxe rooms, nonsmoking and pet
    rooms available. Cable TV, sauna,
    whirlpool, fitness room.

Fort St. John Motor Inn
10707 102nd Street
1-888-988-8846 or 250-787-0411
96 air-conditioned rooms, laundry, winter
    plug-ins. Pets welcome.

Four Seasons Motor Inn
9810 100th Street
1-800-523-6677 or 250-785-6647
Air-conditioned rooms, kitchenettes and
    nonsmoking available. Cable TV, winter
    plug-ins. Pets allowed. Close to
    shopping, restaurants.

Mackenzie Inn
9223 100th Street
1-800-663-8313 or 250-785-8364
113 rooms; nonsmoking, kitchenettes,
    wheelchair-accessible. Winter plug-ins.

Northgate Motor Inn
10419 Alaska Road
250-787-8475
43 air-conditioned units. Satellite TV,
    laundry services, health club, swimming
    pool. Free breakfast. Winter plug-ins.
    Restaurant, pub.

Pioneer Inn
100th Avenue and 98th Street
1-888-663-8312 or 250-787-0521
125 rooms, suites, cable TV. Fitness facility,
    swimming pool, sauna, whirlpool.
    Restaurant, lounge, pub.

Ramada Ltd.
10103 98th Avenue
250-787-0779
74 deluxe rooms, suites, kitchenettes. Cable
TV, data ports, voice mail, guest
laundry. Fitness facility, winter plug-
ins. Free airport shuttle.

Campgrounds

Ron's RV Park
5 miles (8 km) north of Fort St. John
250-787-1569
Shaded sites with full and partial hookup,
pull-throughs, tenting area, picnic
tables. Showers, laundry, rest rooms,
phone. Boat rentals, fishing information.

Rotary RV Park
6 miles (9.5 km) north of Fort St. John
250-785-1700
40 sites with full or partial hookup, pull-
throughs. Showers, laundry, dump
station. Boat dock on Charlie Lake. Open
May 1—September 30.

Sourdough Pete's RV Park
Mile 45 Alaska Highway
250-785-7664
Full hookups, pull-throughs. Next to family
amusement park.

The province manages two easy-access
parks north of Fort St. John. For
more information, contact the Parks District
Office in Fort St. John at 250-787-3407.
The parks are:

Beatton Provincial Park
2 miles (3 km) north, then 5 miles (8 km)
east of Fort St. John
37 RV and tent sites, with Charlie Lake
access. Swimming, playground, fishing,
boat launch.

Charlie Lake Provincial Park
7 miles (11 km) north of Fort St. John
58 sites with picnic tables, outhouses,
dump station. Playground, short hiking
trail to Charlie Lake.

Restaurants

Charlie Lake General Store
Mile 50.6 Alaska Highway
250-787-0655
Take-out chicken and ribs.

Dairy Queen
10032 101st Avenue
250-785-6316
Burgers, fries, ice cream confections.

Also stop by major local hotels, which
feature full lunch and dinner menus in their
dining rooms.

Road Notes

The next major city, Fort Nelson, is 235 miles (378 km) away. That's the longest
segment of the Alaska Highway without a town of 1,000 residents or more.
Nonetheless, on this wilderness drive you'll find the occasional roadhouse, gas
station, restaurant, or campground tucked in quaint little places along the way, so
don't worry about heading into the unknown. Services are available at Shepherd's
Inn (Mile 72), Wonowon (Mile 101.5–102), Pink Mountain (Mile 143–147), Sikanni
Chief (Mile 159), Buckinghorse (Mile 175), and Prophet River (Mile 233). Plus, there's

so much beauty to behold: This country is crisscrossed with rivers, and the Rocky Mountains to the west will keep you company.

Also through this stretch, you'll come across a couple of historical stops on the **Northwest Staging Route**, the series of airstrips that were used during World War II to deliver supplies and Lend-Lease Program airplanes to Fairbanks. From there, Russian pilots ferried the planes over the Bering Sea. One such historical site is at Mile 146 (236.5 km), the Sikanni Chief flight strip on the east side of the road. This was the southernmost end of the Northwest Staging Route. Another abandoned airstrip can be seen near Mile 217 (349 km), where a side road crosses the old airstrip.

As you drive, you'll notice segments of the original road that have been abandoned to the weeds through the years as the route has been straightened (and shortened).

The **Muskwa Bridge** at Mile 281 (452 km), just a couple of miles before Fort Nelson, is the lowest point on the Alaska Highway, at an elevation of only 1,000 feet (305 m).

$\mathcal{F}$ORT NELSON

From Fort St. John: 235 miles (378 km)
To Muncho Lake: 153 miles (246 km)
To Watson Lake: 330 miles (531 km)

Fort Nelson boasts that it has the longest main street in the world: the Alaska Highway. And the city's address is Historical Mile 300 (483 km)—a reference to the town's distance from Dawson Creek on the original Alaska Highway. (Road realignment now puts Fort Nelson just 282 miles from Dawson Creek.)

Established in 1905 as a fur trading post, this community in the northeast corner of British Columbia was named for Admiral Nelson. About 6,400 people live in the area near the convergence of four rivers: the Muskwa, Prophet, Sikanni, and Fort Nelson. The extraction of natural resources fuels the local

The Chadwick Ram at Fort Nelson.

economy, with diverse industries represented on the city's snowflake-shaped emblem: gas and oil, mining, lumber, wildlife, agriculture, tourism, and trapping.

Like other small towns of the north, the emphasis is on opportunity and friendliness. Each Monday through Thursday at 6:45 P.M., travelers are invited to stop by the **Phoenix Theatre** in the town square for a free welcome-visitor program. For information: 250-774-7469. Visitors are free to use computers at the **public library** on the town square to check their e-mail accounts on any service that does not require long-distance dialing. For more information, call 250-774-6777. **The Elks Club** hosts a steak fry every Saturday at 6 P.M. and invites everyone to come, members or not.

This town is a good place to restock the RV with groceries and other necessities. We followed up on a tip to check out the bakery department of the local **IGA store**, and it paid off. The fresh apple fritters were so wonderful that we bought a half-dozen and froze the extras for later.

At the **Fort Nelson information center**, located inside the recreation center at Mile 284 Alaska Highway, you can have a free cup of coffee and browse through the printed materials about things to see and do in the Northern Rockies. The center's number is 250-774-6400. Cash machines and U.S. currency exchanges are available at banks located along the frontage road of the highway.

For the flavor of the past, visit the **Fort Nelson Heritage Museum**, in a log cabin across from the information center. The museum features a mounted white moose in its display of local wildlife. Film footage taken during the building of the Alaska Highway can be seen in the museum's Muskwa Theatre. On the grounds are a trapper's log cabin, gift shop, and an old-time general store. Call 250-774-3536.

Golfers can play a nine-hole, par-35 course at **Poplar Hills Golf and Country Club**, just outside town. Take advantage of the midnight sun and play from dawn to dusk in summers. Call 250-774-3862.

Winter visitors will marvel at the northern lights in these parts. Aurora borealis displays above Fort Nelson draw scientists who observe and record the events. The northern lights can occur year-round, but are easiest to see during the winter months.

Lodging

Almada Inn
5035 51st Avenue
250-774-2844
Kitchenettes, cable TV, office services, free continental breakfast, hot tubs.

The BlueBell Inn
3907 50th Avenue South
250-774-6961
46 air-conditioned rooms, kitchenettes, some nonsmoking. Cable TV, self-service laundry, store, cash machine, winter plug-ins. Restaurant. Fuel station.

Coach House Inn
4711 50th Avenue South
250-774-3911
Modern rooms, plus laundry service, office services, winter plug-ins. Sauna, whirlpool. Small pets welcome. Restaurant, dining room, lounge with TV and fireplace.

Fort Nelson Hotel
5110 50th Avenue North
250-774-6971
145 air-conditioned rooms, kitchenettes.
Cable TV, gift shop, indoor pool, saunas.
Dining room, cocktail lounge,
entertainment and dancing.

Mini Price Inn
5036 51st Street
250-774-2136
Air-conditioned rooms, kitchenettes.
Provides for daily, weekly, or monthly
stays. Cable TV. Downtown location.

Pioneer Motel
5207 50th Avenue South
250-774-6459
12 units; kitchenettes and cabins available.
Cable TV, movie channel, laundry
facilities. Senior rates. Pets welcome.

Provincial Motel
4103 50th Avenue South
250-774-6901
37 air-conditioned rooms, kitchenettes,
extra-long beds. Cable TV, laundry
facilities. Winter plug-ins. Senior
discount.

Woodlands Inn
3995 50th Avenue South
250-774-6669
90 rooms, suites, kitchenettes. Cable TV,
coin-operated laundry, steam bath, hot
tub, fitness room. Restaurant, sports
lounge.

Campgrounds

Husky 5th Wheel Campground
5 miles (8 km) south of downtown Fort
Nelson on Alaska Highway
250-774-7270
55 RV sites with full hookups, some pull-
throughs, 14 tent sites. Showers,
laundry, store, fuel, restaurant. Cable
TV, Internet access. Llama viewing.

Westend RV Campground
Next to Heritage Museum
250-774-2340
140 sites with full and partial hookups, pull-
throughs, tent sites, free firewood.
Showers, laundry, cable TV, dump
station. Gift shop, free car wash.
Walking distance to local attractions.

The province manages two easy-access
parks west of Fort Nelson. For more information, contact the Parks District Office in
Fort St. John at 250-787-3407. The parks are:

Testa River Provincial Park
48 miles (77 km) west of Fort Nelson, then
south for 1 mile (1.5 km)
25 campsites, tenting area, firewood,
outhouses, water, wheelchair access.

115 Creek Provincial Campsite
57.5 miles (92.5 km) west of Fort Nelson
8 campsites, water, picnic tables, garbage
barrels. Fishing nearby in 115 Creek and
MacDonald Creek.

Restaurants

The Bistro
Dan's Neighborhood Pub
South end of town
250-774-3929
Daily lunch specials.

Dixie Lee
Downtown Fort Nelson
250-774-6226
Hamburgers, chicken, fish and chips, ice
cream.

Fort Pizza
5148 Laird Street
250-774-2405
Pizza, fast food, ice cream.

Northern Deli
Landmark Plaza (downtown)
250-774-3311
Subs, sandwiches, salads, deep-fried foods,
lunches to go.

Subway
Main Street
250-774-SUBS
Hot and cold deli sandwiches.

Also stop by major local hotels, which
feature full lunch and dinner menus in their
dining rooms.

Road Notes

As you continue north, you'll generally find fewer mileposts and kilometerposts along the road. Some of the ones you do encounter give figures that represent the distance from Dawson Creek on the original Alaska Highway—they are the Historical Miles. These mileposts do not take into account the road improvements and shortening that have taken place over the years. So be aware that the mileposts won't necessarily jibe with mileage showing on your odometer.

Many of the historical mileposts were erected in 1992, the road's 50th-anniversary year, as a way to provide markers with historical information about the significance of various places. Over the years, many towns and businesses have refused to give up their historical addresses when the road was shortened, so they now refer to themselves as being at Historical Milepost such-and-such, further muddying the question of just exactly where you are. And as British Columbia and the Yukon work on the road, milepost markers may be missing or out of date.

Mileage and kilometer figures used in this text are based on the actual current number of road miles from Dawson Creek.

Thirty-four miles (54.5 km) past Fort Nelson, at the summit of 3,500-foot (1,067-km) **Steamboat Mountain**, you'll gain spectacular views of the Muskwa River Valley and the Rocky Mountains. Looking at the shape of Steamboat Mountain, you'll see how it got its name.

Another 8 miles (13 km) along, you'll catch the first views of a classic Indian profile in the high, craggy rocks. Stop for a photo at the turnout in another mile. Drive another couple of miles to Teetering Rock viewpoint, another turnout with litter barrel and trailheads.

The highest point on the Alaska Highway (4,250 feet) occurs at **Summit**, 90 miles (145 km) from Fort Nelson.

$\mathcal{M}$UNCHO LAKE

From Fort Nelson: 153 miles (246 km)
To Watson Lake: 177 miles (285 km)

With the crown of the Rocky Mountains towering above, and the jewel-colored waters of Muncho Lake at roadside, the highway here lies at an elevation of 2,680 feet. The province has developed campgrounds right along the lake, allowing you a wake-up view that will be indelible in your vacation memories. Copper oxide leaching into the lake is what creates these dramatic deep greens and blues.

Muncho means "big lake" in Tagish, the aboriginal language. At 7.5 miles (12 km) long, it is one of the largest natural lakes in the Canadian Rockies. To the west lies the

Stone sheep may be seen in the Muncho Lake area, where they are drawn to salt licks.

Terminal Range. "Terminal" refers to geographic position of the range—the northernmost section of the Rocky Mountains. Total length of the Rockies is almost 1,850 miles, from here to Santa Fe, New Mexico.

At **Double G Service** at the south end of Muncho Lake, you can book a guided, narrated tour on the lake aboard the MV *Sandpiper*. Call 250-776-3411 for information.

Lodging/Campgrounds/Meals

Muncho Lake is 437 miles (699 km) from Dawson Creek, but its Historical Milepost number is 456. For the locations of the following four businesses, we provide the actual distances from Dawson Creek. However, some of them prefer to use their Historical Milepost distances in advertising. Just be aware that all of these places lie along a 7-mile stretch of road on the eastern shore of the lake.

Double G Service
Mile 436.5 Alaska Highway
250-776-3411
Motel rooms, store, café.

Northern Rockies Lodge/Highland Glen Lodge
Mile 442 Alaska Highway
1-800-663-5269 or 250-776-3481
Rooms, wilderness cabins. Can arrange for fly-in fishing, photo safari tours, floatplane service. Restaurant, bakery.

J & H Wilderness Resort
Mile 444 Alaska Highway
250-776-3453

Motel rooms, free continental breakfast, store, gift shop, restaurant. Lakeside RV sites with full hookups, pull-throughs. Dump station, showers, laundry, fire pits, and firewood. Tour packages available.

Muncho Lake Lodge
Mile 444 Alaska Highway
250-776-3456
Hotel rooms, kitchenette cabins, restaurant, café, lounge. 75 campsites with full or partial hookups, dump station, showers. Senior discount.

Road Notes

The Trout River follows the road beyond Muncho Lake, with swift, clear water that foams over the rapids. For several miles, this part of the highway seems to echo the old days: It's paved, but it's curvy. Left, right, left, right. And then, for a while, the route is unpaved. On a rainy day, the wet mud sounds like gushy soup under the tires.

Just north of Coal River at Mile 514 (823 km), the road narrows and loses its shoulders, and the legal speed is reduced dramatically. This is an old section of the highway, with no shoulders, and blind hills and corners. I feel for anybody on a bicycle. Within a few miles, a couple of rest areas provide good views of rapids along the **Liard River** and of surrounding vistas. In the miles that follow, note several sections of the old Alcan where the former roadbed is buckled, broken, and overgrown with weeds.

You may encounter extensive roadwork in these far-north reaches of British Columbia. A large realignment project is expected to continue for several summers. Get ready for a little flying mud and occasional delays while flaggers hold back traffic for heavy equipment. Farther ahead a solid, gravel roadbed is maintained with graders.

Liard River Hotsprings Provincial Park

Consider making time for a visit to Liard River Hotsprings Provincial Park, some 42 miles beyond Muncho Lake. If you're planning to spend the night, check in early. The 53 campsites are on a first-come, first-served basis, and they fill up quickly. Interpretive programs about area wildlife and the Liard (pronounced LEE-ard) hot springs attract large number of campers each night.

The big attraction here: the wondrous hot springs, which lie at the end of a boardwalk that crosses a superheated marsh. On either side of the walk, you can see the slow bubbling action of the mud beneath a clear layer of warm water. At the swimming hole, there's a changing room with benches and hooks. Outside, more benches and a wooden deck overlook naturally heated pools. Take care on the slippery steps leading into the water. Depending on how hot you like it, you move around to different levels of the pool until you are sufficiently cooked. The experience was heavenly after a day on the road.

This is bear country, and on the day we visited, another pool farther up the walkway was closed because of bear activity. A park ranger with a noisy popgun was headed in that direction to encourage the bears to move out. Bears that are regularly fed by humans lose their natural fear and, in fact, become demanding to the point of being dangerous. Many have to be shot simply because they've been "trained" to come to people for food. Signs at the campground read, "A fed bear is a dead bear."

After our wonderful soak, we crossed paths with a black bear—a little fellow that ran across the road at full tilt and headed into the woods on the other side. I remember thinking how awkward he looked, like a guy in a bear suit.

About 150,000 people come through this campground each year, park ranger Stacy Wall told us. However, the government is drawing the line at too much development, she said. The plan is to keep the boardwalk and campground in good shape, but the facilities will not be enlarged or upgraded. There is no electricity, no running water.

"Trapper Ray's has showers," she said, referring to a private lodge farther down the road. "I live on site and there's no electricity for us either.

"I have a shower, though," she added, smiling, "because we have to deal with the public, after all."

Muncho Lake is among the loveliest places on the Alaska Highway.

Muncho Lake Lodge.

A boardwalk leads to Liard Hotsprings.

North of Mile 551 (887 km), we saw big piles of brush alongside the road where land had been cleared for more work. Evidence of a long-ago forest fire and regrowth was visible in the distance.

At the **Hyland River Bridge**, pullouts on the north side lead to the river's edge. Locals say there's good fishing here for rainbow trout, Dolly Varden, and arctic grayling. Pavement picks up again around Mile 576 (922 km), at **Iron Creek Lodge**. A motel, RV campground, and café are tucked away in these north woods. Call 867-536-2266. The trees are shorter, with pine and shrubby deciduous trees. Their uniform height suggests regrowth from a fire.

At Historical Mile 588 (946 km) is **Contact Creek**, with a plaque that remembers September 24, 1942, a key day in construction of the Alaska Highway. On that day, soldiers from two regiments, one working from the north and one working from the south, met here. The southern segment of the highway was completed. In 1942, this place was 588 miles (946 km) from Dawson Creek; road improvements now put it 568 miles (961.5 km) from Dawson Creek. Nearby Contact Creek Lodge sells fuel, coffee, souvenirs, fishing licenses, and groceries; 867-536-2262.

After Contact Creek, the Alaska Highway crosses the British Columbia–Yukon border seven times, ducking in and out of the Yukon before it finally plunges fully into that immense northern territory—home to some 50,000 moose, 10,000 black bears, and 4,500 wolves.

$\mathcal{W}$ATSON LAKE, Yukon Territory

From Fort Nelson: 330 miles (531 km)
From Muncho Lake: 177 miles (285 km)
To Teslin: 163 miles (262 km)
To Whitehorse: 274 miles (441 km)

Welcome to Canada's Gateway to the Yukon. Driving through Watson Lake, you'll see the Stars and Stripes and the Maple Leaf paired on light-posts down the main drag. That may be a surprising sight to some, but it is reflective of the spirit of cooperation between Canada and the United States, not only in building the Alaska Highway, but also in using it for the last half-century. Watson Lake also is the junction city for the Alaska Highway and Campbell Highway 4, a northbound unpaved highway.

Stop by the **Alaska Highway Interpretive Centre** at the heart of the **Watson Lake Signpost Forest** (see sidebar) for information about the birth of the signpost forest and to see a small exhibit that details the building of the Alcan in pictures and artifacts. You'll find free coffee, use of rest rooms, and lots of printed material on towns and attractions still ahead.

Across the highway, check out the **Northern Lights Centre**, decorated outside with banners that simulate the aurora borealis. Inside, learn about the myth and science behind it. Contact 403-536-STAR or www.yukon.net/northernlights.

Leaving One's Mark

The **Watson Lake Signpost Forest** began with a single sign placed by Carl K. Lindley, a homesick Illinois soldier, during construction of the Alaska Highway. By 1978, when I first came by this place, the addition of signs through the years had expanded to cover a row of telephone poles at a pullout along the road. Each pole was studded with signs from all corners of the world.

In 1999 I was astonished to walk along the many trails of a true forest of poles covered with more than 42,000 signs. A thousand had been added in the previous year alone. There was so much to see that it was hard to take in all of the colors, words, and messages that were meaningful to somebody, somewhere, at some time in this road's history.

An Alaska license plate caught my eye, but it was nailed sideways and low to the ground. Someone had dated it and posted it just a week earlier. "Going back to Alaska," somebody had written around the plate's letters and numbers with a thick black marker. "Samantha, Sandi and Roger, Scooby Doo, Hobbes, Patches. Never to leave again!" It was a declaration that nearly brought tears to my eyes, representing not one trip but two, a leaving home and a going home.

It made me think about the realm of human emotion represented by all of these signs—the grief, sorrow, anger, and gladness that this road has known since the 1940s when young soldiers were missing home, worrying about the battlefront, and wondering if the labor would ever end. Through the years, the highway has seen the bright anticipation of new life in a new land, the tears of a bride who fears what lies ahead, and the joy of this unknown family who is returning to the place they call home. The signpost forest, as garish as some may think it is, has become a testament to the living, a guest book for people who want to tell the world: I WAS HERE.

Truck and RV service and repairs are available in Watson Lake. You can also arrange to go fishing, take a helicopter ride, or play a round of golf at Greenway's Greens. Local shops sell art and jewelry pieces in gold, jade, and ivory.

Lodging

Belvedere Motor Hotel
On the Alaska Highway
867-536-7563
48 rooms, suites, cable TV, whirlpools, in-room coffee. Cocktail lounge, coffee shop, dining room.

Big Horn Hotel
On Frank Trail, 1 block south of Alaska Highway in Watson Lake
867-536-2020
Rooms, wheelchair-accessible suite, cable TV, phones, coffee.

The Watson Lake Sign Forest in Yukon Territory is known far and wide, as each year passersby add their own "signature" sign to the upright posts that have sprouted all around the visitor center.

Cedar Lodge Motel

Junction of Adela Trail and Stubenberg
   Boulevard
867-536-7406
14 rooms, suites, kitchenettes, in-room
   coffee.

Gateway Motor Inn

Junction of Frank Trail and 8th Street South
867-536-7744
50 rooms, kitchenettes, in-room coffee.
   Restaurant.

Watson Lake Hotel

Next to Signpost Forest
867-536-7781
48 rooms, suites in historic building,
   nonsmoking available. Coffee shop,
   dining room. Senior discount.

Campgrounds

Downtown RV Park

Lakeview Avenue and 8th Street north, at
   center of town
867-536-2646
Full hookups, pull-throughs, showers,
   laundry, RV wash. Walking distance to
   shopping, restaurants, visitor
   information.

Gateway to the Yukon RV Park &
Campground

Mile 632.5 Alaska Highway
867-536-7448
140 full and partial hookups. Laundry, food
   mart, RV wash, RV repairs, fuel.

Green Valley RV Park

Just south of the Liard River bridge

867-536-2276

Full or partial hookups, riverside camping
in the shade, tenting area. Showers,
laundry, groceries, souvenirs. Boat ramp
and fishing.

Watson Lake Provincial Campground

2.5 miles (4 km) west of town center via
Alaska Highway

50 tent campsites, camp kitchen, boat
launch.

Restaurants

Pizza Palace

867-536-7744

Take-out pizza.

Sign Post Tempo-Tags

Corner of Alaska and Campbell Highways

867-536-7422

Breakfast, lunch, dinner, baked goods. Dine
in or take out.

Road Notes

Just past Watson Lake, we spotted a "dog truck," a dog-mushing term for a vehicle that transports sled dogs. The trucks are capped with a row of dog boxes, each with an individual door, on each side of the truck bed. You'll see these vehicles all over the northland, usually with a dogsled strapped on top of it all. The musher driving this dog truck had his sled on top, and he was towing a trailer loaded with an all-terrain vehicle. Here was the classic setup for exercising dogs in the summer: running them in front of a four-wheeler. We were looking forward to heading back into the north country, and this was a welcome, familiar sight.

West of Watson Lake on the Alaska Highway is the junction with Canada Highway 37, which leads southbound to Dease Lake and the Cassiar Highway. This is the way to the coastal communities of Stuart, B.C., and Hyder, Alaska. (See the section on the Yellowhead-Cassiar Highways in Chapter 7, Western Canada's Northbound Byways.)

As you journey north, you'll see another form of the signpost forest idea on the slopes along the highway, at a point about 630 miles (1,014 km) from Dawson Creek. For the last decade, "natural" graffiti artists have been writing messages using lines of small rocks.

You'll find several day-use or recreation sites and viewpoints in the beautiful miles between Watson Lake and Teslin. **Rancheria Falls Recreation Site** at Mile 695 (1,118.5 km) is a park-and-rest area with a boardwalk trail that leads to a waterfall.

About 3 miles farther along is the **Continental Divide**, and as you approach this point, the peaks become sharper, more visibly mountainous. At the crossing, a pullout includes signs with points of interest, maps, and outhouses. There are several lodges and visitor services through this section of the road. On the way to Teslin, the highway moves in gentle, winding curves through forest. Just before Teslin, you'll cross the longest bridge on the Alaska Highway, the **Nisutlin Bay Bridge**, which spans the Nisutlin River where it enters Teslin Lake. This is a gorgeous body of water—narrow, but long: 86 miles (138 km).

Teslin

From Watson Lake: 163 miles (262 km)
To Whitehorse: 111 miles (179 km)

Teslin is an inland Tlingit village of fewer than 500 people, many of whom are related to members of the Alaskan coastal Tlingit tribes. Although it is a small town, it offers much in the way of visitor services. You'll find a couple of major motels with in-house restaurants and lounges, groceries and general merchandise, RV parks, gift shops, a trading post, and the George Johnston Museum, named for a resourceful Tlingit man who lived from 1884 to 1972. Find out more about Johnston, Teslin, and the area's natural and cultural history in the museum, operated by the Teslin Historical Museum Society. Call 867-390-2550.

Lodging/Campgrounds/Restaurants

Dawson Peaks Resort & RV Park

Mile 770 Alaska Highway
867-390-2310
www.yukonweb.com/tourism/dawsonpeaks
Lakefront cabins with private baths and decks. Campsites with pull-throughs, water, dump station, showers. Tenting area. Free firewood. Restaurant featuring steak, seafood, Mexican food. Fishing charters, boat rentals.

Yukon Motel and RV Park

Mile 804 Alaska Highway
867-390-2443, office; 867-390-2575, restaurant
Rooms with satellite TV. 40 pull-through RV sites with full hookups, RV wash, fuel. Restaurant, lounge, gift shop, liquor store. Fishing charters. Wildlife μgallery of mounted animals.

Road Notes

A longtime landmark business 9 miles (14.5 km) north of Teslin, **Mukluk Annie's Salmon Bake**, offers hearty meals, motel rooms, cabins, free camping, and free RV wash. Call 867-667-1200.

A mile later, you'll cross the **Teslin River Bridge**, which is 1,770 feet (539.5 m) long and high enough to accommodate the steamers that once navigated the river between Whitehorse and Teslin. At the north end of the bridge, **Johnson's Crossing** offers camping opportunities, as well as souvenir shopping, fishing, canoeing, and wildlife-watching. Johnson's Crossing Campground Services claims that its cinnamon buns are world famous.

We decided to put in a few more miles before choosing our campsite and ended up at **Squanga Lake**, a Yukon government campground at Mile 821 (1,366 km). It's said to have good fishing for northern pike, grayling, burbot, rainbow trout, and whitefish (which are called *squanga* in the local Native language). The setting sun cast a brilliant pink across the sky and the lake's surface, silhouetting the spruce trees in black. That late-August night was dark, superbly quiet, and cool—a great

Kids and Bears

Cindy Birdwise had just driven between the province of Manitoba and Whitehorse, Yukon, with two children, ages 5 and 3, camping out of a 1997 four-wheel-drive Aerostar. She'd done it two years before that, too, when the kids were even younger and she had moved to the Yukon. So I figured she would be a good person to ask about advice for travelers on Canada's highways.

Birdwise, a human resources adviser for Parks Canada, had some advice for traveling with young ones: "Don't rush. We didn't have any particular destination in mind with a 5-year-old and a 3-year-old, and we found it best to drive between 1 P.M. and midnight.

"One really nice place to visit is Liard Hotsprings," she said. "Try to make it by 2 P.M. and reserve ahead for a place to park your RV. They go very quickly. There are three different levels of heat [at the hot springs]. You feel like you're right in nature, and you are. Beware of bears there. Watch out for bears at Pink Mountain, too [at Mile 140]. They're moving into the campground." ●

combination for sleepy Alaskans. The next morning we saw loons out on the lake in the rain.

Farther up the highway comes an opportunity for an exciting side trip to the historic Alaska community of **Skagway** (see photo on next page). To drive there, leave the Alaska Highway at Jake's Corner (Mile 874.5) and go west on Yukon Highway 8 for 34 miles (55 km) to Carcross and Klondike Highway 2. Skagway is then a scenic 66 miles (106 km) to the south. For details on the highway and on the history, attractions, lodging, and restaurants of Skagway, see the section on Klondike Highway 2 in Chapter 8, Alaska's State Highways.

Whitehorse

From Watson Lake, Yukon: 274 miles (441 km)
From Teslin, Yukon: 111 miles (179 km)
To Haines Junction, Yukon: 98 miles (158 km)
To Alaska–Yukon border: 303 miles (488 km)

The beautiful capital of the Yukon Territory is situated on the banks of the Yukon River, along the route of the gold seekers who were bound for riches a century ago. One of the first things you'll see as you enter the city is a lovely giant: the 210-foot SS *Klondike*, a restored paddlewheeler that is dry-docked on the west bank of the Yukon. Named a National Historic Site, the *Klondike* is a tangible reminder of this region's history—a retired workhorse left from a fleet of more than 250 riverboats that

Headed for Skagway on Klondike Highway 2, also known as the Skagway-Carcross Road, which climbs the infamous White Pass. Thousands of gold seekers traversed this trail in the 1898 gold rush.

reigned until construction of the highway. Fully restored to its 1937–1940 appearance, the *Klondike* remains a figure of elegance and grace. Come aboard for a tour of the decks, cargo holds, and passenger accommodations; a gift shop and a visitor center are located nearby.

More than 24,000 people live in Whitehorse year-round, and it also serves as the economic base for outlying communities. This is an economy that was built on mining and transportation services, and those industries remain important, along with tourism and government. Major airlines connect Whitehorse to the rest of the world, and the Alaska Highway brings thousands of visitors to its doorstep, mostly during the summer.

As is the case in other far north cities, living in Whitehorse sometimes means sharing the streets with wildlife. As we drove through a Whitehorse neighborhood, we spotted a small family of coyotes trotting across mowed lawns. One of the local constables said he'd seen them often, that they were part of the urban landscape. Almost every morning, he said, they were out and about at the same early hour. You could almost set your clock by them.

The **Visitor Reception Centre**, downtown at 2121 2nd Avenue, offers advice and printed materials on attractions throughout the area, as well as films, maps, and displays. There's easy access for RV parking, and it's a good place to plan your day. For the active set, you'll find golfing, fishing, nature hikes, trail rides, swimming, biking, canoeing, kayaking, and more.

Downtown Whitehorse retains much of its old-time charm, with log structures and false-front buildings sharing city blocks with more modern stores and offices. Park your vehicle and join in on a **Heritage Walking Tour**, which leaves Donnenworth House, next to Lapage Park, on a regular basis. Learn about local characters and the city's history, and view architectural marvels such as the Old Log Church, built in 1900, and the Log Skyscraper. For information, call 867-667-4704.

A hydroelectric dam built in 1958 created **Schwatka Lake**, which is now a floatplane base. Beneath this stretch of deep water, there still exists the boulder-strewn river bottom once known as **Whitehorse Rapids**. The town was named after those rapids—the plumes of foamy water were as white as the mane of a white horse. For gold seekers on the trail to the Klondike, this was the most perilous stretch of the Yukon River. Ill-prepared stampeders had to maneuver through the rapids, often aboard homemade boats that shattered against the rocks. Those who were successful were next met with the Devil's Punchbowl, a swirling mess of confused current, then the roaring water and hundred-foot sheer rock walls of Miles Canyon. After such a frightening river run, shaken and no doubt relieved, the miners often pulled ashore to dry out their goods and rest.

Entrepreneurs arrived with the miners, eager to find ways to make money without digging in the ground. In 1897 two men devised a way around the natural obstacles by building tramways on either side of the rapids and canyon. During a short-lived boom, a tent city called **Canyon City** sprang up, with businesses such as a saloon and roadhouse to further mine the pockets of the thousands who passed through.

The Yukon River sternwheeler S.S. Klondike in Whitehorse, Yukon, has been lovingly restored.

North-West Mounted Police arrived to maintain order as more than 20,000 stampeders used this gateway to the Klondike.

The historic site of Canyon City is accessible by walking trail, and interpretive signs mark the way. To get there, take Miles Canyon Road from Mile 910 (146.5 km) of the Alaska Highway. At the lookout, enjoy a spectacular view, then drive down to the suspended footbridge and walk over the bridge to the site where Canyon City once stood.

With completion of the **White Pass & Yukon Route** railway in 1900, stampeders could travel in comfort to a point beyond the rapids. However, by then, all claims had been staked and the rush was in decline. Whitehorse is still connected by bus service to the railway, which offers service from Skagway, Alaska. The historic depot stands near the river in downtown Whitehorse. The White Pass & Yukon Route remains the only operating narrow-gauge railroad in North America, and riding in the restored railcars is a rare treat. For tickets and reservations, call 1-800-343-7373 or 867-668-RAIL.

MacBride Museum, at 1st Avenue and Wood Street, provides mining displays, natural history, First Nations culture, artifacts from the gold rush, and geology of the area. Exhibits teach about different kinds of gold deposits, where they are found, and how they are taken from the ground. You can pan for gold here, too. Call 867-667-2709.

The Yukon Transportation Museum, off the Alaska Highway near Whitehorse Airport, features displays on the various modes of transportation used on the Trail of '98, then and now. Murals painted by Yukon artists serve as backdrops. Call 867-668-4792.

Beringia Centre, at Mile 915 (1,473 km) on the Alaska Highway, features prehistory displays that offer insight into a time when this land belonged to mastodons, saber-toothed cats, and lions. Call 867-667-8855.

The Frantic Follies has entertained audiences for 30-plus years, so we expected a corny, tired stage show. Instead we discovered a first-class vaudeville show by talented performers. On the bill: ragtime piano, can-can girls, red-hot-mama singing, banjo extravaganzas, magic, family-oriented comedy—and some wild Robert Service poetry. You've never heard "The Cremation of Sam McGee" quite like this. The revue shows nightly from mid-May through mid-September. The box office is in the Westmark Whitehorse, 2nd Avenue and Wood Street. Call 867-668-2042 or e-mail ffollies@yknet.yk.ca.

The Whitehorse Fishway features the world's longest wooden fish ladder and three underwater viewing windows. Watch the migration of the Yukon River chinook salmon and other species, including trout and arctic grayling. The aquarium and fishway is open from June through August, and admission is free. Take 2nd Avenue from downtown, cross the bridge over the Yukon River to Lewes Boulevard, then follow the signs to Nisutlin Drive and the fish ladder. Call 867-633-5965.

Yukon River tours are available through several operators, including rides on the MV *Anna Maria* through Pete Fox Tours at 867-668-6132; A Taste of '98 Yukon River Tours at 867-633-4767; or Canadian Yukon Riverboat Family at 867-668-1898. One of the most popular river excursions is aboard the **MV** *Schwatka*, which offers a 2-hour cruise that begins at Schwatka Lake. The dock is 5 minutes from the city center via Miles Canyon Road on the north side of town. Just follow the signs. The lake serves as a floatplane base, so you'll see lots of traffic in the air and on the water. The route takes you through Devil's Punchbowl and into Miles Canyon. You can wave to the foot traffic above you on the Robert Lowe Suspension Bridge. Points of interest include an old fox farm and the historic site of Canyon City. This trip is popular, so advance tickets are recommended. Call 867-668-4716.

Takhini Hot Springs, with its naturally heated outdoor swimming pool, is a star attraction any time of year, but it's especially popular when the temperature drops below freezing. To get there, drive several miles north of Whitehorse, turn right onto the North Klondike Highway (Highway 2), and follow it for about 4 miles to the turnoff to the hot springs; follow the 6-mile spur road to the west. This mini-resort also offers camping, trail rides, and lodging. Out of the ground, the source water is 117°F, so it is mixed with cool water to maintain a temperature around 100°F for the swimming pool. While it is rich in minerals such as calcium, magnesium, and iron, no sulfur is present to foul the air or your swimsuit.

Advice from a Mountie

Constable Serge Stewart, Royal Canadian Mounted Police, was in a police car, not on a horse, when I greeted him in a Whitehorse parking lot. I told him we had seen a group of coyotes in a city neighborhood that morning. Yes, he nodded, that family of four is around every day about the same time.

Stewart said that every summer the population of Whitehorse nearly triples, from about 18,000 to 50,000 people, but the crime rate does not soar with the influx. It's a good mix of people, he said, and they have respect for each other.

"I guess the people up here just like it a little slower. Whitehorse itself seems to be the focal point for people to come in from the bush: trappers, miners."

His advice for highway travelers: "Keep your car full of gas and take your time. It's not a race. If you try to drive too fast, a lot of people push it, and we then have single-vehicle rollovers."

Customized gold-nugget jewelry is a local specialty, and several shops will sell you raw nuggets or fashion a piece just for you. Two such places are Gold Originals by Charlotte, at 204 Main Street, and Murdoch's Gem Shop, at 207 Main Street. Murdoch's also is something of a mini-museum, with displays of gold rush artifacts and photos, Klondike Kate's silver belt, and mastodon tusks that were unearthed in local mining districts.

Yukon Gallery is the shopping outlet for original art, prints, pottery, and crafts, as well as fine jewelry. The gallery is at the corner of Lambert and 2nd Avenue downtown, across from the Visitor Reception Centre. Or stop by **North End Gallery**, at 1st Avenue and Steele Street, for scrimshaw, Inuit sculpture, and other original art. Your art purchases may be shipped anywhere in the world.

Get a Whiff of This

The marriage of fly-fishing and cigar smoking is ordained in Whitehorse's **Learning to Fly Shop**, *where Al Green works as a fishing guide.*

What you don't know about area lakes and streams, Green does. And he'll take you there for a half-day or day on the water. This fly shop at 407A Ogilvie Street is loaded with high-tech tackle and outdoor clothing, and offers casting classes, cabins, licenses, ice, and fishing equipment rentals. The shop has bait and bear spray and float tubes. It has hand-drawn maps and topo maps and secret in-your-head-only maps for the holes in the Yukon and Ogilvie Rivers.

But it is the glass-topped humidor that attracts me again and again, and I don't even smoke. These are Cuban cigars, unavailable to American retailers, laid out in tidy rows in a temperature-controlled environment, like little mummies in a tiny Egyptian museum. I keep wondering what is it about fish and cigars that fishermen love so much? Must be the stink.

To make myself useful, I ask Green what he knows that he can share. He says local lakes are stocked with rainbows and other fish including char, grayling, lake trout, and whitefish. It's hard to fish from shore, he says, so he recommends float tubes on lakes. On rivers you'll need waders if you're not fishing from a boat.

I take his picture holding a Cuban cigar, which is legal to sell in Canada, and we head back to the RV, where there's a dog waiting who loves to fish as much as any man. And he stinks most of the time, too. Am I onto something?

Al Green displays a Montecristo Habana that's normally kept in a 66-degree humidor. Only four cigars in the world are rated above 96 in Cigar Aficionado. This is one of them, Green says.

Services and parts for autos and RVs are available in Whitehorse. Twenty-four-hour cash machines may be found at the Bank of Montreal, the CIBC, or the Royal Bank of Canada, all on Main Street. The Thomas Cook Foreign Exchange, 2101A 2nd Avenue, is open 7 days a week during summer.

For information on city attractions and services, write the City of Whitehorse, 2121 2nd Avenue, Whitehorse, Yukon, Canada Y1A 1C2, or call 867-668-TOUR.

In Whitehorse, a favorite family-oriented show is "The Frantic Follies," which combines Klondike history with singing, fiddling, can-can dancing, and some great Robert Service poetry.

Lodging

Airline Inn Hotel
16 Burns Road (across from the airport)
867-668-4400
30 rooms, laundry, lounge, restaurant. Adjacent to convenience store and gas station.

Airport Chalet
91634 Alaska Highway
867-668-2166
Hotel and motel, offering gas, diesel, RV dump, and self-service laundry for guests. Restaurant and lounge.

Best Western Goldrush Inn
411 Main Street
867-668-4500
101 rooms, suites, spas, barber shop, beauty salon. Gold Pan Saloon and Casca Dining Room.

Capital Hotel
103 Main Street
867-667-2565
Rooms in historic downtown setting, restaurant, entertainment.

The Edgewater Hotel
101 Main Street
1-877-484-3334 or 867-667-2572
30 deluxe rooms and suites, restaurant. Downtown location.

High Country Inn
4051 4th Avenue
1-800-554-4471 or 867-667-4471
Executive suites and kitchenettes available. Guest laundry, whirlpools.

Stop In Family Hotel
314 Ray Street
867-668-555
44 air-conditioned rooms. Self-service laundry, hair salon, sauna, hot tub.

202 Motor Inn
206 Jarvis Street
867-668-4567
60 rooms, dining room, lounge with entertainment. Discount for miners.

Westmark Klondike Inn
2288 2nd Avenue
867-668-4747
Deluxe rooms, suites. Gift shop, restaurant,
    lounge.

Westmark Whitehorse
2nd Avenue and Wood Street
867-393-9700
Deluxe rooms, suites. Gift shop, restaurant,
    lounge, box office of The Frantic Follies.

The Yukon Inn
4220 4th Avenue
1-800-661-0454 or 867-667-2527
92 luxury guest rooms, suites, kitchenettes.
    Laundry, dry cleaning, hair salon, office
    services, winter plug-ins. Gift shop,
    exercise facilities. Moose Café, two
    lounges, big-screen TVs. Walking
    distance to local attractions

Area Campgrounds

Whitehorse:
Hi Country RV Park
91374 Alaska Highway
1-877-458-3806 or 867-667-7445
Roomy sites with power. Showers, self-
    service laundry, cable TV, store, gift
    shop. Close to downtown.

Trail of '98 RV Park
117 Jasper Street, just off Two Mile Hill at
    Industrial Road
1-800-377-2142 or 867-668-3768
150 sites with full or partial hookups, tent
    camping, self-service laundry, gift
    shop.
Desk can set up city tours, tickets to
    attractions.

West of Whitehorse:
Sourdough Country RV Park
Mile 904 Alaska Highway
867-668-2961
Sites with power, satellite TV, car wash, tent
    camping available.

Pioneer RV Park
Mile 911 Alaska Highway
867-668-5944
144 sites, including full and partial hookup,
    some pull-throughs. Showers, laundry,
    rest rooms, store, gift shop. Car and RV
    wash, some automotive services,
    windshield chip repairs. Tickets and
    reservations for local attractions.

MacKenzie's RV Park
Mile 922.5 Alaska Highway
867-633-2337
79 roomy sites with full or partial hookups;
    22 tent sites. Cable hookup, showers,
    laundry, store. Playground, horseshoe
    pit, free gold panning. Wheelchair
    access. Vehicle wash. On city bus route.

Restaurants

The Cellar Dining Room
101 Main Street
In Edgewater Hotel
1-877-484-3334 or 867-667-2572
Fine dining, specializing in salmon, crab,
    halibut, arctic char, prime rib.

China Garden
309 Jarvis Street
867-668-2899
Chinese and western menus; lunch buffet,
    dinners, takeout.

G & P Steak House & Pizza
Mile 918 Alaska Highway
867-668-4708
Greek and Italian specialties, seafood,
    pasta.

Giorgio's Cuccina
206 Jarvis Street
Next to the 202 Hotel
867-668-4050
Italian cuisine.

Klondike Rib and Salmon BBQ
2nd Avenue and Steele Street
Across from Westmark Whitehorse
Fresh local fish, Texas-style BBQ ribs,
    caribou and musk ox Stroganoff.

Moose Café
4220 4th Avenue
In the Yukon Inn
867-667-2527
Klondike and southwestern cuisine.

Pandas
212 Main Street
867-667-2632
European fine dining, without the dress
    code. Northern seafood specialties,
    steaks, schnitzels, pasta.

Sam 'n' Andy's
506 Main Street
867-668-6994
Mexican and Canadian food; outdoor patio.

Tim Hortons
Two locations:
2101B 2nd Avenue (6 A.M.–11 P.M., no
    smoking)
2210 2nd Avenue (open 24 hours, smoking
    allowed)
Eat in or take out; soups and sandwiches;
    donuts and other pastries.

Tung Lock Chinese Restaurant
404 Wood Street
867-668-3298
Casual dining, specializing in seafood,
    daily lunch and weekend dinner buffets.

Yukon Mining Co.
4051 4th Avenue
In the High Country Inn
867-667-4471
Barbecue on the deck, local beer specialties.

Road Notes

Just north of Whitehorse, the Alaska Highway connects with the North Klondike Highway (Highway 2), which heads north to Dawson City. (See the section on the North Klondike Highway in Chapter 7, Western Canada's Northbound Byways.)

It's 98 miles (158 km) between Whitehorse and Haines Junction. In 1958, more than 1.5 million acres of forest burned in this region, and you can still see evidence of that fire in the landscape around you.

About halfway to Haines Junction, the road leads through the Native village of **Champagne**, where it winds past picturesque log homes. Visitors are asked to be respectful of the villagers' private property and of their cemetery, which is not open to visitors. If you'd like to learn more about the Champagne-Aishihik Indian Band, you

In parts of the Alaska Highway, especially the farther north you travel, the road narrows and the shoulders disappear.

are welcome to visit the **Kwaday Dan Kenji** traditional camp at Mile 939.5 (1,512 km). Native interpreters will discuss what life was like for their ancestors, and you will visit a replica of a First Nations campsite. Dry camping is available for RV travelers who wish to overnight at Champagne.

Pay close attention to the junction at **Haines Junction**, at Mile 985 (1,585 km). To continue on the Alaska Highway, you must make a right turn, the first in many miles. Hundreds of wayward travelers have ignored the turn and ended up instead on Highway 3, heading south toward Haines, Alaska, instead of Fairbanks, Alaska. Canadian customs officials at the border before Haines reported 356 wrong-turners in 1994, 96 in 1996 (an improvement credited to bigger signs), and about 75 in 1999 (even with bigger signs). (See the section on the Haines Highway in Chapter 8, Alaska's State Highways.)

After Haines Junction, the Alaska Highway crosses **Bear Creek Summit**, elevation 3,294 feet (1,004 m), and **Boutillier Summit**, elevation 3,293 feet (1,003 m), en route to the memorable **Kluane Lake**. The Alaska Highway skirts this vast and beautiful body of water for more than 60 miles (96.5 km), making this drive worthy of a few extra lines in your travel journal. On the way to the communities of Destruction Bay and Burwash Landing (where all services are available), take a few minutes to pull over at Mile 1,061 (1,707.5 km), the historical wayside for **Soldiers Summit**. This was the site of the Alaska Highway's official opening ceremonies, on November 20, 1942.

A forest fire in 1999 blackened the landscape near **Burwash Landing** and beyond it for several miles. Stop by the local museum, just off the highway, and you'll see how close the fire came to burning down this structure and many others in the town. The fire line came within 30 feet of the museum's back door. For unexplained

Burl wood is the raw material for special creations such as this bizarre man made of burls, which are the result of fungus distorting a tree's growth.

Burwash Landing, Yukon, boasts the world's largest gold pan.

reasons, the winds changed direction and the town was spared. Ask about the fire at local businesses; residents are glad to share their stories.

The northernmost town on the Alaska Highway in the Yukon Territory is **Beaver Creek**. As at Contact Creek, this was a place where construction crews in 1942, working from opposite directions, met and completed a stretch of the Alaska Highway.

𝒜LASKA–YUKON BORDER

From Whitehorse: 303 miles (488 km)
From Haines Junction: 205 miles (330 km)
To Tok: 92 miles (148 km)
To Fairbanks: 298 miles (480 km)

Crossing into Alaska is an achievement, and you're due for another round of photos. There's a wonderful place to pull over and record this moment, right at the demarcation line that separates the United States and Canada. Alaska and the Yukon

Local Boy Makes Good

Mike Larson runs **Scottie Creek Services**, in Alaska within sight of the Alaska–Yukon border. Typical of entrepreneurs along the Alaska Highway, Mike runs a multifaceted business. He pumps gas, sells T-shirts and postcards, offers RV parking, and sells "first- and last-chance liquor." And, no surprise, he's bothered when he sees traffic pass by his place to buy fuel at a neighboring business.

A former trucker, Mike was born in Anchorage. He's also lived in Tok and Northway, places that record some of the coldest temperatures in Alaska. So I know he's tough.

Mike built his business on hard work and endurance, and knowledge of local history is threaded through his conversations. He points out a nearby cabin, moved here from the border, that was the Canadian customs station from 1948 to 1953. He made the metal barriers out by his gas island with remnant pipe from a line that transported fuel from Haines to Fairbanks during the 1950s and '60s.

I should have known what Mike would say when I asked him for a travel tip: "Fill up here."

Territory have each erected impressive welcome signs, massive wooden affairs that are beautifully painted. Between them is a parking area with a gazebolike structure over the international border marker. Stand here and look north, then south, and you'll see the border as a brushed-out band in the scrubby trees, signifying the 141st meridian. At this wayside, most people like to pose with a foot in each country or sit on the nearby bench that's divided by a carved line with the word Yukon on one side, Alaska on the other.

Just ahead is the U.S. **Customs and Immigration station**, which is open 24 hours a day. Turn your watch back an hour to reflect the Alaska Time Zone.

Gas, RV camping, and tire services are available at the border, and beyond it at Scottie Creek Services.

Road Notes

For the first 65 miles (104.5 km) into Alaska, the highway follows the border of 730,000-acre **Tetlin National Wildlife Refuge**, a sparsely treed region of marshes and lakes that attract thousands of nesting waterfowl and migrating sandhill cranes. Watch for other birds, too, including ptarmigan, trumpeter swans, loons, and some species of raptors. Mammals include black and brown bears, moose, caribou, and smaller furbearers such as lynx, red foxes, and coyotes. The Forest Service maintains two campgrounds, Lakeview and Deadman Lake, along the Alaska Highway, both before Northway Junction.

Eighty miles (129 km) from the border, at **Tetlin Junction** (not to be confused with Tetlin, Yukon), you'll find the northbound turnoff to Alaska Highway 5 (the Taylor Highway), an unpaved road that's closed in winter. This route leads to the Alaska villages of Chicken and Eagle, and connects with the Yukon's Top of the World Highway, the northern route to Dawson City. (See the section on the Taylor Highway in Chapter 8, Alaska's State Highways. Also see the section on the Top of the World Highway in Chapter 7, Western Canada's Northbound Byways.)

Twelve miles (19 km) beyond Tetlin Junction is Tok, which was a construction camp during construction of the Alaska Highway.

Tok

From Alaska/Yukon border: 92 miles (148 km)
To Delta Junction: 108 miles (174 km)
To Fairbanks: 206 miles (330 km)

Surrounded by stands of spruce trees, Tok (TOKE) is a junction city. Motorists can continue northwest on the Alaska Highway toward Fairbanks, or veer southwest onto the Glenn Highway (locally known as the Tok Cutoff). This shortcut for southbound drivers leads to Glennallen or Valdez on the Richardson Highway, or to Anchorage at the end of the Glenn Highway.

With a population of about 1,400, Tok is geared toward travelers' services and stays, and is especially busy in the summer months. **Alaska's Mainstreet Visitor Center** is housed in a beautiful log structure at the junction of the two highways. Cultivated flower beds around the center and elsewhere in town flourish in the long, sunny days of Alaska's Interior. At the center, you can learn about Tok's strategic role during the building of the Alaska Highway and about area wildlife, events, and attractions.

Say hello at the visitor center to Sid Venne, who greets visitors, offers directions, and enjoys answering questions, even the most bizarre ones. In her self-published humor book *If It's Tourist Season, Why Can't We Shoot Them?* Venne tells about the man who gave her a $20 bill and asked for change in "Alaskan money." She said OK, opened her register, and handed over a ten, a five, and five ones. He seemed satisfied. He pocketed the money and walked away, ready to spend his "Alaskan money" in Alaska.

Every evening at 7:30, except Sundays, **Burnt Paw Gift Shop** stages a free dog show. A team of dogs waits patiently in harness as lecturers talk about ideal physical and mental characteristics for a sled dog, about mushing gear, and about travel in the deep cold. Burnt Paw is located next to the post office along the Alaska Highway. Inside the log cabin shop with the sod roof, you'll find exceptional Alaska souvenirs.

Take the kiddies to **Mukluk Land** at Mile 1317 of the Alaska Highway, just 2 miles (3 km) west of the highway junction. You'll find a lovely Alaska garden (mixing cabbages and flowers), videos on the trans-Alaska pipeline and the northern lights,

Tetlin National Wildlife Refuge lies to the south of the Alaska Highway as you enter the state.

Even in summers, sled-dog demonstrations take place in Tok, Alaska, where visitors can learn about racing, gear, and what makes a sled dog tick.

dogsled rides, golf, and a chance to do some gold panning (Mukluk Land guarantees the gold). Call 907-883-2571.

Tok is a great place to rest and restock. You'll find many choices here for comfortable accommodations, meals, gifts, groceries, and filling up the gas tank. Some campgrounds even offer a free breakfast for their guests.

Lodging

Golden Bear Hotel
Just south on the Tok Cutoff
907-883-2561
60 rooms, private baths. Cable TV, gift shop, Alaska displays, restaurant. Senior discount.

Snowshoe Motel
Mile 1314 Alaska Highway
907-883-4512
www.alaskaoutdoors.com/eagle
24 units, satellite TV, phones. Continental breakfast, picnic area.

Tok Lodge
Near junction of Alaska and Glenn Highways
1-800-883-3007 or 907-883-2851
www.alaskan.com/toklodge
10 rooms in historic building; 38 motel units. Gift shop, café, lounge.

Westmark Tok
Junction of Alaska and Glenn Highways
1-800-544-0970 or 907-883-5174
92 deluxe rooms, nonsmoking available. Dining room, lounge. Adjacent to visitor center.

Young's Motel
Mile 1313 Alaska Highway
907-883-5023
43 rooms, private baths, nonsmoking available. Satellite TV, phones. Restaurant.

Campgrounds

Golden Bear Motel & RV Park
Just south on the Tok Cutoff
907-883-2561
Full and partial hookups, pull-throughs, tent sites. Showers, laundry, restaurant, gift shop, phone. Senior discount.

Rita's Campground and RV Park
Mile 1316 Alaska Highway
907-883-4342
Full and partial hookups, tent sites.

Sourdough Campground
1.5 miles (2.5 km) south on Tok Cutoff
907-883-5543
Full hookups, shaded area. Breakfast 9 A.M. to 11 A.M. Sourdough slide show nightly. Gift shop.

Tok RV Village
Mile 1313.5 Alaska Highway
907-883-5877
95 sites, full and partial hookups, pull-throughs. Showers, laundry, dump station, vehicle wash. Connection to check e-mail. Fishing licenses.

Tundra Lodge & RV Park
Mile 1316 Alaska Highway
907-883-7875
78 sites with full or partial hookups, tent sites, dump station, RV wash. Connection to check e-mail. Cocktail lounge.

Restaurants

Fast Eddy's Restaurant
Mile 1313 Alaska Highway
Next to Young's Motel
907-883-4411
Steaks, seafood, pasta, burgers, pie.

Golden Bear Restaurant
Just south on the Tok Cutoff, adjacent to
motel and RV park.
907-883-2561
Luncheon and dinner specials. Senior
discount.

Tok Gateway Salmon Bake
Mile 1313 Alaska Highway
907-883-5555

King salmon, halibut, reindeer sausage,
buffalo burgers. Shuttle pick-up
available.

Tok Lodge & Café
Near junction of Alaska and Glenn Highways
1-800-883-3007 or 907-883-2851
Breakfast, lunch, dinner: prime rib, salmon,
halibut, daily specials.

Young's Café
At highway junction
907-883-2233
Breakfast all day. Lunch specials, dinner,
beer and wine, baked goods.

Road Notes

From Tok to Delta Junction is 108 miles (174 km) of almost unpopulated wilderness.
The road follows or crosses several streams, the biggest of which is the Tanana River.
Many of these streams were formed by runoff from glaciers in the Alaska Range.
That's why the water tends to be a cloudy gray; in it are particles of suspended rock,
called rock flour, carried by glaciers. The forest here is largely of spruce. Watch for
moose and caribou.

*D*ELTA JUNCTION

From Dawson Creek: 1,422 miles (2,288.5 km)
From Alaska–Yukon border: 200 miles (322 km)
From Tok: 108 miles (174 km)
To North Pole: 83 miles (134 km)
To Fairbanks: 98 miles (157 km)

At Delta Junction, the Alaska Highway joins the Richardson Highway—marking
the official end of the Alcan. Stop by the End of the Road milepost for a photo to
add to your travel scrapbook. (This may be the official end, but for most travelers,
Fairbanks is still the destination that marks completion of their journey up the Alaska
Highway.)

Addresses for Delta Junction are Mile 1422 Alaska Highway or Mile 266
Richardson Highway. This crossroads town is an agricultural community where hardy
strains of barley flourish in the short growing season and long hours of sunshine.

Other crops include oats, wheat, grass seed, canola, and potatoes. Local farmers raise dairy cows, Tibetan yaks, elk, and reindeer.

In Alaska, Delta Junction may be best known for its buffalo herd. Twenty-three plains bison, or buffalo, were transplanted to the area in 1928, and they flourished. A 90,000-acre **bison range** was established in 1978, with enough habitat to support between 400 and 500 animals. An annual hunt by permit keeps the population in line and helps feed families. New calves arrive in spring. In early summer you're most likely to see the herd browsing on the west side of the Delta River, but they move back over to the bison range in August. The Alaska Department of Fish and Game plants barley, oats, and hay on the range to keep the animals there and out of private fields. (Fences, as you can imagine, do not work when a headstrong herd wants to cross to the other side, especially if a meal is waiting.)

A historic roadhouse along the Tanana River has been restored by the Bureau of Land Management and put to good use, along with the adjacent BLM campground and picnic areas. **Rika's Roadhouse** is a favorite community gathering spot and houses museum displays, a gift shop, restaurant, and bakery. Annual events in town include the Buffalo Wallow Square Dance in late May, the Buffalo Barbecue in July, and the Deltana Fair in late July and early August. A quirky mid-July event is the Mud Drags, when Alaskans pull out their snowmobiles in midsummer and race them through the mud.

In the Delta Junction area, you can go horseback riding, take a wildlife tour with Do It In Delta Tours at 907-895-4762, or sample smoked buffalo and reindeer sausage at Delta Meat & Sausage Co. at Mile 1413 Alaska Highway; 907-895-4006. Or try fishing in one of the more than 40 stocked lakes in the area. You can also view the **trans-Alaska pipeline** at the **Tanana River Bridge**, which spans 1,200 feet between its two towers. The bridge was built to withstand an earthquake measuring up to a magnitude of 7.5 and temperatures as low as -60°F.

Check in at the **Delta Junction Visitor Information Center** at the junction of the Alaska and Richardson Highways for more on what to see and do. While you're there, don't forget to ask for your end-of-the-road certificate. You can call the center at 1-877-895-5068 or 907-895-5069 or visit www.alaska-highway.org.

Lodging

Alaska 7 Motel
Mile 270 Richardson Highway
907-895-4848
Rooms; kitchenettes available. TV, full
 baths. Daily and weekly rates.

Alaskan Steak House & Motel
Mile 265 Richardson Highway
907-895-5175

Rooms, with cable TV. Adjacent restaurant.
 Walking distance to downtown visitor
 center.

Kelly's Country Inn
1616 Richardson Highway
907-895-4667
Rooms with private bath, phone, TV,
 kitchenettes.

Campgrounds

Bergstad's RV Park & Camp Sites
Mile 1421 Alaska Highway
907-895-4856
Open year-round.

Cherokee Lodge
Mile 1412.5 Alaska Highway
907-895-4814
Campsites, rooms, restaurant, lounge.

Clearwater Lodge
End of Remington Road
907-895-5152
RV and tent camping, cabins, restaurant
open for dinner 7 days a week.

Smith's Green Acres RV Park & Campground
Mile 268 Richardson Highway
1-800-895-4369 or 907-895-4110
Full and partial hookups, pull-throughs,
tent sites. Showers, self-service laundry,
rest rooms, phone, vehicle wash. Can
arrange here for a pipeline pump
station tour.

Restaurants

Alaskan Steak House & Motel
Mile 265 Richardson Highway
907-895-5175
Breakfast, lunch, dinner. Specializing in all-
you-can-eat barbecue rib dinners.

Buffalo Center Diner
Across from IGA
907-895-5089
Family dining: breakfast, lunch, dinner.

Clearwater Lodge
End of Remington Road
907-895-5152
Open for dinner 7 days a week; live music
on weekends.

Pizza Bella
Across from visitor center
907-895-4841
Pizza, pasta, sandwiches, salads.

Rika's Roadhouse & Landing
Big Delta State Historical Park
907-895-4938
Baked goods and meals.

Trophy Lodge
1420 Alaska Highway
907-895-4685
Fine dining, cocktails. Closed Sunday and
Monday.

Road Notes

The Richardson Highway between Delta Junction and Fairbanks is a four-lane route, but it remains a challenging road because much of it was built over permafrost. With Interior Alaska's extreme seasonal cycles of hot and cold damaging the road, you've got a roller-coaster ride in places.

About 7 miles (11 km) before you reach the town of North Pole, you'll pass by **Eielson Air Force Base**, a major military installation named for Carl Ben Eielson, an early-day Fairbanks pilot. A few miles later, note the eastbound turnoff for **Chena**

Lakes Recreation Area. This popular park includes 80 campsites and dozens of picnic sites. Swimmers enjoy the sandy beach at Chena Lake; canoeists can navigate the lake or the Chena River, which flows through at one end. Boat rentals are available, and there's fishing, biking, hiking, and nature walks for outdoor fun. The Fairbanks North Star Borough charges a nominal use fee.

*N*ORTH POLE

From Delta Junction: 83 miles (134 km)
To Fairbanks: 15 miles (24 km)

It's Christmas all year long in North Pole. That's because Santa doesn't disappear after Christmas Eve. On December 26, you can track him to his house and tell him what you want for next Christmas. This small community was founded in the 1950s, when several homesteading families sold their property for town lots. One far-thinking woman among them decided that a North Pole theme would likely help sell more lots, and maybe attract industry to their fledgling town.

The cheerful, candy-striped exterior of **Santa Claus House** is an invitation to any age, and the king-size cutout of Santa is a great photo opportunity. Mail your letters from here for that impressive North Pole cancellation. Inside the gift shop is a kiddie toyland. You can buy Christmas ornaments and order up a personalized Christmas letter for your favorite little ones. Santa makes regular appearances and greets children in his throne room. To order a Christmas letter, mail $5 along with the child's address to Santa Claus House, 101 St. Nicholas Drive, North Pole, AK 99705. Call 1-800-588-4078 or 907-488-2200. Santa has a website too: www.santaclaushouse.com.

Motels and RV camping are nearby, and other North Pole businesses invite you to drive around town and enjoy all that the city of 1,620 people has to offer. Stop by the **Visitor Center Log Cabin** at 2550 Mistletoe Drive, or call 907-488-2242.

Lodging

Beaver Lake Resort Motel
2555 Mission Road, No. 1102
907-488-9600
Quiet setting; close to Santa Claus House.

Jolly Acres Motel
3068 Badger Road
907-488-9339
Rooms, kitchenettes, close to downtown.

Campgrounds

Riverview RV Park & Seafood Cookout
1316 Badger Road
907-488-6392
160 RV sites with hookups, pull-throughs. Tent camping. Showers, laundry, water, dump station.

Road's End RV Park
Mile 356 Richardson Highway, halfway between North Pole and Fairbanks
907-488-0295
Full hookups, showers.

Looking for the End of the Alaska Highway

No confusion exists about where the Alaska Highway begins: Mile 0, Dawson Creek, British Columbia. But far away in Alaska, two cities claim the distinction of being the end of the Alaska Highway: Delta Junction and Fairbanks. And in a way, they're both right. The former is the official end; the latter is the practical end.

Military convoys that used the Alcan in the 1940s were destined for installations in Fairbanks. But in constructing the highway, builders didn't have to lay new road all the way to the city limits. The new Alaska Highway simply joined the already existing Richardson Highway at Delta, 1,422 miles (2,288.5 km) from Dawson Creek, and almost 100 miles short of Fairbanks. That made Delta the official end of the Alaska Highway.

Delta was originally a construction camp for builders of the north-south Richardson Highway in 1919, and the town took its name from the nearby Delta River. As the joining place of two major highways, however, the name was changed to Delta Junction.

Now here's where it gets confusing: The State of Alaska did not assign the same route number to the entire length of the Richardson Highway. It is Route 4 from Valdez to Delta Junction, and it is Route 2 (same as the Alaska Highway) for those last hundred or so miles from Delta Junction to Fairbanks, thus implying, on road maps at least, that the Alaska Highway ends at Fairbanks.

Today you can have your picture taken at Delta Junction next to a monument inscribed with the words "Crossroads of Alaska" and "End of the Alaska Highway." The monument is flanked by flags of the United States, Canada, Alaska, and the Yukon Territory.

Fairbanks has a nearly identical monument, which also proclaims "The End of the Alaska Highway." It's just a few steps outside the front door of the Fairbanks Convention and Visitors Bureau log cabin, along the Chena River, where tourists by the thousands stroll each summer. Not surprising that a majority of them have their pictures taken here, too, adding to the belief that this is the end of the Alaska Highway.

The reality is that the end of the road is where you set your sights. It's wherever you stop, turn around, and head back. If you come as far as Delta Junction, you'll probably have your picture taken, and then continue on to Fairbanks—where you'll have your picture taken again. Then, back home, you'll be able to say without hesitation: "Yes, I've been to the end of the Alaska Highway. Wanna see my pictures?"

Santaland RV Park & Campground

125 St. Nicholas Drive

85 RV sites with full hookups and pull-
   throughs, 9 tent sites. Shower, laundry,
   water, dump station. Tour
   arrangements.

Sled Dog RV Park & Campground

1160 Badger Road

907-488-2136

20 RV sites with hookups and pull-
   throughs, 20 tent sites. Showers, dump
   station.

Restaurants

The Elf's Den

On Mistletoe Drive, next to visitor center

907-488-3268

Family dining, pizza, cocktail lounge.

Riverview RV Park & Seafood Cookout

1316 Badger Road

907-488-6392

Grilled salmon and halibut.

Road Notes

It's a short hop from North Pole to Fairbanks, and the Richardson Highway continues
as a four-lane route bordered by spruce, aspen, and birch trees as it heads toward
town. Then it ends without fanfare, joining the Steese Highway near the entry to **Fort
Wainwright**, which lies on the eastern edge of town. An army post today, Fort
Wainwright was Ladd Air Field during World War II. Military spending has often
stabilized or boosted the Fairbanks economy during the past 60-plus years.

*F*AIRBANKS

From Delta Junction: 98 miles (157 km)
From Alaska–Yukon border: 298 miles (480 km)
From Dawson Creek, British Columbia: 1,488 miles (2,395 km)

Welcome to another end of the road! You are standing at 64.8° north latitude. The
Arctic Circle is only 66 air miles north.

Fairbanks was founded in 1901 by a trader named **E. T. Barnette**, who really
didn't want to settle here. As a passenger aboard a stern-wheel riverboat, he had
intended to set up shop in a place that was more accessible to the gold miners in the
area. But following the tip of a local Native, he directed the captain up the Chena
River, which he thought was a shortcut to his destination. The Chena was too shallow,
and the summer was ending. In a hurry to return without his argumentative
passenger, the captain ordered Barnette and his party, and his trade goods, off the
ship. They landed at a spot that's marked today with a low rock monument, by the
Fairbanks Convention and Visitors Bureau log cabin on 1st Avenue near the
Cushman Street Bridge.

Luck was with Barnette. Within hours, he and his group had their first paying
customers in the form of a couple of miners who had spotted the ship's plume of

steam. One of the miners was **Felix Pedro**, an Italian immigrant who struck gold less than a year later. His find ignited a rush to Alaska's Interior, drawing miners from the goldfields of Fortymile country and the Klondike.

The long-term health of this fledgling community was cinched when Barnette struck a deal with federal district judge **James Wickersham**, who was stationed in Eagle, Alaska, a gold-mining town northeast of Fairbanks. Wickersham wanted to feed the ego of a political friend by naming a town after him. **Charles W. Fairbanks** was then a U.S. senator from Indiana; later he would be vice president under Theodore Roosevelt. In exchange for naming the town after Fairbanks, Wickersham promised Barnette that he would move the judicial seat from Eagle to Fairbanks—which he did, ensuring that the town was firmly rooted.

The people of Fairbanks today commemorate Felix Pedro's gold discovery with a weeklong festival called **Golden Days**. Held in mid-July, the festival includes sourdough pancake feeds, gold-panning demonstrations and mining lectures, dances, historical exhibits, and an old-fashioned community parade. The winner of the Pedro look-alike contest leads the parade, and he walks the downtown route with his gold poke full of nuggets.

Fairbanks has grown from the days of E. T. Barnette to a hub city for all of Alaska's Interior communities. It's also a major jumping-off point for flights into the bush. Overnight tours are available by air, and in fly/drive packages, to Barrow, the Arctic Circle, Nome, Kotzebue, and Anuktuvuk Pass. A crossroads city, Fairbanks is the hub

Californians Barbara Dudl and Phyllis Weiss pose by the official–unofficial end of the road milepost in Fairbanks.

The Cushman Street Bridge crosses the Chena River in Fairbanks near the spot where founder E. T. Barnette established his first trading post.

for the Elliott, Dalton (via Elliott), Steese, Richardson, and Parks Highways. Before you leave town for any of these highway trips, you can call for road conditions at 907-456-7623. A statewide weather recording is at 1-800-472-0391.

Other annual events include a **summer solstice celebration** in late June. That's when the Fairbanks semipro baseball team, the Goldpanners, hosts the Midnight Sun Baseball Game beginning at 10:30 P.M., without artificial lights. The **World Eskimo-Indian Olympics** are held in late July. In winter, mushing fans gather by the thousands for the start or finish of the **Yukon Quest International Sled Dog Race**, which follows a 1,000-mile route between Whitehorse, in the Yukon, and Fairbanks. Around town, you'll find movie theaters, shopping opportunities, art galleries, and outdoor adventures.

While you're in Fairbanks, visit some of these local attractions:

University of Alaska Museum. Gallery exhibits include dinosaur fossils, ivory carvings, historical photos, totem poles, natural history dioramas, and lots of gold. Be sure to visit Babe the Blue Bison, a 36,000-year-old bison mummy that was excavated by a Fairbanks scientist. Videos on the northern lights explain the scientific reason for the phenomenon. The museum store offers books, gifts, clothing, and Native art. The museum is on the University of Alaska Fairbanks campus, at College Road and University Avenue. Call 907-474-7505 for 24-hour information.

Creamer's Field Waterfowl Refuge. What was once the northernmost dairy farm in the country was converted to a waterfowl refuge many years ago, but the old

Adventurers of the Road

During the mid-1980s, I was features editor of the Fairbanks Daily News-Miner, *and our offices were sought out by many end-of-the-roaders. They trickled in each summer, having traveled the Alaska Highway on horseback, on motorcycles, on bicycles; on trans-Canada trips, trans-America excursions, Pan-American global drives; walking, skipping, hopping, one-legged, backward, with their dogs, with their walking sticks, with their sidecars, with tattoos and signs and duct tape-patched sneakers.*

The travelers would inevitably march into the newspaper offices and announce: "I MADE IT, I'm here! Write an article about me!"

The reporting staff, who that summer might already have interviewed a half-dozen or more adventurers of this type, would smile and mutter, "Here's another one." This is not to make little of a great thing. It's just that when you live at the end of the road, after a while, it doesn't seem so novel. But we usually obliged the adventurers with a photo, at the least.

buildings remain. Anna and Charlie Creamer's farmhouse is now headquarters for the Alaska Department of Fish and Game offices that oversee this property. Signs along trails at the refuge describe the migratory birds that feed in great numbers here each spring and fall. Most are Canada geese and sandhill cranes.

Birch Hill Recreation Area. In winter this area in the northeast corner of the city is a great place for cross-country skiing, snowmobiling, and snowshoeing. In summer, hikers enjoy the place, and a Shakespearean troupe performs in an outdoor theater. Call 907-456-5774 for information.

Historical walking tour. Meet at the Fairbanks Convention and Visitors Bureau log cabin on 1st Avenue near the Cushman Street Bridge. Guided or unguided walking tours of notable historic sites begin there. Call 907-456-5774 for information.

Golden Heart Park. The focal point of this downtown park is a sculpture titled "The Unknown First Family," which portrays a northern family, either Native or non-Native. Plaques around the statue include names of people who helped build this town during its first century. This is a place for relaxing by the fountain or enjoying outdoor concerts on summer afternoons.

Ice Art. March is the best time to visit Fairbanks if winter is your favorite season. On the bill: the annual Winter Carnival, sled-dog races, and Ice Art, the international ice-carving competition. You can walk through a park filled with ice statuary, all of it lit with colored lights that sparkle through the nearly clear ice. But even summer visitors can get a glimpse of the "coolest show in town" at the Ice Art Museum, in the Lacey Street Theater on 2nd Avenue. You'll stay warm; the ice sculpture is behind glass in a 20-degree display case. For information, call 907-451-8222.

Alaskaland. This spacious theme park, at Airport Way and Peger Road, was built in 1967 to commemorate the centennial of Alaska's purchase from Russia. The Centennial Exposition grounds were divided into themes that echoed Alaska history. In one section, replicas of Native villages were constructed. In another, a gold rush town was re-created by relocating some of the oldest cabins and businesses of Fairbanks. The Palace Saloon is still operating as a bar and dance hall. A gold-mining "valley" was created to demonstrate the ways that gold was extracted from the ground. And one of the region's hardworking sternwheelers, the riverboat *Nenana*, was dry-docked here after retirement. It has since been beautifully restored.

Riverboat **Discovery.** Follow the signs off Airport Way that lead to Discovery Landing. A star attraction for decades, a cruise on the riverboat *Discovery* is a must for every summer visitor to Fairbanks. Your hosts are the Binkley family, whose members have been cruising Alaska rivers for five generations. The *Discovery* is an authentic paddlewheeler that follows the Chena and Tanana Rivers on a narrated cruise. Disembark at a replica of an Athabascan Indian fish site to learn more about the area's first residents and their ways of life. Meet Iditarod champion musher Susan Butcher and see her dogs in action. Reservations are a must. Call 907-479-6673.

For more information about local attractions and events, contact the Fairbanks Convention and Visitors Bureau at 1-800-327-5774 or 907-456-5774.

Lodging

Alaska Motel
1546 Cushman Street
907-456-6393
Rooms and kitchenettes. Cable TV, laundry facililties. Senior discount; weekly rates.

Bridgewater Hotel
1501 Queens Way
907-452-6661
www.mosquitonet.com/fountain
94 units, dining, cocktails. Downtown location. Airport/train shuttle.

The Captain Bartlett Inn
1411 Airport Way
1-800-478-7900 or 907-452-1888
197 units, laundry, restaurant, cocktails. Airport/train shuttle.

College Inn
700 Fairbanks Street
1-800-770-2177 or 907-474-3666
www.mosquitonet.com/akhotel
100 units, laundry, pets allowed.

Comfort Inn Chena River
1908 Chena Landings Loop
1-800-201-9199 or 907-479-8080
74 units, laundry, pets allowed. Shuttle service.

Fairbanks Golden Nugget Hotel
900 Noble Street
907-452-5141
36 units, restaurant. Downtown location.

Going for the Gold

Here are some golden opportunities for fun:

Eldorado Gold Mine. This family attraction is located about 12 miles (19 km) north of Fairbanks, just past Fox on the Elliott Highway. You can ride the narrow-gauge rails of the old Tanana Valley Railroad through a permafrost tunnel to the cook shack. Afterward, look on as two local miners, a husband-and-wife team, demonstrate modern mining. Then it's your turn to grab a gold pan and get some gold for yourself. You get to keep what you find. For reservations, call 907-479-7613.

Ester Gold Camp. Just west of Fairbanks off the Parks Highway, the Ester Gold Camp was once a gold-mining community with a saloon, roadhouse, and other support businesses. The camp is still a hot spot with dinner and a show every evening from late May to early September. Dig into a buffet-style dinner featuring baked halibut, reindeer stew, and country chicken. Then enjoy a fun-filled evening at the Malemute Saloon, with melodrama, Robert Service poetry, honky-tonk piano, and free-flowing beverages for any age. Ester Gold Camp is on the National Register of Historic Places. Call 1-800-676-6925 or 907-479-2500 or visit www.alaskabest.com/ester.

Yellow Eagle Gold Mining Tours. In Ester, some 5 miles (8 km) west of Fairbanks on the Parks Highway, a working gold mine offers daily guided tours. View a gold dredge, watch the excavation processes used today, then pan for gold in special water troughs. There's a gift shop, and you can have your picture taken with thousands of dollars' worth of gold. Call 907-479-0470 or visit www.yegoldminingtours.com.

Gold Dredge No. 8. In the 1930s and 1940s, great gold-processing dredges moved many tons of soil in this area. And while most of them are gone or broken-down, Gold Dredge No. 8 has been renovated for public touring. Located just north of Fairbanks, off the Steese Highway near Fox, Dredge No. 8 is a multistory giant operated by Gray Line of Alaska. Learn about this amazing operation, and pan for gold. Food service is available, too. For reservations or information, call 907-452-6835. ⬤

Gold has been a great motivation for get-rich-quick people from all over the world. Most of the thousands who flooded into the northland during the gold rush of 1898 did not even make it to a claim. A fraction got rich.

Fairbanks Hotel

517 3rd Avenue

1-888-329-4685 or 907-456-6411

www.alaska.net/fbxhotl

36 units in Fairbanks's oldest hotel, now restored to an art deco style. Downtown location. Airport/train shuttle.

Fairbanks Princess Hotel

4477 Pikes Landing Road

1-800-426-0500 or 907-455-4477

200 deluxe units. Gift shop, health club, restaurant, lounge. Along the Chena River. Airport/train shuttle.

Fairbanks Super 8 Motel

1909 Airport Way

1-800-800-8000 or 907-451-8888

www.super8motel.com

77 units, laundry, pets allowed.

Golden North Motel

4888 Old Airport Way

1-800-447-1910 or 907-479-6201

www.akpub.com/goldennorth

62 units, free continental breakfast. Pets allowed. Shuttle service.

Northern Lights Hotel - Fairbanks

427 1st Avenue

1-800-235-6546 or 907-452-4456

134 units, dining, cocktails. Tallest building in Fairbanks, overlooks Chena River. Shuttle service.

Ranch Motel

2223 South Cushman Street

1-888-452-4783 or 907-452-4783

www.expage.com/page/ranchmotel

31 units, cable TV, coffee. Pets allowed. Restaurant.

Regency Fairbanks Hotel

95 10th Avenue

1-800-348-1340 or 907-452-3200

www.regencyfairbankshotel.com

130 rooms, suites, nonsmoking available. Laundry, whirlpools, dining, cocktails. Airport/train shuttle.

Sophie Station Hotel

1717 University Avenue

1-800-528-4916 or 907-479-3650

www.mosquitonet.com/fountain

147 suites, kitchens, laundry. Dining, cocktails. Airport/train shuttle.

Westmark Fairbanks Hotel

813 Noble Street

1-800-544-0970 or 907-456-7722

www.westmarkhotels.com

244 well-appointed rooms, laundry. Restaurant, cocktails. Airport/train shuttle.

For more information about local bed-and-breakfasts, contact the Fairbanks Convention and Visitors Bureau, 1-800-327-5774 or 907-456-5774.

Campgrounds

Chena Marina RV Park

1145 Shypoke Drive

907-479-4653

www.gocampingamerica.com/chenarv

40 sites with hookups and pull-throughs. Showers, water, dump station.

River's Edge

4140 Boat Street

1-800-770-3343 or 907-474-0286

www.riversedge.net

180 sites with hookups and pull-throughs, tent camping. Showers, water, laundry, dump station. Free shuttle to attractions.

Tanana Valley State Fair
1800 College Road
907-452-3750
32 RV units with hookups and pull-
    throughs. Showers, laundry,
    fireplace/grills, dump station.

Restaurants

Ah Sa Wan Chinese Restaurant
600 Old Steese Highway
907-451-7788
Chinese buffet lunches, dinner menu.

Alaska Salmon Bake
3175 College Road, in Alaskaland's Mining
    Valley
1-800-354-7274 or 907-452-7274
Salmon, halibut, ribs, steaks over a fire.

The Bakery Restaurant
College Road near Old Steese Highway
907-456-8600
Breakfast anytime; lunch, dinner. Great
    cinnamon rolls.

Bear 'N Seal Grill & Bar
813 Noble Street
In Westmark Fairbanks
1-800-544-0970 or 907-456-7722
Pacific Rim cuisine; open for breakfast,
    lunch, dinner.

Denny's of Alaska
1929 Airport Way
907-451-8950
Open 24 hours for family dining.

Gambardella's Pasta Bella
706 2nd Avenue
907-456-3417
Italian cuisine for lunch, dinner. Outdoor
    seating available.

Ivory Jack's
Mile 1.5 Goldstream Road
907-455-6666
Alaska dinner specialties: king crab, Nome
    reindeer.

Jennifer's
3535 College Road
907-456-3805
American cuisine, fine wines, seasonal
    menu.

Pike's Landing Restaurant & Lounge
4438 Airport Way
907-479-7113
Brunch, lunch, dinner along the Chena
    River. Outdoor seating available.

The Pump House Restaurant
796 Chena Pump Road
907-479-8452
Alaskan specialties, steak, seafood. Historic
    site with outdoor seating along Chena
    River.

The Vallata
2.5 Mile Goldstream Road
907-455-6600
Italian cuisine; open for dinner.

Wolf Run Dessert and Coffee House
3360 Wolf Run
907-458-0636
Homemade desserts.

Chapter 7

Western Canada's Northbound Byways

$\mathcal{P}$erhaps you are one of those people who resist following the most-traveled path. You want a customized itinerary. In western Canada, you have plenty of options for exploring even more backcountry than where the Alaska Highway roams. From the well-developed, high-speed trans-Canada route to the narrow gravel byways that reach into the Yukon's northernmost regions, choose which route suits your sense of adventure. Spur roads and loops lead through pastureland or tundra, across mountains, or down to the sea. Along them lie ghost towns, industrious small towns, farms, and glittering cities. Use this chapter to discover what lies along the bends of western Canada's beautiful byways.

$\mathcal{N}$ORTH KLONDIKE HIGHWAY

Part of the Klondike Loop
Alaska Highway (near Whitehorse) to Dawson City: 327 miles (526 km)

The Alaska Highway skirts along the southern reaches of the Yukon Territory from Watson Lake to Whitehorse to Haines Junction, then crosses the international border and moves on to Tok, Alaska. But there's another way to reach Tok—a way that gives you more time in the Yukon.

From Whitehorse, you can drive north to Dawson City (via the North Klondike Highway), west to cross the Alaska border (via the Top of the World Highway), and then back south to Tok (via the Taylor Highway). Together, these three northerly highways are called the Klondike Loop.

If you have the yearning to see some of the Yukon Territory's most scenic vistas and experience even more gold-rush charm, take the Klondike Loop. Better yet, on the way to Alaska, take the Klondike Loop, and on the way back, take the Alaska Highway. You'll get the best of both.

Travelers will find the beginning of the Klondike Loop several miles north of Whitehorse, where the Alaska Highway (Highway 1) continues west and the North Klondike Highway (Highway 2) heads north. Highway 2 is paved for all of its 327 miles (526 km) to Dawson.

About 4 miles north of the highway junction, watch for the left turn to **Takhini**

Dawson City has been restored to its glory of a century ago.

Hot Springs, 6 miles west on a spur road. There you can bask in a naturally heated outdoor pool, winter or summer. Hiking and trail rides are other summertime options. Unlike most hot springs, Takhini's water does not contain sulfur, so it doesn't have that lingering, unpleasant odor. Meals and overnight accommodations are available.

Continuing north on Highway 2, you'll soon spot **Lake Laberge**, made famous in "The Cremation of Sam McGee," by Yukon poet Robert Service. The lake is among the bodies of water, big and small, that make up the headwaters of the Yukon River. On the west, the road soon begins paralleling long, narrow Fox Lake, its pristine waters sparkling in the long summer days. While it appears to be an autonomous body, the lake is connected to Lake Laberge by Fox Creek. Watch for signs that indicate where you can go fishing or find a campsite in one of the Yukon's government-operated campgrounds. They are clean and modestly priced.

The entire North Klondike Highway is a pleasure to drive, but one of the greatest pleasures may be found at Mile 55 (88.5 km) in the kitchen of the **Braeburn Lodge**: their world-famous giant cinnamon rolls. These folks even named their landing strip after the dinner plate-size delicacy: Cinnamon Bun Airstrip. There are other items on the menu, believe it or not, and the lodge also offers necessities such as fuel, souvenirs, and tips on local fishing holes. Canoe rentals and campsites are available here, too. Braeburn Lodge is open year-round; its most famous winter guests are the mushers and the doggie athletes competing in the 1,000-mile (1,609-km) Yukon Quest International Sled Dog Race.

The historic **Montague House**, one of the earliest roadhouse stops on the old stagecoach line, lies along this route, about 80 miles (128.5 km) north of the Alaska Highway junction.

Up ahead, Carmacks and Pelly Crossing are towns of fewer than 500 people. Each year the villages host throngs of mushers and their dog teams, who stop at these checkpoints along the trail of the Yukon Quest. The race starts or finishes in Whitehorse, alternating with Fairbanks on the other end of the route. Carmacks and Pelly Crossing both feature a First Nations interpretive center, where you can learn more about the area's archaeology and cultural history.

Fuel, groceries, and campsites are available in **Carmacks**, 103 miles (165.5 km) from the junction, where the road crosses the Yukon River. This riverside town has long served as an important stopping point for steamboats on the Yukon.

Fifteen miles (23 km) north of Carmacks is an interpretive sign and viewing area for **Five Finger Rapids**—among the most treacherous places for stampeders to pass during the gold rush of 1898.

Pelly Crossing marks the halfway point of the North Klondike Highway—about equal in distance from the Alaska Highway junction and Dawson City. Pelly Crossing is a community of First Nations people. Penny's Place serves burgers and shakes and sells locally made crafts. Call 867-537-3115.

In the final 158 miles (253 km) to Dawson City, the road parallels or intersects numerous creeks and rivers, such as Crooked Creek, Moose River, McQuesten River, and Clear Creek. The streams of this gold-mining region continue to pique the interest of placer miners for their proximity to the great discovery by George Carmacks. His find on Bonanza Creek, just outside of Dawson City, incited the Klondike Gold Rush of 1898.

Apart from Stewart Crossing, you will find few settlements along the remainder of the road. A handful of businesses offer accommodations, sundries, and fuel. Rest areas and pullouts provide the basics of a level surface and a garbage can.

Dawson City

In 1897, when news of a great gold discovery in the Klondike reached the outside world, more than 100,000 people resolved to pack up and head north, the mayor of Seattle among them. Only about 40,000 actually made it to the Klondike, and of those, a mere fraction made it rich, but the get-rich-quick compulsion was too great to ignore. Tens of thousands made uninformed decisions, not realizing that the way was hazardous, the cold could break a person's body and spirit, and the work was murderously difficult. Some men literally worked themselves to death, never enjoying the fruits of their labor. What remained was the romance—stories of men drinking champagne from ladies' slippers while gold nuggets spilled from their pockets. Most of it was bunk.

The gold rush still lingers in Dawson City, along with the refurbished and modernized historic buildings that are so attractive. But in little niches off the main

On the Silver Trail

At Stewart Crossing, 45 miles (72 km) north of Pelly Crossing, you can begin a side trip along Yukon Highway 11 to visit the historic silver- and gold-mining communities of **Mayo**, **Keno**, and **Elsa** on the Silver Trail. In the early 20th century, Mayo was a major settlement and river port. You will also pass through the traditional territory of the Na-Cho Nyak Dun people.

The Silver Trail is partially paved and leads to areas for swimming, camping, and hiking, and stunning views of glaciated mountains. Government campgrounds, as well as privately owned motels, are available in Mayo and in Keno, which is 69 miles (111 km) east of Stewart Crossing. Investigate the placer gold mine operation at Duncan Creek Golddusters in Mayo, and be sure to see the Keno City Mining Museum, which documents an era through artifacts, photographs, and written histories. Call 867-995-2792.

streets are the derelict structures that have seen human dramas we can only imagine. Dawson was nearly falling down several decades ago when, in a drive to save historic buildings, city leaders began fund-raising in earnest. Today Dawson is an imaginative slice out of time. One of its favorite sons, Pierre Berton, is a trusted storyteller who uses books and videos to share the true story of Dawson's riotous beginning, its years of quiet retirement, and its rebirth as a major visitor attraction. Berton's books and videos are available in gift stores throughout Dawson City, including the Dawson City Museum gift shop (or through your favorite Internet bookstore).

Gold is still king in Dawson, and you can pan for some yourself. Or buy a hunk of the yellow metal at one of several jewelry stores. You can have your nuggets made into a special piece of jewelry at The Gold Claim, on 3rd Avenue, or at the Klondike Nugget and Ivory Shop, at the corner of Front and Queen Streets, which has been in business since 1904. At the Nugget, gold samples from more than 50 creeks are on display.

Unlike refined gold, nuggets are slightly dull, dimpled, and irregular. They possess a compressed, raw beauty that still strikes a note of discovery in your chest. The metal and its shape remind you of the powerful forces that made it centuries ago under this very ground.

From the vantage point of **Midnight Dome** above the city, you can look out over this countryside that miners have tried to strip of its gold. Across the confluence of the **Yukon** and **Klondike Rivers**, the land below looks as if giant earthworms had burrowed beneath the surface. These peculiar marks are telltale signs of gold dredges, which operated like mechanical soil-eaters. These multistory gold-processing ships floated on small ponds and worked efficiently. Using a conveyor belt of steel buckets, a dredge would eat at the earth in front of it, sort out the gold from the useless rock and soil, then dump these tailings out the back. The dredges slowly moved forward, opening up the pond in front and filling it in behind the dredge. The machines followed the veins of gold, operating until the early 1960s and leaving behind these unique signs that are still visible today. Visit **Gold Dredge No. 4** on Bonanza Creek for a tour of the largest wood-hull dredge in the world. Call 867-993-7200.

Mining remains the most important industry in the Yukon Territory, and tourists are invited to try their hand at gold panning, or digging with a shovel and pick ax, at **Gold Claim No. 6** above Discovery Claim on Bonanza Creek. This venture is operated by the Klondike Visitors Association, and there is no charge. Bring your own gold pan or rent one in town. From Dawson Creek, take the North Klondike Highway 2 east to Bonanza Road for 13 miles (32 km). You'll drive past Dredge No. 4 and Discovery Claim. Signs will lead the way from there.

The year 2000 marked the 100th anniversary of the day the first bucket-line dredge began work on Discovery Claim. It also marked 100 years since construction of the post office on King Street and the White Pass & Yukon Route railway.

The year 2001 is the centennial year for many of Dawson's historic buildings, among them the old Territorial Administration Building, the Commissioner's Residence, the Territorial Courthouse, and the Arctic Brotherhood Hall. The year 2002 promises the biggest party yet when Dawson City celebrates its 100th birthday. This is a formal designation, recognizing Dawson's incorporation as a Canadian city, even though it existed as a wild-and-woolly boomtown prior to that.

Dawson attractions include:

George Black Ferry. This ferry across the Yukon River is a free service, 24 hours a day, except between 5 and 7 on Wednesday mornings, when the vessel is serviced. Commercial businesses hold special passes for priority boarding, so make sure you enter the correct lane for boarding your vehicle. Rush hours for tourists are as predictable as those for a big-city workforce. Between 7 A.M. and 11 A.M., most drivers are outbound tourists. Peak times for those headed into Dawson are between 2 P.M. and 8 P.M. Work around those rush hours and you'll have a shorter wait.

Dawson City Museum. The features of this museum on 5th Avenue in the Old Territorial Administration Building include goldfield exhibits, a First Nations Collection, films, a Klondike history library, and steam locomotives. A gift shop and coffee shop are on site. Open Victoria Day to Labour Day. Call 867-993-5291.

Robert Service Cabin. One block south of Mission Street and 8th Avenue is the site of the Robert Service cabin, a Klondike National Historic Site. It was here that Service wrote such classics as "The Cremation of Sam McGee" and "The Shooting of Dan McGrew." Every day from mid-May to September, you can hear free recitals of works written by the Yukon bard.

Just one block farther south on 8th Avenue, you can visit the **Jack London Cabin and Interpretive Centre.** The former Dawson City bank teller who became a famous author lived in this cabin when he first made his way to the Yukon. (The cabin has

From Midnight Dome, the confluence of the Klondike and Yukon Rivers is spread before you.

Robert Service lived in this cabin when he penned some of his best-known poems.

Ice sculptors created this statue at the door of Diamond Tooth Gerties one winter.

been moved to this site from its original location in the backcountry.) Among London's most famous books are *White Fang* and *Call of the Wild*. Like other visitor offerings in Dawson, the Interpretive Centre is open from late spring to early fall.

Palace Grande Theatre. Another Klondike National Historic Site, the Palace Grande continues to host top-flight entertainment such as the *Gaslight Follies*. Nightly family shows are performed throughout the summer. Call 867-993-5575.

Gold City Tours. See Dawson City aboard an antique car, visit the goldfields, or take in the view from atop Midnight Dome. Call 867-993-5175.

Ancient Voices Wilderness Camp. Come along for an evening barbecue, or take a day trip and learn about First Nations traditions from local interpreters. For tickets or information: 867-993-5605 or www.yukon.net/avwcamp.

Diamond Tooth Gerties Casino. The casino at 4th Avenue and Queen Street offers three different shows every night. A cover charge gets you in the door for can-can entertainment and gambling until 2 A.M. Call 867-993-5575.

Top of the World Golf Course. This is Canada's northernmost golf course, with grass greens, nine holes, a driving range, and a pro shop. Take the Top of the World Highway for 5 miles (8 km) out of Dawson City and follow the signs. Shuttle service from Dawson City is available; golfers arriving by RV are permitted to dry camp overnight. Call 867-667-1472.

Yukon River Cruises. Cruise the Dawson City waterfront and along the Klondike River. Stops include the Yukon Native village of Moosehide, and lunch or dinner at

Pleasure Island Restaurant. Tickets include an all-you-can-eat buffet featuring barbecued king salmon or, by request, chicken or steak. Learn about the favorite winter sport of sled-dog racing, too. Get information and tickets from Birch Cabin Gift Shop, on Front Street, 867-993-5482.

Two highways extend beyond Dawson: the Dempster Highway, which heads north, and the Top of the World Highway, which goes west to Alaska. See the sections on these two highways, in this chapter.

Lodging

Bonanza Gold Motel

1 mile (1.5 km) from downtown, just past
   Bonanza Road
867-993-6789
Rooms, suites, nonsmoking available,
   wheelchair-accessible suites. Cable TV,
   fax, modem access, whirlpool.
   Restaurant.

Downtown Hotel

2nd Avenue and Queen Street
1-800-661-0514 or 867-993-5346
www.yukonweb.com/tourism/downtown
59 modernized rooms in a historic building.
   Cable TV, whirlpool, winter plug-ins.
   Gift shop, restaurant, saloon. Airport
   shuttle.

The El Dorado Hotel

3rd Avenue and Princess Street
867-993-5451
www.yukon.net/eldorado
Modern rooms in a historic building, suites,
   kitchenettes. Laundry, winter plug-ins.
   Dining room, lounge. Open year-round.

Midnight Sun Hotel

3rd Avenue and Queen Street
867-993-5495
Historic property in downtown Dawson City
   location.

Triple J Hotel

5th Avenue and Queen Street
1-800-764-3555
Rooms, executive suite, kitchenette cabins.
   Laundry, restaurant, lounge. Free airport
   limo.

Westmark Inn

5th Avenue and Harper Street
1-800-544-0970 or 403-993-5542
www.westmarkhotels.com
Nicely appointed rooms, restaurant, lounge.

Campgrounds

Bonanza Gold RV Park

1 mile (1.5 km) from downtown Dawson City
867-993-6789
Full hookups, dry camping, tenting,
   laundry, car wash.

Dawson City RV Park and Campground

1 mile (1.6 km) south of town, across
   Klondike River
867-993-5142
Full and partial hookups, tent campsites,
   showers, phone. Dining, gold panning.
   Adjacent to gas and diesel station.

Gold Rush Campground / RV Park

5th Avenue and York Street
867-993-5247
Full hookups, downtown, close to most
   attractions.

GuggieVille
On Bonanza Road
867-993-5008
Full hookups available along Bonanza
 Creek. Showers, self-service laundry,
 gift shop, car wash. Gold panning.

The **Yukon Territory** government operates
two campgrounds near Dawson City:
Yukon River Territorial Campground
From downtown Dawson City, take the ferry
 across the Yukon River to reach this
 campground next to the ferry access
 road.
98 campsites for RV or tent camping. Partial
 hookups.

Klondike River Territorial Campground
Near the airport, southeast of Dawson City
38 campsites for RV or tent camping. Partial
 hookups.

Restaurants

**Bonanza Dining Room and Sluice Box
 Lounge**
3rd Avenue and Princess Street
In the El Dorado Hotel
867-993-5451
Steaks, ribs, chicken, northern specialities.

Jack London Grill and Sourdough Saloon
2nd Avenue and Queen Street
In the Downtown Hotel
867-993-5346
Barbecue, steaks, seafood.

Klondike Kate's Restaurant & Cabins
3rd Avenue and King Street
867-993-6527
Breakfast, lunch, and dinner featuring
 Canadian and ethnic foods.

Pleasure Island Restaurant
Tickets: Birch Cabin Gift Shop, Front Street
867-993-5482
Lunch or dinner restaurant cruises with
 Yukon River Cruises feature all-you-can-
 eat king salmon buffet; steak or chicken
 by request.

$\mathcal{T}$OP OF THE WORLD HIGHWAY

Part of the Klondike Loop
Dawson City to Alaska–Yukon border: 66 miles (106 km)

From Dawson to the Alaska–Yukon border, the Klondike Loop continues west on Highway 9 (the Top of the World Highway) for 66 miles (106 km). Before you leave Dawson, check on current road conditions by calling 867-993-5566.

The Top of the World cuts into mountainsides and crosses peaks, dipping and rising hundreds of feet, while just beyond the edge of the road, a beautiful valley beckons. Above tree line, the view is so broad and inspiring that you suppress a loud "Wow!" (or maybe you don't). Seal-coated in some sections, dusty and gravelly in others, the road is less inspiring when you are traveling behind a truck or slow-moving RV. But take heart, the next pullout may offer a view that's too great to pass up.

Cruise ships share the Inside Passage with Alaska's ferries, commercial fishing vessels, pleasure boats, and floatplanes.

This region is known as Fortymile country, for the Fortymile River that wends its way nearby. It was a place of uncertain possession when American miners thought they were mining U.S. soil. With the arrival of the North-West Mounted Police and officials who certified the international demarcation line, some of the miners left for more golden opportunities. Others settled in to live as Canadians.

This highway is unplowed in winter months, leaving it to snowmobilers who gladly use this major road as their trail. Each year in late February and early March, snowmobilers travel this highway and Alaska's Taylor Highway for their Trek Over the Top event, a dash between Tok, Alaska, and Dawson City, Yukon.

The winter that I traveled in the pack of Trekkers, we were headed east from Alaska to the Yukon when, shortly after crossing the border, we spied a large hump in the deep snow. Mounties had placed sticks and pink flagging around the unusual rise on the side of the road. It was a car, completely snowed over, with only a few windows still slightly visible.

I remembered the story: Just a couple of months earlier, a man had tried to drive from Alaska to the Lower 48 via this closed road and had become stuck in the snow. He tried walking out for help. A few weeks later, snowmobilers found his body. The car would stay there until late spring, when the snow released its grip and the road reopened.

Between Dawson City and the border, there is little man-made clutter—just miles and miles of awe-striking scenery. The handful of buildings at the border are for customs officials only. There are no facilities, no rest rooms, no currency exchange. And the customs station is open summers only, from 9 A.M. to 9 P.M. Yukon Time (or 8 A.M. to 8 P.M. Alaska Time).

From the border, the road continues into Alaska for a dozen miles before reaching the Taylor Highway.

*T*AYLOR HIGHWAY

Part of the Klondike Loop

For details on this section of the Klondike Loop, see the section on the Taylor Highway in Chapter 8, Alaska's State Highways.

*D*EMPSTER HIGHWAY

North Klondike Highway (near Dawson City) to Inuvik: 460 miles (740 km)

Meant for only the most dogged motorists, this undeveloped highway wends north from the Dawson City area to the upper reaches of the Yukon, across untamed wilderness and into the **Northwest Territories**. Completed in 1979, the route begins from the North Klondike Highway at a point 25 miles (40 km) east of Dawson and ends in the village of Inuvik, 460 miles (741 km) later.

This gravel road was named for Cpl. W. J. Dempster, a member of the North-West Mounted Police, who led the search for the famous Lost Patrol. The party had become lost near Fort McPherson in the winter of 1911 and froze to death.

This is wilderness at its finest, with humans few and far between as you drive over mountains and onto vast river floodplains. The only service stations are at Eagle Plains, Fort McPherson, and Inuvik. You'll cross the **Arctic Circle** at Mile 250 (402 km), at latitude 66° 33' N. Free ferry service is available at two crossings: the Peel River and the Mackenzie River.

Gold City Travel in Dawson City can arrange for you to ride along in the Dempster Highway van or in a chartered bus so you can cross the Arctic Circle without the extra wear on your own vehicle. Gold City Travel is on Front Street across from the SS *Keno*. Call 867-993-6424.

Hotel accommodations, fuel, dining, camping, and other services are available at Eagle Plains Hotel, Mile 231 (371.5 km). Yukon government campgrounds may be found at Tombstone Mountain, Mile 45 (72.5 km); Engineer Creek, Mile 120.5 (194 km); and Rock River, Mile 278 (447 km). The Dempster Highway Interpretive Centre, at the Tombstone Mountain campground, is open from mid-June to early September.

In the Northwest Territories, you can camp at Mile 340 (547.5 km) at the **Nitainlaii**

Campground and Information Centre, operated by the territory government.

For Inuvik-area travel information, contact the Western Arctic Tourism Association in Inuvik at 867-777-4321.

CAMPBELL HIGHWAY

Watson Lake to North Klondike Highway (near Carmacks): 373 miles (600 km)

Motorists on their way to Dawson City can shorten their drive by taking the alternate route around Whitehorse: the Campbell Highway (Highway 4). The road heads northwest from Watson Lake and, after 373 miles, connects with the North Klondike Highway (Highway 2) just north of Carmacks.

You accomplish three things by taking this route to Dawson City: You save 20 miles on your odometer; you miss out on all the fun that's waiting in Whitehorse; and you eat a lot of dust. On the other hand, you also see some beautiful land as you follow the route of early-day fur traders who worked for the Hudson's Bay Company. Robert Campbell himself was sent here in the 1840s to explore on behalf of the company.

Completed in 1968, the Campbell is mostly unpaved, and this road less traveled wends through the communities of Ross River and Faro, where you can buy gas, food, and groceries, as well as find a place to stay with or without an RV.

YELLOWHEAD-CASSIAR HIGHWAYS

Prince George to Alaska Highway (near Watson Lake): 744 miles (1,197 km)

Alaskabound travelers can shave some 100 miles (161 km) off the drive between Prince George and Watson Lake by taking westbound Yellowhead Highway 16 and then northbound Cassiar Highway 37. Some motorists are less concerned about time, but still take the Yellowhead-Cassiar route for a change of scenery through British Columbia's outstanding **Skeena Mountains**. Most portions of this route are paved, but drivers should stay alert for sections of washboard in gravel stretches of the Cassiar.

Yellowhead Highway 16 is a trans-Canada route that extends from southern Manitoba and trends westward and north across Saskatchewan, Alberta, and British Columbia. In western Canada, it is a primary east-west route linking Edmonton with Prince George. Through mountain passes, along glacial lakes, and into canyons, the Yellowhead promises stunning vistas and plenty of wildlife-watching.

The Yellowhead continues west to the coastal city of **Prince Rupert, B.C.** From there, travelers may connect with the British Columbia ferry system and the Alaska Marine Highway System. (See Appendix 1, Alaska Marine Highway System.)

The junction of the Yellowhead and Cassiar Highways is 298 miles (480 km) west of Prince George near the village of **Kitwanga**. From here, the Cassiar trends north for 446 miles (718 km) to its junction with the Alaska Highway 13 miles (21 km) west of Watson Lake.

From the Cassiar Highway, motorists can access the coastal communities of **Stewart, B.C.**, and **Hyder, Alaska**. The turnoff to these towns is at Mile 96 (155 km) on the Cassiar Highway, at Meziadin Junction. Stewart and Hyder straddle the international border 41 miles (66 km) west of the junction.

The Yellowhead Highway got its name from the story of an Iroquois-Caucasian trapper who was called Tête Jaune, or Yellowhead, for the blond cast to his hair. He led fur traders through the Rocky Mountains and opened the way for a trade route across western Canada.

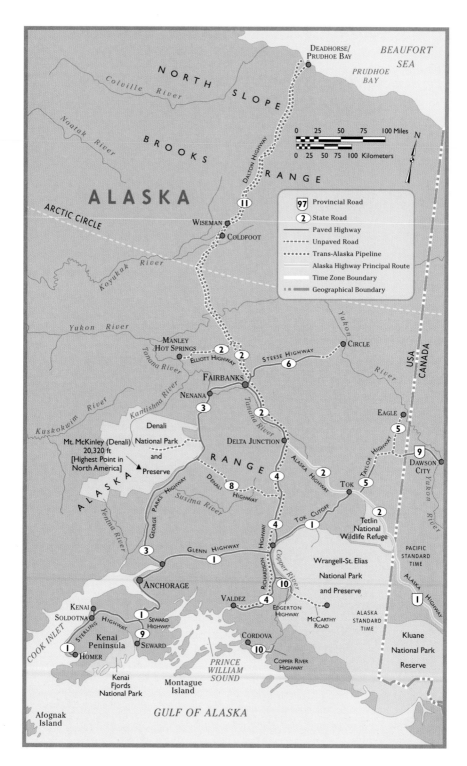

- DEADHORSE/PRUDHOE BAY
- BEAUFORT SEA
- PRUDHOE BAY
- NORTH SLOPE
- Colville River
- BROOKS RANGE
- Noatak River
- ALASKA
- DALTON HIGHWAY
- ARCTIC CIRCLE
- 11
- WISEMAN
- COLDFOOT
- Koyukuk River

Legend

97	Provincial Road
2	State Road
	Paved Highway
	Unpaved Road
	Trans-Alaska Pipeline
	Alaska Highway Principal Route
	Time Zone Boundary
	Geographical Boundary

- 0 25 50 75 100 Miles
- 0 25 50 75 100 Kilometers
- N
- Yukon River
- MANLEY HOT SPRINGS
- 2
- 2
- CIRCLE
- ELLIOTT HIGHWAY
- STEESE HIGHWAY
- 6
- Tanana River
- Yukon River
- USA CANADA
- FAIRBANKS
- NENANA
- 3
- 2
- EAGLE
- Kantishna River
- Tanana River
- 5
- Kuskokwim River
- Denali National Park
- DELTA JUNCTION
- Mt. McKinley (Denali) 20,320 ft [Highest Point in North America]
- and Preserve
- RANGE
- ALASKA HIGHWAY
- TAYLOR HIGHWAY
- 9
- DAWSON CITY
- Yukon River
- ALASKA
- DENALI HIGHWAY
- 8
- 4
- TOK
- 5
- George Parks Highway
- Susitna River
- 2
- Yentna River
- 4
- TOK CUTOFF
- 1
- Tetlin National Wildlife Refuge
- 3
- GLENN HIGHWAY
- 1
- RICHARDSON HIGHWAY
- Copper River
- Wrangell-St. Elias National Park and Preserve
- PACIFIC STANDARD TIME
- ALASKA HIGHWAY
- ANCHORAGE
- 10
- KENAI
- SOLDOTNA
- STERLING HIGHWAY
- 1
- SEWARD HIGHWAY
- VALDEZ
- 4
- EDGERTON HIGHWAY
- McCARTHY ROAD
- ALASKA STANDARD TIME
- 1
- Kluane National Park Reserve
- COOK INLET
- 1
- 9
- SEWARD
- CORDOVA
- 10
- Kenai Peninsula
- HOMER
- PRINCE WILLIAM SOUND
- COPPER RIVER HIGHWAY
- Kenai Fjords National Park
- Montague Island
- Afognak Island
- GULF OF ALASKA

Chapter 8

Alaska's State Highways

𝒟*riving Alaska.* Most visitors to Alaska are accustomed to choosing from a vast menu of roads, reading and following maps, and watching for their exits. When they ask directions, they commonly refer to route numbers. So when they arrive in Alaska, they might ask, "Where is the exit for Route 9?" The puzzled Alaskan will answer with another question, "Where do you want to go?" Choices are so few that decision-making is made easy. Name your destination and there's usually only one way to get there.

Portage Glacier is such a place. Located about 45 minutes south of Anchorage off the Seward Highway, the glacier is counted among Alaska's top tourist attractions, along with the Inside Passage and Mount McKinley. Its popularity is due in part to its accessibility by road. Each summer, thousands of people take a 1-hour cruise to the

The Glenn Highway wends above treeline and down again as you travel from Anchorage toward Glennallen.

Highway Name	Length	Number	Route Description
Copper River Highway	48 miles 77 km	10	Disconnected from highway system. Connects Cordova, on Prince William Sound, with the derelict Million Dollar Bridge to nowhere; mostly unpaved.
Dalton Highway	414 miles 666 km	11	Splits northbound from Elliott Highway (north of Fox) to Deadhorse, where it dead-ends at the Arctic Ocean; mostly unpaved; almost no services.
Denali Highway	136 miles 219 km	8	Road between Richardson Highway and Parks Highway; connects Paxson and Cantwell; unpaved; few services.
Edgerton Highway	33 miles 53 km	10	Connects Richardson Highway (south of Glennallen) to Chitina, 33 miles (53 km) east on paved road; from there, unpaved McCarthy Road travels east for 60 miles (96.5 km) almost to McCarthy; few services; not maintained in winter.
Elliott Highway	152 miles 244.5 km	2	From Fox (north of Fairbanks) to Manley Hot Springs, where it dead-ends at the Tanana River; partially paved; few services.
Glenn Highway	328 miles 528 km	1	Connects Anchorage with Glennallen and the Richardson Highway, and connects Gakona Junction with Tok via the Tok Cutoff; paved; sections often under repair; services at regular intervals. *(continued)*

glacier's face on a custom-built icebreaker named the MV *Ptarmigan*. I was selling tickets there one summer when a man stopped by after his cruise, an Alaska map in his hand. "We came down here on Route 1 in our rental car," he said as he smoothed his creased map on the counter, "but we'd like to go back to Anchorage another way and see some different country. What do you recommend?"

"Well, sir," I told him, "the Seward Highway out there is your only road, and it runs north-south. You're south right now, so just turn the car around and keep driving until you bump into Anchorage." He could hardly believe it until I showed him on his own map. He was driving in the country's biggest state, with fewer roads per square mile than Rhode Island. I knew the trip back wouldn't disappoint him, though. The fabulous Seward Highway is among only 53 roads in the United States chosen for the federally designated title of National Scenic Bypass.

A separate issue entirely is the Alaskan preference of calling highways by name, not route number: the Steese, the Parks, the Seward. You'll hear the names regularly, the route numbers rarely. Most of the highways dead-end at small towns along a major body of water. Consequently, the term "end of the road" applies to several

Highway Name	Length	Number	Route Description
Haines Highway (Via Yukon Route 3 and B.C. Route 4)	152 miles 245 km	7	Connects Alaska Highway at Haines Junction, Yukon, with Haines, Alaska, where it dead-ends on Lynn Canal; paved.
Klondike Highway 2 (Yukon road)	99 miles 159 km	2	Connects Alaska Highway just south of Whitehorse, Yukon, with Skagway, Alaska, where it dead-ends on Lynn Canal; paved.
Parks Highway	358 miles 576 km	3	Connects Anchorage with Fairbanks via the Glenn Highway. Completely paved; services at regular intervals.
Richardson Highway	364 miles 568 km	4 & 2	Connects Valdez with Fairbanks. Paved; services at regular intervals.
Seward Highway	127 miles 204 km	1 & 9	Connects Anchorage with Seward, where it dead-ends on Resurrection Bay off the Gulf of Alaska; paved; services at regular intervals.
Steese Highway	162 miles 260.5 km	6	Connects Fairbanks with Circle City, where it dead-ends on the Yukon River; mostly unpaved; few services.
Sterling Highway	143 miles 230 km	1	Branches off the Seward Highway for south-bound travelers to Homer, where it dead-ends on Cook Inlet; paved; services at regular intervals.
Taylor Highway	160 miles 257 km	5	Connects Alaska Highway at Tetlin Junction (southeast of Tok) with Eagle, where it dead-ends on the Yukon River; unpaved; few services. Not maintained in winter.

communities around the state, although one, in particular, was made famous by author/humorist Tom Bodett. He put his hometown of Homer, Alaska, on the map with his national radio program *The End of the Road Show.*

If you want to drive northwest, west, or southwest from this narrow, north-south cluster of blacktop, you can forget it. Most of Alaska remains accessible only by air or, along Alaska's Panhandle (Southeast Alaska), by marine highway (see Chapter 9, Alaska Marine Highway System).

In 1942, when the Alaska Highway was built and attached to the existing Richardson Highway at Delta Junction, there were even fewer roads. Alaska's busiest highway between Anchorage and Fairbanks, the Parks, didn't even exist. Travelers had to use the longer, roundabout way via the Richardson and Glenn Highways. The pipeline was still 30 years in the future, so the Dalton Highway (also known as the Haul Road for pipeline construction) hadn't been conceived. Nor had the Sterling Highway, which wends down the Kenai Peninsula. If you wanted to go to Homer, you took a ferry.

What are now considered major transportation routes (by Alaska standards) weren't much more than improved trails that had been used by early-day settlers, traders, and miners. A century ago and more, the pioneering Europeans simply traveled along the ancient trading routes of Alaska's first people, who were familiar with the passes through the mountains, and who graciously showed the newcomers the way.

Today, although Alaska's roads are called highways, a few remain rustic and unpaved; in winter, four of them (the Copper River, Edgerton, Taylor, and Denali Highways) are not plowed, so they are impassable except to snowmobilers. Even if a road is regularly plowed, wise winter travelers will check the local phone book and call the Department of Transportation's recorded information line to obtain road conditions before setting out. (See the section on Driving in Winter in Chapter 1, Getting Ready.)

Generally speaking, most of Alaska's major roads are in great shape. The paved roads are well-marked, two-lane routes with ample shoulders. Unpaved sections are graded regularly, and sometimes serve better than the broken-down parts of paved roads. Small towns, gas stations, and other services appear at regular intervals, and restaurants and lodging aren't hard to find, either. That can't be said for all of Alaska's "highways," though, so read up on your route before you embark.

Road maintenance workers have a particular challenge in Alaska, considering what they have for a subsurface. In many parts of the state, they contend with an underground enemy called permafrost: permanently frozen sections of soil that are riddled with ice. When the insulating overgrowth is scraped away to create a road, the ground begins to melt and sink. Adding a layer of weighty, heat-conductive blacktop creates more subsurface problems. With the freeze and thaw of seasonal change, some roadbeds suffer, and an army of maintenance workers sets out to make repairs each year in the short summer construction season. As a motorist, plan for one or two delays, because flaggers, pilot cars, dust, and lumbering trucks are virtual guarantees. Please be patient. If they weren't out there doing their jobs, you wouldn't be willing (or able) to set out on these passageways into some of America's most magnificent places.

Of course, one must include gawking time in any Alaska road trip. When the evening light turns the sky pink-orange above a mountain range, the view can be distracting. Glacier-fed rivers merge and divide across a broad floodplain, and low clouds drag across the vivid, white mountain peaks. Wild animals step out onto the pavement ahead, or pause to feed along the shoulder, and your camera is at the ready. In the midst of such beauty, "making good time" loses its appeal.

Since 1995, the Alaska Department of Transportation and Public Facilities has named 11 transportation routes as Alaska Scenic Byways. To qualify for the designation, a byway must possess some or all of these intrinsic qualities: scenic or natural beauty, cultural importance, recreational value, or archaeological or historic significance. Not all 11 are paved roadways, however—the Alaska Railroad and the Alaska Marine Highway System are among the names on the list. Others are the Dalton Highway, Haines Highway, Parks Highway (from Denali State Park to Healy),

Richardson Highway (from Glennallen to Valdez), Seward Highway, Steese Highway, Sterling Highway (from Wye to Skilak, and Anchor Point to Homer), and the combination of the Taylor and Top of the World Highways. For more information and photos of Alaska's Scenic Byways, visit the following website: www.dot.state.ak.us/scenic.

This chapter features Alaska's highways, in alphabetical order, and includes the cities, services, access, recreational opportunities, and attractions that you'll find along this exceptionally scenic road system.

$\mathcal{C}$OPPER RIVER HIGHWAY

Cordova to Million Dollar Bridge: 48 miles
Travel Opportunities: *Scenic fishing village; flightseeing over Wrangell–St. Elias National Park; Prince William Sound cruises; rafting on the Copper River; chartered fishing for salmon or halibut; Childs Glacier; Million Dollar Bridge; bird-watching.*

Among Alaska's unique roads, the Copper River Highway is a standout—a mere fragment of a highway that's disconnected from the rest of the highway system, but still official enough to merit a route number: Alaska Highway 10. To drive this road, you'll need to fly in and rent a car at Cordova on Prince William Sound. Or bring your vehicle along on the Alaska Marine Highway System and disembark at Cordova (see Chapter 9, Alaska Marine Highway System). Pay heed to the return schedule if you choose to cruise, or you may stay longer than you had planned.

For centuries, Native Alaskans have lived in this region, moving with the seasons to fish and hunt as they drew life from the land. The ways of the early Native people are not just in museum displays today. In this area, you'll find many Athabascan Indians and Chugach Eskimos who still follow the cultural practices of their ancestors in dance, song, and art, as well as through a subsistence lifestyle of hunting and fishing for food. Throughout the small Native villages of Southcentral Alaska, people live in log or wood-frame houses, drive cars, go to work, and follow the same television "soaps" as anybody else in the country. Some of them, however, have great-grandmas who remember the moment they saw a white person for the first time.

Explorers, gold seekers, and traders brought the stamp of the Western world to the Copper River Delta, especially during the 19th century. In 1902 geologists made the first major oil discovery in Alaska—at Katalla, southwest of Cordova. In 1907 entrepreneur Michael J. Heney began building the Copper River & Northwestern Railway to transport the ore mined from the Kennecott Copper Mine, to the north. The mine and railroad flourished for more than 20 years, closing in the late 1930s. In the mid-1940s, builders of the Copper River Highway chose to follow the railway's bed and planned to join Cordova with Chitina and the Richardson Highway. In 1964, a natural disaster thwarted the project, and the work stalled out. That year, the Good Friday Earthquake devastated Cordova and many Southcentral coastal communities.

The earthquake originally was measured at a magnitude of 8.6 and later was upgraded to an unbelievable 9.2.

The state's Department of Transportation is still interested in completing the road from Cordova, but protests from residents and others have further delayed the project. It turns out that a majority of the Cordovans like their insulation and don't want more road traffic. As a result, the Copper River Highway sees little use from anyone other than the locals.

The first 12 miles (19 km) are paved, followed by a gravel surface that threads for another 36 miles (58 km) through awesome beauty to the **Million Dollar Bridge**, which crosses the Copper River. One section of the bridge collapsed in the 1964 earthquake. Even though the bridge looks impossibly damaged, it is still usable. A crude road extends another 10 miles (16 km) beyond the bridge, but only four-wheel-drive vehicles should give it a go. Near the bridge, you'll get a panoramic view of **Childs Glacier**. Plan a picnic here amid unforgettable surroundings.

In the course of its 48 miles (77 km), the highway crosses a number of glacially fed streams and the multifingered Copper River Delta. Magnificent glaciers are visible on the north side of the road as you drive east. And all around you, for miles and miles, is **Chugach National Forest**, close to 6 million acres of it. On this drive, you'll find viewpoint turnouts with informational plaques, trailheads, and developed recreation areas at **Cabin Lake** and **Alaganik Slough**. Fishing, wildlife-watching, hiking, biking, and camping are popular activities around here, and the Copper River is famed for its annual runs of salmon. Freshwater and saltwater fishing takes place in an angler's paradise. Learn about local regulations and closures when you obtain your fishing license at any number of retail outlets in Cordova.

Cordova is a photogenic town with a population of about 2,500 people. Because its economy is largely based on fishing, commercial fishing vessels outnumber pleasure boats in the harbor, and a U.S. Coast Guard vessel is moored just outside the small-boat harbor. It's fun to walk the docks and read the names of the vessels and to watch the fishermen gear up or down from a trip. The catch may be salmon, halibut, or herring, depending on season. In town, nearly everything you need lies within walking distance. North of Cordova, the Alaska Marine Highway ferry terminal offers scheduled service aboard the MV *Tustumena* and the MV *Bartlett* on the Southcentral/Southwest Alaska ferry route (see Chapter 9, Alaska Marine Highway System).

Located on a major flyway for 2 million waterfowl and 40 million shorebirds, Cordova hosts the **Copper River Delta Shorebird Festival** in early May each year. Birders come from all over the world to view the millions of birds that nest and feed in the delta. So vital to the birds' survival, this portion of the Chugach National Forest gained added protection in 1978 when it was named a Critical Habitat Area.

The favorite party of the winter season is the **Cordova Iceworm Festival**, set each year on the first weekend of February. Events include a parade, entertainment, an arts and crafts show, skiing events, a best-beard contest, and selection of a king and queen. Call 907-424-5756 for more information.

Cordova Museum and Library offers exhibits on the rich Native cultures of this region, as well as its exploration in 1778 by Captain James Cook, the gold rush, and more recent copper-mining history. Also inside are art displays, a fishing diorama, gift shop, and a modest bookstore. At the U.S. **Forest Service** office, in a historic 1925 building at 612 2nd Street, you can learn about the Chugach National Forest and local natural history.

Other options from Cordova include rafting the Copper River, a fly-in fishing trip, a cruise on Prince William Sound, or a flightseeing excursion above the fabulous Wrangell–St. Elias Range. For more information on what to see and do in Cordova, contact the Chamber of Commerce at P.O. Box 99, Cordova, AK 99574-0099, call 907-424-7260, or visit www.ptialaska.net/~cchamber.

Lodging

Cordova Rose Lodge
1315 Whitshed Road
907-424-7673
Historic setting of landlocked barge offers
  rooms with a view and breakfast.

The Northern Nights Inn
P.O. Box 1564
907-424-5356
Rooms with a view of the inlet; kitchens,
  laundry, freezer for your fish.

Prince William Motel
2nd and Council Streets
1-888-796-6835 or 907-424-3201
16 rooms and kitchenettes. TV, microwaves,
  refrigerators, laundry, store.

Campgrounds

Odiak Camper Park
Whitshed Road off Copper River Highway
907-424-6200
24 sites, tenting area, showers; operated by
  the city.

U.S. Forest Service
1-877-444-6777
17 cabins available in this district; most
  accessible only by boat or plane. Three
  are on the trail system.

Restaurants

Power House Bar and Restaurant
Mile 2 Copper River Highway
907-424-3529
Soups, sandwiches, seafood. Eat in or
  take out.

$\mathcal{D}$ALTON HIGHWAY (Haul Road)

From Elliott Highway to Deadhorse: 414 miles (666 km)
Travel Opportunities: *Trans-Alaska pipeline views; Coldfoot; Wiseman gold-mining village; Brooks Range continental divide; Arctic Circle crossing; guided tours to Prudhoe Bay oil operations.*

The Dalton Highway originally was called the Haul Road because it was built for one purpose: to haul goods and supplies for the building of the trans-Alaska pipeline. The road was named for James William Dalton, a principal player in North Slope oil development. Although experimental ice roads, seasonal at best, had been built in the Arctic, the Dalton was the first planned and engineered roadway into the farthest north reaches of the state. Even though the Dalton was finished in 1974, its entire length wasn't opened to the public until 1995.

You will share the road with mostly truckers headed to or from Deadhorse and Prudhoe Bay at the top of the state, a small number of hardy souls like yourself, and a handful of tourism operations. As far as services go, this route remains largely undeveloped. With a few exceptions—such as businesses at the Yukon River Bridge, Coldfoot and Wiseman, and a couple of wayside stops—you'll encounter long stretches of no towns, no gas stations, no rest rooms, and few other travelers. The last-chance public toilet and garbage drop may be found at a wayside 200 miles (322 km) south of Deadhorse.

As you head north, the terrain changes in degrees of beauty: from sparsely treed rolling hills, to lofty mountains, to limitless undulating tundra. Your most constant companion is the nearby pipeline, visible only in the stretches where the permafrost in the soil was so bad that builders put it up on supports and ran it above ground. The 48-inch-diameter pipeline was built between 1974 and 1977. Its 800-mile (1,287.5-km) length stretches from Mile 0 at Prudhoe Bay to its terminus at Valdez on Prince William Sound. South of Fairbanks, most of the pipeline route parallels the Richardson Highway.

Salmon drying in the sun is a common sight in Native fish camps along Alaska's rivers. Learn more about the Athabascan culture at the Stevens Village fish camp, accessible by boat from the Dalton Highway.

The old log post office in Wiseman, Alaska, off the Dalton Highway.

A wide, unpaved wilderness road with a good roadbed, the Dalton extends from Mile 73 of the Elliott Highway, north of Fox, all the way to Deadhorse and the working oil fields of Prudhoe Bay. Don't expect to waltz in anywhere at will. Most of these places are off-limits to the traveler. In Deadhorse you'll find an airport, general store, filling station, and a couple of hotels, which are the best places to line up a guided tour of the area. With a guide, you may dip your toes in the frigid Arctic Ocean, view Mile 0 of the pipeline, and learn about how the vast oil reservoir beneath Alaska's North Slope was discovered and developed.

Consider the following option for less wear-and-tear on your vehicle and your sensibilities: Take a fly-drive combo tour with an operator such as Princess Tours or Northern Alaska Tour Company out of Fairbanks. I did this once and found the trip very worthwhile. Even though you begin the trip with strangers, within hours you'll find fast friends in the group. A shuttle bus will pick you up from your Fairbanks campground or hotel. Pack an overnight bag, but don't worry about food. You'll be well fed throughout the trip.

After a 45-minute flight from Fairbanks to **Deadhorse**, we boarded an 18-passenger van and cruised around the oil fields, with permitted access to places where we would not have been allowed as independent visitors. Naturally this is a high-security area, and tourism is only a recent development. The population of Deadhorse is officially 25—plus 2,500 transient workers. Most work a fluctuating schedule of two-weeks-on, two-weeks-off, or something similar. You won't see many people, actually. Most work indoors.

The trans-Alaska pipeline parallels the Dalton Highway for the entire route to Deadhorse.

Around the low buildings and ground-level maze of pipes, the road meanders among the oil-company installations and enclosed drilling rigs. We saw numerous caribou, waterfowl, and wildflowers in what I considered unexpected places. In one spot, we saw a group of caribou resting under a raised part of the pipeline. Without trees to block the view, they were easy to spot. At the **Arctic Ocean,** I handed off my camera to a fellow traveler and asked him to take my picture standing ankle deep in the water. (I threw my arms in the air and said "Hurry!" through a clenched smile. The water was piercing cold.)

Our driver had packed lots of good food in coolers, and we had plenty of water, coffee, and soft drinks. Driving south that day, he told us all about the unique forces of nature here, the climate, the geology, and the wildlife. We learned how to pronounce "Sagavanirktok River," and understood instantly why everybody calls it the Sag.

Farther south we spied a hunter who had bagged a caribou with bow and arrow, and some of us tried walking out to him over the tundra. It was like trying to walk on and between underinflated basketballs that are covered with mossy, leafy growth.

We stopped again to share our drinking water with a British couple on a bicycle journey from Fairbanks to Prudhoe Bay, then visited the century-old mining town of Wiseman. A woman behind the counter in the general store told us that in the last couple of days, a local miner had uncovered a record-size gold nugget: flat and big enough to eclipse a saucer.

After an overnight at Coldfoot, in buildings that once housed pipeline construction workers, we continued our southbound trip and later came upon the only structure around for a hundred miles: the tour company's private, off-road outhouse, placed there just for our comfort. Next stop was the Arctic Circle, marked by a sturdy sign showing your place on the globe. Our driver asked us to wait a moment, then literally rolled out a red carpet and shook our hands, welcoming us across the invisible line. That evening, we pulled in to Fairbanks, tired but thrilled to have seen such rare sights.

My advice is to go with a tour guide if you want the best experience and the least worry. It was a privilege to have someone drive, especially when a good-size piece of gravel damaged the tour van's windshield (and not mine).

Places of note along the Dalton Highway, from south to north:

Yukon River Bridge. The highway crosses the bridge at Mile 56 (90 km), where many travelers are happy to encounter the businesses of Yukon Ventures Alaska: motel rooms, gas station, tire repairs, gift shop, and restaurant. You may launch your boat on the Yukon River.

From the bridge, you can visit an Athabascan Indian fish camp, as a guest of Yukon River Tours and the people of **Stevens Village**. Native guides will transport you from the bridge in their modern, enclosed jetboat to an upriver site. This area lies within the Yukon Flats National Wildlife Refuge, which supports moose, caribou, bears, millions of migrating birds, and small furbearers such as lynx, snowshoe hares, foxes, and beavers. On shore, observe as Native Alaskans work to put up fish for the coming winter, a tradition that continues as part of the annual rhythms of the Athabascans. At the Stevens Village Cultural Center, you'll learn about Native history through artifacts, ancient tools, and weapons. Plan an overnight stay or spend a few hours. To arrange your Stevens Village trip, call 907-452-7162.

A cow moose crosses the Dalton in the treeless area north of the Brooks Range.

Arctic Circle. At Mile 115 (185 km), an expansive wayside with viewing platform, outhouses, and great signs is worth a stop to record your momentous crossing of the Arctic Circle—that invisible boundary that encircles the globe at the southernmost latitude where the sun never sets on the day of the summer solstice (June 21 or 22). Likewise, at this latitude the sun does not rise on the day of the winter solstice (December 21 or 22). Nearby, the Bureau of Land Management offers undeveloped camping.

Coldfoot. This former pipeline construction camp was given this name for obvious reasons. Winter temperatures plunge well below zero all along the Dalton Highway. The farther north you go, the deeper the plunge. I once visited Coldfoot with a television crew in January, and I still remember the heartbreaking sound of an expensive and important part of the camera when it went crraack! in the –50°F air. In summer, Coldfoot is pleasantly warm, but be advised that mosquitoes and other biting insects are a nuisance. There is no town here, but rather a welcome stop in the road at Mile 175 (282 km), where truckers and tourists refresh and refill. Fuel, a restaurant, and overnight accommodations are available.

Wiseman. Gold miners gather where there's gold to be found. Towns are created by the people who follow: the scores who offer services and supplies for those miners. That's how Wiseman came to be, nearly a century ago here in the Koyukuk Mining District. Disconnected from the rest of the world as it was, the town nearly died out before the Haul Road was built. Now located about 3 miles (5 km) off the Dalton Highway (at Mile 188) and populated by a scant two dozen people, it has managed to cling to life as gold and tourism now feed the town. Pay mind to private property as you walk among the log homes—it's easy to imagine this as a Disney set, but people do live and work here! Visit the **Wiseman Museum** to learn more about local and regional mining history. It's located in the historic Carl Frank cabin in north Wiseman. On the south end of town, cross the river to reach the Wiseman Trading Co. in the two-story log cabin for unique gift shopping. Ask permission and directions to the old cemetery on a beautiful hillside above town, where many area pioneers have gone to rest.

Continental Divide. Drive through the majestic Brooks Range and cross the northernmost Continental Divide in the United States, at Mile 245. Atigun Pass, at 4,739 feet, is the highest point on the 800-mile north-south route of the pipeline.

The North Slope. To oil company workers, this name—or its abbreviated version, the Slope—is synonymous with Prudhoe Bay. It is derived from a geographical feature. On the north side of the Brooks Range, this country takes its time returning to sea level. It is that slow, almost unrecognizable slope toward the Arctic Ocean that is referred to in "North Slope."

Deadhorse. End of the line. Stop at the Prudhoe Bay General Store (and U.S. post office) to send a postcard from the top of the world. The store features its own little museum, too, along with sales of souvenirs, sweatshirts, outdoor gear, hats, and more. Call 907-659-2412.

Lodging/Meals

Yukon River Bridge:
Yukon Ventures Alaska
Mile 56 Dalton Highway
907-655-9001
40 rooms, plus service station, tire repair,
   boat launch, gift shop, restaurant.

Coldfoot:
Arctic Circle Bed and Breakfast
Mile 175 Dalton Highway
907-452-0081
Lodging, plus gift shop, fishing and
   canoeing adventures.

Slate Creek Inn
Mile 175 Dalton Highway
907-678-5201
80 rooms, plus service station, post office,
   gift shop, restaurant. RV hookups and
   dump station.

Wiseman:
Arctic Getaway Bed and Breakfast
Mile 189 Dalton Highway
907-796-9001
Located in a historic building: Pioneer Hall,
   Igloo No. 8.

Deadhorse:
Arctic Caribou Inn
907-659-2368
75 rooms with private or shared baths. Near
   restaurant, gift shop, airport. Tours
   available: oil field; Mile 0 of the
   pipeline; Arctic Ocean walk.

Campgrounds

Coldfoot:
Slate Creek Inn
Mile 175 Dalton Highway
907-678-5201

RV hookups, dump station. Adjacent to
   motel, with service station, restaurant,
   gift shop, post office.

Deadhorse:
Arctic Caribou Inn
907-659-2368
RV parking is available adjacent to this
   hotel.

Deadhorse–Prudhoe Bay Tesoro
907-659-3198
This service station permits overnight
   parking. Phone, rest rooms, and free
   area maps. Fuel available 24 hours a day.

The Bureau of Land Management oversees
four camping areas along the Dalton
Highway. For more information, contact the
Northern Field Office in Fairbanks at 907-474-
2302 or visit the bureau's website at www.
ak.blm.gov/ ndo. The camping areas are:

Sixty Mile Site
Mile 60 Dalton Highway
Undeveloped 5 acres with water, outhouse.

Arctic Circle Site
Mile 115 Dalton Highway
Undeveloped 5 acres above wayside,
   outhouse.

Marion Creek Campground
Mile 180 Dalton Highway
Developed 1.5 acres with campsites, water,
   toilets.

Galbraith Lake Site
Mile 275 Dalton Highway
Undeveloped 5 acres, outhouse.

$\mathcal{D}$ENALI HIGHWAY

From Richardson Highway to Parks Highway: 136 miles (219 km)
Travel Opportunities: *No towns, just fabulous mountain vistas; hiking, biking, berry picking; fishing at lakes and stream crossings; wildlife-watching and bird-watching.*

The Denali Highway first opened in 1957 as the only road access to what was then called Mount McKinley National Park. The George Parks Highway, finished in 1972, made the park even more accessible. Using a grand scale, visualize the Richardson Highway and George Parks Highway as parallel uprights in the letter H. Then the Denali Highway is the crossbar that joins them. Connecting **Paxson** on the Richardson Highway to **Cantwell** on the Parks Highway, this mostly unpaved wilderness road is a 136-mile shortcut through an awesome landscape.

Three major peaks dominate the skyline in this section of the Alaska Range: **Mount Deborah**, at 12,339 feet; **Mount Hess**, at 11,940 feet; and **Mount Hayes**, at 13,892 feet.

In 1980 the national park's name was changed to reflect local use of the name for the highest peak in the continent: Denali. In the Athabascan language, the word means "the high one." The park became **Denali National Park and Preserve**, though the official name for the peak remains **Mount McKinley**.

The park attracts thousands of visitors who most often arrive via the Alaska Railroad or with major tour operators, such as Gray Line of Alaska and Princess Tours. But the road travelers are many as well. From June through early August, RV and tent campers often fill up every available spot in the park's camping areas. (See the section on the Parks Highway, in this chapter, for tips on securing a campsite reservation.)

The **Tangle Lakes, Tangle River,** and a dozen other lakes and streams along the Denali Highway are popular destinations for anglers. Typical in these waters are grayling, whitefish, burbot, and lake trout. Inquire in Paxson or Cantwell for licensing and tips on what is biting. Consider hiring a guide for a more fulfilling experience. Denali Highlands Adventures operates out of Mile 18.5 (30 km) Denali Highway, with rentals of boats, canoes, and all-terrain vehicles, and offers guided or unguided trips. Call 1-800-895-4281.

The Denali Highway is a wonderful drive, particularly during sunny days that offer boundless views of the Alaska Range. RV travelers take heed that while the road out of Paxson is paved and broad, after 20 miles (32 km) it is a gravel road that gradually narrows as it journeys west. The maximum recommended speed, even when no one is around, is 30 mph.

There are few services along its length, but plenty at each end. Milepost addresses are measured from Paxson, on the Richardson Highway. And, of course, keep your eye out for moose and caribou. This is their kind of country.

Lodging/Meals

Tangle River Inn
Mile 20 Denali Highway
907-822-7304 or 907-822-3970
www.alaska.net/tangle
Rooms, cabins, liquor store, bar, restaurant
overlooking Tangle Lakes. Canoe rentals.

Tangle Lakes Lodge
Mile 22 Denali Highway
907-688-9173
www.alaskan.com/tanglelakes
Rooms, log cabins, dining room. Guided
fishing, canoe rentals, birding and
wildlife-watching.

Gracious House Lodge & Flying Service
Mile 82 Denali Highway
907-333-3148 or 907-822-7307
www.alaskaone.com/gracious
Rooms, with or without private bath. Fuel,
café, bar.

Adventures Unlimited Lodge
Mile 99.5 Denali Highway
907-561-7723
Rooms, breakfast, lunch, dinner. Fishing,
hiking, mountain biking, dogsled tours.

Campgrounds

The Bureau of Land Management oversees
three campgrounds along the Denali
Highway. For information, call the
Glennallen Field Office at 907-822-3217 or
visit the bureau's website at www.ak.blm.
gov/gdo. The campgrounds are:

Tangle Lakes Campground
Mile 21.5 (from Paxson)
60 acres for RV or tent campsites with
water, wheelchair-accessible toilets,
boat launch, fishing.

Tangle River Campground
Mile 21.5 (from Paxson)
3 acres for RV or tent campsites with water,
toilets, boat launch, fishing.

Brushkana Campground
Mile 104.5 (from Paxson)
20 acres for RV or tent campsites with
water, toilets, picnic shelter.

*E*DGERTON HIGHWAY

From Richardson Highway to Chitina: 33 miles (53 km)
From Chitina to McCarthy (on McCarthy Road): 60 miles (97 km)
***Travel Opportunities:** Athabascan Indian culture in Tonsina and Chitina; fishing
or rafting the Copper River; salmon dip-netting in the Chitina River; McCarthy,
historic copper-mining town; derelict Kennecott Copper Mine.*

Named for a former member of the Alaska Territorial Road Commission, U.S. Army
Major Glenn Edgerton, the Edgerton Highway is an eastbound spur road off the
Richardson Highway at a point 32 miles (51.5 km) south of Glennallen, or 83 miles
(133.5 km) north of Valdez. You're on pavement for 35 miles (56 km)—to the village
of Chitina—and there the Edgerton officially ends.

This village lies at the edge of **Wrangell–St. Elias National Park and Preserve,** 13.2 million acres of some of the most beautiful, glaciated mountain wilderness you've ever seen from ground level. From a plane, its mountain peaks and hanging valleys are even more breathtaking.

This region is the traditional homeland of the Athabascan Indians, and along the Edgerton Highway or in Chitina, take advantage of opportunities to purchase locally made Native art, as well as to visit with descendants of the first Alaskans. Roam around **Chitina** (CHIT-na) to view evidence of a boomtown grown old. A few buildings have been restored and placed on the National Register of Historic Sites.

In the early part of the 20th century, when the Kennecott Copper Mine was in its heyday, Chitina was a busy center of commerce, with hotels, restaurants, saloons, and even a movie theater. Today's Chitina, population 84, is no longer essential to the defunct copper mine, but neither is it a ghost town. As the gateway to Wrangell–St. Elias National Park, the village sees hundreds of visitors annually.

In summer, the tiny population really swells when the salmon are running in the **Copper River** and the Alaska Department of Fish and Game declares a "subsistence opener." This is a great time to come and watch the fishing action. Monitoring fish numbers throughout each run, the state opens the river to Alaska residents who depend on fish to feed themselves and their families. They hold a special permit for subsistence fishing. Dip-netting is the fast and preferred method of harvesting the fish. It's a partylike atmosphere as men and women don waders and walk into the river with billowy nets attached to a frame with a long handle. The fishing is as simple as dipping into the water and walking back to shore with the fish. It's that easy, or hard. These are weighty fish, ranging from 15 to 35 pounds or better.

You may see places along the river where local Athabascan Indians have set up a fish wheel to capture fish using the river current to turn the net-covered arms of the contraption. Beneath the surface, a fish is swept up and out of the water by the net and, as the wheel turns, the fish then drops into a holding box.

Stop at the National Park Service visitor information office, housed in one of Chitina's historic cabins, for publications, videos, and slide shows about Wrangell–St. Elias Park. The office also is a good place to ask about weather and road conditions in the park. Call 907-823-2205.

From Chitina, the unpaved, 60-mile (96.5-km) McCarthy Road leads to the village of **McCarthy** within the park. From there you may take a van or bus ride to visit the old Kennicott town site and the remains of a once-great copper operation: the **Kennecott Mine.** (The spelling of both place-names is correct. The mine and town names don't match due to a century-old spelling error!)

The McCarthy Road is so rugged, however, that big-rig RVs would be advised to think twice about making this adventure drive. Even family-car drivers have to stay under 25 mph to keep their hubcaps on! Because the road follows the stripped railbed of the defunct Copper River & Northwestern Railway, drivers should watch out for old railroad spikes, along with potholes, washboard, or slippery sections in the rain. This isn't to say don't go—just know that it will be slow going. Also know this: Few places outside of heaven are this beautiful.

So think about letting someone else do the driving. **Backcountry Connection** at 907-822-5292 offers scheduled van service between Glennallen and McCarthy, and on to Kennicott. Or you can arrange a fly-in day trip between Chitina and Kennicott with **Wrangell Mountain Air**, based in McCarthy. Call 1-800-478-1160 or visit their website at www.alaskaone.com/wma. Other charter air services may be arranged out of Gulkana, Glennallen, or Valdez.

The payoff for putting up with the McCarthy Road is getting to the village of McCarthy, population 28, in an incredible mountain-rimmed setting. But bear in mind that you can't just drive into the town itself. The McCarthy Road ends in a parking area on the west side of the Kennicott River. Overnight parking is permitted for RV travelers. To reach McCarthy, you still must cross the river via two footbridges and travel another mile on land (shuttle service is available). The footbridges here are still a fairly new development. For some, they are a most welcome replacement for the hand-operated cable tram that once spanned the river. Others believe that losing the tram was a blow to what makes McCarthy so charming. You decide.

This quaint little village was founded in 1910 at the height of the copper rush. Several historic buildings are still standing and still doing business. In summer, the little community buzzes with activity as wilderness guides, bush pilots, anglers, photographers, mountain climbers, and tourists drift in and out of town.

Arrange for a rafting excursion on the Kennicott River with the Copper Oar; call Wrangell Mountain Air for a flightseeing expedition; book a shuttle ride to the ghost town of Kennicott and wander amid the ruins of a once-great copper mine. All businesses are within walking distance, and the locals will have answers to your questions.

Lodging/Camping/Meals

Kenny Lake:
Kenny Lake Hotel & RV Park
Mile 7 Edgerton Highway
907-822-3313
Rooms with shared baths. Store, fuel, fishing licenses, RV parking for dry or partial hookups. Tent sites, dump station, self-service laundry, showers, pay phone, café.

Chitina:
Chitina Motel
Mile 53 Edgerton Highway
907-823-2211

Rooms, fuel, groceries, fishing licenses. Water and showers.

Silver Lake Campground
Mile 11 McCarthy Road
RV and tent sites along Silver Lake. Fishing; boat and canoe rentals.

McCarthy:
McCarthy Lodge
Downtown McCarthy
907-554-4402
All-Alaskan decor in 1916 hotel with modern fixtures, lodge, saloon, dining room.

Kennicott:

Historic Kennicott Bed & Breakfast

No. 13 Silk Stocking Row

907-554-4469

One of the few renovated buildings in the

  ghost town.

Kennicott Glacier Lodge

Kennicott's main street

1-800-582-5128

25 rooms, dining room, spacious porch,

  overlooking Kennicott Glacier and

  Chugach Mountains. Open May 15–

  September 20.

*E*LLIOTT HIGHWAY

Fox to Manley Hot Springs: 152 miles (245 km)
Travel Opportunities: *Gold panning at Eldorado Gold Mine; viewing the pipeline;*
views of Minto Flats; wildlife-watching; soaking in Manley Hot Springs.

The Elliott Highway begins a short 11 miles (17.5 km) north of Fairbanks, at the town of Fox. At the only intersection in Fox, continue driving straight ahead and you'll be on the Elliott. Travelers who want to stay on the Steese Highway have to take a sharp right. The Elliott is paved at its start, but the asphalt is lumpy-bumpy from the damaging work of freeze-thaw action.

Just a mile from the intersection, on the left, is one of the most popular attractions in the Fairbanks area: the **Eldorado Gold Mine.** The Eldorado tour begins and ends with a ride on a narrow-gauge railroad, on tracks that were recycled from a railway that once operated among the gold-rich fields of this area. The train's engineer is a fiddler, too, and his entertainment and narration make for an enjoyable ride as you pass an old sourdough's cabin, enter a permafrost tunnel, and watch antique mining equipment at work once again. Round a bend to an old-time cook shack, where you are greeted by Yukon Yonda and Dexter Clark, a husband-and-wife mining team that has been extracting gold from Interior streams and valleys for more than 20 years. Through their demonstration and banter, you learn about modern mining practices. Next, everybody enters the panning area with a gold pan and a poke to try it for themselves. Every pan holds glitter. Visitors carry their finds into the mining store to have them weighed and assayed. And, if you like, you can have your gold made into a piece of jewelry on the spot, or just buy a sizable nugget for bragging rights when you get home. (Go ahead and lie—all miners do.)

At Mile 66 (106 km), you'll find a comfort stop at **North Country Mercantile,** where you can buy an ice cream cone or a cup of coffee, get a tire fixed, and gas up the car. Hunting and fishing licenses are available here, too.

A few miles down the road is a turnoff that leads to the old mining camp known as **Livengood.** Although you may want to read that as "livin' GOOD," this place-name is actually pronounced "LIVE-en-good" for one of the two men who discovered gold near here in 1914. There are no visitor services here. While the old town hints at the millions in gold that was taken out of the Livengood-Tolovana Mining District, large-

Each summer, thousands of visitors learn how to pan for gold from longtime miners Yukon Yonda and her husband, Dexter, at the Eldorado Gold Mine, just north of Fairbanks on the Elliott Highway.

scale gold-mining operations have ceased. The Livengood region is home to about 100 people who drive into Fairbanks when they need to stock up on supplies.

The Elliott Highway parallels the trans-Alaska pipeline for part of its path through the paper birch and spruce forests. You'll catch views of the above-ground stretches of the pipeline flashing silver through the trees. At Mile 73 (117.5 km), watch for the fork in the road. Here is Mile 0 of the Dalton Highway, which trends north while the Elliott veers west toward the Tanana River.

The Elliott's unpaved sections rise above tree line and grant breathtaking vistas of valleys on either side of this ridge. Beyond them lay the White Mountains. At Mile 110 (177 km), a spur road leads to the Athabascan Indian village of **Minto**, where you can refuel your car, then eat at the Village End Café. This village is centrally located in Minto Flats, through which flows the Tolovana River. The area is exceptionally rich in fish, waterfowl, big game, and small furbearers. It is only natural that Alaska Natives would choose this location for its abundant resources. As were their ancestors, residents of Minto are dependent upon hunting and fishing to feed their families. Natives of contemporary times supplement their diets with store-bought groceries. You may be able to buy locally made Athabascan crafts, such as a birch-bark basket or beaded moosehide slippers.

Even though the Elliott is unpaved and dusty, up and down, the exceptional views and the prize at the end of the road make it all worthwhile. The highway dead-ends at **Manley Hot Springs**, a modest, mini–resort town that has offered comfort to miners and travelers for more than a century. It's even more historically significant if you consider that the Athabascans of the Interior knew and loved these springs long before the first Europeans showed up on the scene.

Manley Hot Springs calls to visitors and Fairbanks residents, winter and summer. A quiet town along the Tanana River, its buildings include a trading post and a roadhouse dating from 1904. To make a reservation to soak in the hot springs, call 907-672-3171, or watch for the signs near the end of the road and inquire at the house. For $5 a person, those seeking a bone-warming soak can choose from three pools.

Winter travelers to Manley are rewarded with exceptional views of the northern lights, dogsled tours, and the opportunity to converse with local mining and dog-mushing folks. Gas and groceries are available at the Manley Trading Post. Roads are spare in town, so it's easy to find your way around.

Lodging/Meals

Minto:
Village End Café
Along the Tolovana River
907-798-7373
Sandwiches, soups, sweets.

Manley Hot Springs:
Manley Roadhouse
End of the road
907-672-3161
Rooms, cabins, dining room, bar. The roadhouse is a historic gem dating from 1906, with historical artifacts on display.

Campgrounds

RV travelers are permitted to dry camp in gravel pullouts along the Elliott Highway.

Olnes Pond Campground
Mile 10.5 Elliott Highway
Campsites, toilets, picnic areas, boat ramp, fishing. In the Lower Chatanika State Recreation Area.

Whitefish Campground
Mile 11 Elliott Highway
Campsites, toilets, picnic areas, boat ramp, fishing. Also in the Lower Chatanika State Recreation Area.

Manley Hot Springs
Across from Manley Roadhouse
Park with campground, playground, picnic area.

GLENN HIGHWAY including the Tok Cutoff

Tok to Anchorage: 328 miles (528 km)
Travel Opportunities: *Glennallen; Matanuska Glacier and River; Musk Ox Farm; Independence Mine; Palmer Visitor Center and Garden; Eklutna; Anchorage-area attractions.*

The Glenn Highway is a well-traveled route because it connects the Anchorage area (where nearly half the state population lives) to the towns and wilderness areas along the Glenn and Richardson Highways. Further, this is the way to Tok, the Alaska Highway, and the most-used route to the Lower 48. Likewise, if you're headed into Alaska from Canada, and Anchorage is your destination, the Glenn is your highway. The Glenn is the single most important east-west road in the state highway grid.

The Glenn's official start is at Tok, at Mile 1314 (2114.5 km) Alaska Highway, where the Glenn branches south and west toward Anchorage, 328 miles (528 km) away. The first 125 miles (200 km) of the Glenn is widely known as the **Tok Cutoff**—a shortcut between the Alaska Highway and the Richardson Highway. In fact, it may come as a surprise to many Alaskans that this section actually is a part of the Glenn.

After leaving Tok, don't expect to find much development or services along this subtly beautiful stretch of road. An exception is the area of the **Eagle Trail State Recreation Site**, about 16 miles (26 km) from Tok, which offers a campground with picnic shelter, water, toilets, and trailhead access. A handful of B&Bs, lodges, and gas stations are tucked into the woods, so watch for their signs. This may seem like a lonely stretch of highway, but you're not alone.

The road crosses **Mentasta Summit** (2,434 feet/742 m) about 45 miles (72 km) from Tok. From here, most of the Tok Cutoff follows the boundary of **Wrangell–St. Elias National Park and Preserve**. These northern lowlands of the park are inhabited by caribou, moose, black and brown bears, coyotes, and numerous other creatures.

The Cutoff connects with the Richardson Highway near the village of **Gulkana**,

Lion Head rock is an easily recognized formation along the Glenn Highway.

Fishin' Tips?

At Glennallen, we stopped for gas at The Hub of Alaska. I decided to stretch my legs and wandered next door to North Star Fireworks, where I met Sourdough Joe of Sourdough Joe's Fish 'n' Flies. He gave me his card so I wouldn't forget him.

The fireworks business was slow, so Joe had time to talk. I figured he'd make time to talk anyway. It looked like a lonely job unless, of course, you had your trusty fly-tying vise at the ready.

"Sourdough Joe" sells dry flies and fireworks at a Glennallen stand near the junction of the Glenn and Richardson Highways.

"I started tying flies 'cause I didn't want to pay three bucks for one I didn't like," Sourdough Joe said. "This summer I tied at least 4,000. That's not a lot compared to the best fly tiers." He tells me that the fly tier for Orvis, the outdoor gear manufacturer, tied 36,000 in one summer.

I asked Joe if he hands out free fishing advice with his flies, especially for RVers who have a little more time on their hands.

"You can't do any serious fishing in an RV, unless you're pulling a car," he told me. "I can send 'em up to Lake Louise, and they'll get bogged down in the mud and gravel."

For some reason, I believe Sourdough Joe just didn't want to share his favorite fishing holes with a stranger. ●

about 15 miles (24 km) north of Glennallen. The most-traveled portion of the Glenn begins at Glennallen, 139 miles (223.5 km) from Tok at the busy junction of the east-west Glenn Highway and the north-south Richardson Highway. For decades, a gas station on this corner has called itself, in large letters, "The Hub of Alaska." It's an active intersection with more than just fuel and snacks for travelers on either road. At roadside is a log cabin **visitor center** that's staffed with informative people, along with the usual brochures and newsletters.

Glennallen is the unofficial capital of this region, situated on the western edge of Wrangell–St. Elias Park and 189 miles (304 km) from Anchorage. As a highway junction city, this town caters to travelers. You'll find campgrounds, restaurants, lodges, and visitor attractions.

This region is the traditional homeland of the Athabascan Indians, who have lived in the Copper River Basin for centuries. When a U.S. military party of explorers came through here in 1885, they were amazed at the accuracy of the hand-drawn maps they received from Natives who assisted them. (Glennallen is named for two of those explorers: Capt. Edwin F. Glenn and Lt. Henry T. Allen.)

Athabascans continue to fish and hunt for food (as do many people of other ethnic backgrounds who have arrived during the past century). Some people trap for furs; others work at local businesses. Sales of locally made craft items such as birch-bark baskets and beaded combs, slippers, and earrings help support a small cottage industry. Watch for parking-lot craft fairs, where you can learn more about local culture as well as pick up some wonderful gifts.

The **Copper River Basin** is especially popular for winter recreation, such as snowmobiling, skiing, and snowshoeing. Flightseeing, mountaineering, hiking, biking, fishing, and rafting are favorite summertime activities. Numerous creeks and lakes are suitable for a fine day of fishing. For fishing regulations and openers, check with the Alaska Department of Fish and Game office in Glennallen, downtown at Mile 186 (299 km) from Anchorage. Licenses are available at most retail outlets.

From Glennallen, the westward way begins flat and fairly straight. On either side of the road, you'll see occasional boggy lowlands and sad, spindly-looking spruce trees that tell a story about survival against the odds. These "used pipe cleaners" are black spruce trees, tenaciously growing in poorly drained soil where permafrost is present. Their root systems are so shallow that they sometimes tip over into each other, hence the name **Drunken Forest**. Because of the seasonal freeze and thaw of permafrost, this road can be wavy or sunken in places. Watch for flagged signs that warn "Dip in Road." They really mean it.

The state maintains four **recreation sites** with camps, water, and rest rooms in the stretch between Glennallen and Palmer. They are Matanuska Glacier, at Mile 101 (162.5 km); Long Lake , at Mile 85 (136.5 km); Bonnie Lake, at Mile 83 (133.5 km), not recommended for motor homes; and King Mountain, at Mile 75 (120.5 km). All distances are from Anchorage.

The land changes as you travel west through dry, treeless uplands and farther still into dazzling mountainous beauty. The road bends, rises, and falls as you follow the **Matanuska River Valley**, which flows between rocky mountains that turn purple in a certain light. This silty, braided river is a head-turner. You'll see it from various angles and elevations along the way, and its beauty is enhanced by the changes in light and weather.

Views of the **Matanuska Glacier** only get better and better. Stop at the marked waysides that offer photo opportunities, or you'll always regret that you didn't. In broad daylight, the glacier is brilliant white with hints of blue, but overcast days are best, when the blue of the glacier seems to glow from within. The **Matanuska River**, which flows from beneath the glacier, is a milky gray color due to the ground "rock flour" that is suspended in its water. Float trips or whitewater adventures can be arranged at sites along the highway (watch for signs) or in Palmer, 42 miles (67.5 km) north of Anchorage.

About 74 miles from Anchorage, watch for a distinctive rock formation called **Lion Head** that looks like it's blocking the road. This striking feature is a mini-mountain shaped by the Matanuska Glacier as it retreated from the area.

Between Glennallen and Palmer, you can stop at remote, family-operated **roadhouses and restaurants**, such as Sheep Mountain Lodge (Mile 113 from Anchorage) or Long Rifle Lodge (Mile 102) to bring even more color to your trip. Hicks Creek Roadhouse (Mile 96) offers food, camping, cabins, and trail rides. Their portable sign along the road reads, "Stop and Eat or We'll Both Starve." A classic old log place, King Mountain Lodge (Mile 76), offers rooms or campsites down by the river, along with good burgers and pizza.

As you approach Palmer from the east, you'll see signs and a right turnoff at Mile 50 (80.5 km) for the **Musk Ox Farm**, a don't-miss attraction. A herd of musk oxen here is the core of a small industry that centers on the gathering, spinning, and knitting of the animals' underwool, called qiviut (KIV-ee-oot). The gift shop features the handiwork of Native women who knit the garments in their home villages and mail them to this cooperative headquarters. Tours introduce you to these unique animals and the wonderfully warm garments made from their qiviut. For information, call 907-745-4151.

If you're interested in the area's gold-mining history, turn north off the Glenn Highway at Mile 49.5 (79.5 km) onto **Hatcher Pass Road** (also known as Fishhook–Willow Road). This is a gorgeous drive where in places you follow the course of a boulder-strewn, fast-moving stream. Watch for pullouts to let faster drivers pass by, or stop for a picnic and stick your toes in these chilly waters. Summit Lake State Recreation Site, 19 miles (30.5 km) up the road, is developed as a trailhead rather than a campground; public rest rooms are available here. **Independence Mine Historical Park** is just over 31 miles (50 km) up the road, at Hatcher Pass (elevation 3,886 feet). Getting there is slow driving for big-rig RVs at times, but the gravel road is generally in good condition. Walking trails lead throughout this extensive mine site, which includes buildings under restoration. Borrow a gold pan from the visitor center and try your hand at panning the stream. Nearby, overnight accommodations and meals are available at Hatcher Pass Lodge. Call 907-745-5897 or visit the lodge's website at www.hatcherpasslodge.com.

Back on the Glenn Highway, **Palmer** is located 42 miles (67.5 km) northeast of Anchorage, or 147 miles (236.5 km) west of Glennallen. During the Great Depression of the 1930s, the federal government offered Midwest farmers the opportunity to move to this valley for a fresh start in a new land, in a program known as the **Matanuska-Susitna Colony Project**. Whole families arrived to find that their free land first needed clearing of trees and rocks, and many spent their first cruel winter in a canvas tent with wood floors and a hungry woodstove. Through their hard work and perseverance, the community took root and thrived.

Ah, the Retired Life

Larry and Darlene Bahensky of St. Paul, Nebraska, had stopped along the Glenn Highway so Larry could try his hand at fishing the Gulkana River. He'd seen the river, thought it looked good, and pulled over. Maybe they would camp here along the river and grill up the salmon he had fished out of the Kenai River. Last night, they had picked a spot along the Kings River. Who knows about tomorrow? This is retirement the way he had planned it.

Between them on the front seat of their truck was a full-to-overflowing box of travel literature. They had been on the road in Alaska for more than four weeks. But before that, they had volunteered for five days as teachers at the Lutheran mission's Vacation Bible School in the village of Wiseman, off the Dalton Highway.

Larry did what a lot of people do before they drive in Alaska: He protected the grill of his truck with a homemade screen.

"We took a few chips in the windshield," he said. "Everybody's quick to blame the truckers, but it's mostly the campers or cars that are going too fast."

I asked if he wanted to share some words of wisdom, having put so many Alaska road-miles on his truck. His answer:

"Don't worry too much. Make sure you top off your tank whenever you go, and just drive a little slower."

Larry Bahensky, of St. Paul, Nebraska, spent five weeks on the road with his wife, Darlene.

The colony project was the settlement seed for what is now the community of Palmer, with a population of nearly 4,000. Many descendants of those settlers still live in the Matanuska-Susitna (or Mat-Su) Valley. As you drive along the Glenn Highway, you'll see farmhouses and barns built in a style reminiscent of the Midwest. Wheat, hay, potatoes, lettuce, tomatoes, carrots, cabbages—the land keeps providing, and the abundance of grain and produce continues to support valley farmers.

Palmer is the seat of the **Alaska State Fair**, where the stiffest agricultural competition is seen in the giant-vegetables category. Under a blessed 22 hours of summer sunlight, Palmer farmers grow cabbages that balloon to between 40 and 60 pounds. Squash, carrots, and other vegetables thrive in the cool soil and long doses of sunlight. If you're in Alaska in late August and early September, stop by the Palmer fairgrounds to see the giants for yourself, and enjoy the midway rides, food booths, and equestrian competitions. Although it's an Alaska state fair, it feels as cozy as a Kansas county fair, until you lift your eyes and take in the peaks of the Chugach Range, which seems to be just a field away.

Streams and lakes in this valley yield world-class fishing in picturesque settings. Anglers routinely land prized king salmon weighing an average of 20 to 30 pounds, but these fish can reach 70 pounds. Other salmon runs include reds, chums, pinks, and silvers. Trout, Dolly Varden, northern pike, arctic grayling, and other species also are found in local waters. Pick up your required license at any number of retail outlets, from grocery stores to sporting goods stores. Call the Palmer office of the Alaska Department of Fish and Game at 907-746-6300 for recorded fishing reports and answers to frequent questions about fishing regulations.

In Palmer, turn east off the Glenn Highway and drive four blocks to the railroad tracks. Near the old railroad depot, you'll see the Palmer Visitor Center, a log building where a history of the colony can be found in photos and artifacts, and a gift shop is stocked with Alaska souvenirs. Ask about a walking tour of Palmer's historic buildings. Call 907-745-3880.

Next door to the visitor center is the **Matanuska Valley Agricultural Showcase**, where local gardeners have done a magnificent job of showing what happens when skilled hands sow seed under the midnight sun. Walk around the garden paths for a peaceful break from traveling.

Just a few miles south of Palmer, the Glenn Highway is joined by the Parks Highway from Fairbanks. The Glenn is in excellent shape from here all the way to Anchorage, with four lanes of traffic and a legal speed of 65 mph. The lay of the land changes as you follow the Glenn around this side of the Chugach Range. The divided highway passes through a broad expanse of wild grasses dotted with tall trees that look like they died a long time ago—which they did. This is the **Palmer Hay Flats State Game Refuge**, which supports a diversity of wildlife, from big game to eagles to waterfowl and more. This entire region dropped several feet during the 1964 Good Friday Earthquake that damaged so much of the Anchorage coastline. Seawater flooded in, killing mature trees and creating wetlands where once there had been hayfields.

Up ahead, two four-lane bridges cross the **Knik** (kuh-NIK) **River**, a popular staging area for local duck hunters. Because Cook Inlet experiences such extreme tides (up to 30 feet), the tidal zone of the Knik River likewise fluctuates dramatically.

Twenty-six miles (42 km) from Anchorage, an exit leads to **Eklutna Historical Park**, which includes a historic Russian Orthodox church and nearby graveyard. Developed by the Athabascan residents of Eklutna village, population 25, this park offers tours and cultural interpretation. The tradition of placing brightly colored "houses" over the graves is neither completely Orthodox nor completely Athabascan. As in other areas of the state, western religions have been integrated into the Native culture, and some practices reflect a unique third culture. Although the residents of

Eklutna live close to Alaska's biggest city, many continue in a largely subsistence-based life, hunting and fishing for much of their diet. Grocery stores supply the rest.

Inside the city limits of Anchorage, the Glenn Highway peters out, unmarked, somewhere along the small-plane airport called Merrill Field. Stay on the same road and it becomes 5th Avenue, which leads you into the downtown core.

Anchorage

Born of necessity, as many Alaska towns were, Anchorage was once a tent city along the muddy banks of Ship Creek. The people who gathered here in 1915 were builders of the Alaska Railroad, their families, hoteliers, restaurateurs, laundry operators, freight haulers, and others who supplied services.

When conditions at the tent city became dangerously overcrowded, threatening disease, Alaska Railroad officials took charge and cleared building lots on the bluff overlooking the creek. In July 1915, town-site lots were auctioned off, and building began immediately. Today, few original homes or businesses exist, mainly because they were wooden and therefore fairly expendable as the town matured. Notable survivors include two side-by-side buildings on the 5th Avenue and E Street corner of Town Square.

Anchorage is Alaska's biggest city, with nearly 270,000 people, almost half of the state's population. It is an international crossroads in passenger and air cargo, as well as headquarters for the biggest names in the oil industry. This modern community is bordered on the north by military installations, on the east by the **Chugach Range**, on the south by **Chugach National Forest**, and on the west by **Cook Inlet**. Options for city sprawl are limited. Its proximity to wilderness means that moose often wander into the streets, making the "Anchorage bowl" a unique urban habitat. Car-moose encounters are causing city officials to ponder the question of what to do as moose numbers continue to multiply.

The **Log Cabin Visitor Information Center** on the corner of 4th Avenue and F Street is operated by the Anchorage Convention and Visitor Bureau. Staffers can answer questions and direct you to a self-guided historical walking tour throughout downtown. If you're interested in bed-and-breakfast accommodations, they have the information. Call 907-274-3531 or visit the website at www.alaska.net/~acvb.

In summer, Anchorage is a tourism hub. Its downtown streets are filled with color and the contagious enthusiasm of people on vacation. Gift shops, restaurants, street vendors, and musicians lend a partylike atmosphere to every summer day. Dining experiences can range from a stop at a fast-food outlet, hot dog stand, grocery-store deli, or burger joint, to elegant dining above Cook Inlet.

As Alaska's biggest city and hub of two major highways, this is an ideal spot to consider renting an RV if you didn't arrive in one. You may contact any number of local businesses for daily or weekly rentals (check the local phone listings). If you are traveling in your own RV, this is a good place to take care of any mechanical or windshield repairs or have your oil changed.

Walking 4th and 5th Avenues on foot, you can stop in and book a day cruise on Prince William Sound or on Resurrection Bay, south of Anchorage. Tour operators usually offer shuttle transportation to harbor cities. Down the street, you can book a flightseeing trip to fly over Mount McKinley and even land on a glacier to walk a bit. Large coaches provide day trips around town, north to the Matanuska-Susitna Valley, south to Portage Glacier, and beyond. At the landmark 4th Avenue Theatre, you can catch a trolley for a city tour and learn more about local history. Or flag down a carriage for a slow-moving ride behind a fine pair of draft horses.

Soak up local color as you stroll around downtown. Especially popular is **4th Avenue**, where in summer every lamppost bears two huge flower baskets of lobelia and marigold, representing Alaska's state colors, blue and gold. In Anchorage's mild temperatures and prolonged light, the flowers are extraordinarily bright and fresh, here and in gardens throughout the city. Due to the low angle of the sun, there is no heat of midday to wilt them. A few years ago, the mayor of Anchorage instituted a program to recognize the exceptional gardening all over town by designating Anchorage the **City of Flowers**. Each year, program leaders announce a new garden theme, such as the state colors, or berry colors, or the colors of fish—reds, silvers, and pinks in the salmon vernacular!

All winter long, as dusk comes earlier and daybreak comes later, the seasonal theme is Anchorage, **City of Lights**. Millions of tiny white lights decorate trees, homes, and businesses, further illuminating the snow and creating a true winter wonderland. Most people agree that the lights have a secondary effect as a true lift to the spirits come winter.

On Saturdays and Wednesdays, follow the crowds to the outdoor markets in downtown Anchorage. These mini-fairs include entertainment, food booths, crafts, and sales of Mat-Su Valley vegetables.

Other attractions of the Anchorage area include:

Anchorage Fur Rendezvous. This is the country's biggest winter carnival, celebrated in Anchorage each February. Events include snowshoe softball, the Outhouse Classic (the race entries are outhouses equipped with skis), and a waiter/waitress competition in which contestants run an obstacle course while carrying a tray of drinks. Craft fairs, a fur auction, carnival rides, snow sculpture competitions, and an Eskimo blanket toss are other highlights. The World Championship Sled Dog Races are another main Rondy event, with dogs and drivers lining up to start the race on 4th Avenue.

Iditarod Trail Sled Dog Race. For more than a quarter-century, Anchorage has been the official starting line for the men, women, and dogs of the 1,000-mile Iditarod Trail Sled Dog Race. Thousands of people jam the sidewalks of 4th Avenue and connecting streets as these champion athletes—human and canine—leave the chute for the trail that leads to Nome. The Iditarod (eye-DIT-uh-rod) begins on the first Saturday of March. The Iditarod headquarters and museum is in Wasilla, north of Anchorage off the Parks Highway. Call 907-376-5155 or visit their website at www.iditarod.com.

From the Glenn Alps, hikers are afforded a magnificent view of Anchorage, Cook Inlet and, in the distance, the Alaska Range.

A statue of Captain James Cook, who explored the waters here, overlooks Cook Inlet in Anchorage's Resolution Park.

Alaska Railroad. Daily north-south rail service between Anchorage, Denali National Park and Preserve, and Fairbanks is available through the Alaska Railroad or through tourism companies that operate specialty railcars on the train. Southbound passengers between Anchorage and Seward can do the same: book a seat with the Alaska Railroad or travel in a luxury railcar operated by Gray Line of Alaska or Princess Tours. The luxury railcars offer a great way to take in the scenery, enjoy bar service and an excellent meal, and stretch your legs regularly while crossing the state in style. In most of the cars, you'll find a knowledgeable guide who can answer questions and provide information on local history and natural history as you travel. Contact the Alaska Railroad at 907-265-2494, Gray Line of Alaska at 907-277-5581, or Princess Tours Rail Operations at 907-278-8038.

Chugach State Park. Serving as a spectacular backdrop for Alaska's biggest city, the Chugach (CHOO-gatch) Range lies along the eastern edge of Anchorage. Here too is Chugach State Park, an extremely popular getaway for hikers, bikers, picnickers, or those who simply want to drive uphill and get a great view of the city and the twin bodies of water around it, Knik Arm and Turnagain Arm.

A Whirlwind Tour

Tom McIntosh of Gladwin, Minnesota, was fly-fishing at Long Lake Recreation Site on the Glenn Highway when we met him and his wife, Becky. They had flown into Anchorage a couple of weeks earlier, picked up a rental car, and took off.

"I read up a lot before we left home," Becky said. "All we did in Anchorage was shop and start driving."

Already the couple had put more than 2,000 miles on the car. They had been to Denali Park, Fairbanks, the Arctic Circle, Valdez, and Anchorage. "And we've still got a week to go!" she said.

For now, the couple was just enjoying a late summer evening on a quiet pond where the trout were rising to meet Tom's dry fly. In Valdez, they had been fishing across from town near the marine terminal when they spotted a bear right on the highway. That was the highlight of their wildlife viewing.

Since they had seen so much of the state, I asked Becky what she thought about car-camping in Alaska.

"The waysides and campgrounds in Alaska are clean and very well kept," she said. "In Fairbanks, we stayed at the fairgrounds and showered there. We've just been meeting very friendly people everywhere we go."

Farther north, off the Dalton Highway, they stayed overnight at a bed-and-breakfast near the Arctic Circle.

"It was a log home with a propane tank and outdoor facilities," Becky said. "It's a revelation for a lot of people, and you wouldn't believe how rustic it is."

A hike up the sawed-off mountain known as Flattop is invigorating, yet suitable for families. Groomed trails lead the way from the Glenn Alps parking area. On clear days, you can see Mount McKinley from here. Park headquarters is in the Potter Section House, just south of Anchorage on the Seward Highway, but the park is accessible from Anchorage's Hillside area as well as from Eagle River. For directions and information, call park headquarters at 907-345-5014.

Alaska Native Heritage Center. One of Anchorage's newest attractions focuses on the wonders and diversity of Alaska's Native cultures. Located near the intersection of the Glenn Highway and Muldoon Road, the Heritage Center features art, music, photography, and a variety of exhibits. The spacious Welcome House at the center offers programs of dancing and singing in the theater, photography and artifact exhibits, and a chance to watch an artist at work. From there, paths lead to five village settings that show traditional home-building methods and tools. Interpreters from each culture are on site too. Call 1-800-315-6608.

Anchorage Museum of History and Art. The museum, at 121 West 7th Avenue, is an architectural beauty that shows Alaska art treasures as well as visiting exhibits. The Alaska Gallery includes exquisite displays from Alaska's Native, Russian, and U.S. history. Other features include a children's gallery, gift shop, café, and special programs in a theater that entertain visitors year-round. For more information, call 907-343-6173.

Town Square Park. An army of gardeners takes exquisite care of this floral showcase. Split by curving paths, with a simple fountain at the center, Town Square Park is the meeting place for businesspeople on lunch break, visitors who gape over the bedding plants, walkers, and people-watchers. In places, inscribed sidewalk bricks pay homage to people and businesses that have helped make Anchorage great. The adjoining **Alaska Center for the Performing Arts** is a venue for national and international talent, from Broadway shows to the Vienna Boys Choir to the best in New Orleans jazz. Anchorage has come a long way since its days as a tent city.

Lodging

The **Mat-Su Chapter** of the **Bed and Breakfast Association of Alaska** has information on rooms, apartments, and cabins from Glennallen to Anchorage to Denali. Call 1-800-401-7444 or visit the association's website at www.alaska.net/~akhosts.

Tok: See listings in the section on Tok in Chapter 6, The Alaska Highway.

Glennallen:
Brown Bear Rhodehouse
Mile 183.5 Glenn Highway
907-822-3663
Motel, cabins, campsites. Restaurant,
lounge. Grizzly bear photo display.

Caribou Hotel
Mile 187 Glenn Highway
1-800-478-3302
Rooms, suites, kitchenettes, wheelchair
access. Satellite TV, whirlpool, gift shop,
Caribou Café Family Restaurant.

Palmer:

Colony Inn
325 Elmwood Street
907-745-3330
Located in historic Teachers' Dorm from the
  Mat-Su Colony.

Fairview Motel & Restaurant
Mile 40.5 Glenn Highway
1-800-745-1505 or 907-745-1505
Rooms, TV, phones, laundry. Dining room,
  lounge.

Gold Miner's Hotel
918 South Colony Way
1-800-7ALASKA or 907-745-6160
Large rooms, restaurant, lounge. Downtown
  location.

Pioneer Motel
124 West Arctic Avenue
907-745-3425
Rooms with cable TV. Daily or weekly
  rentals.

Valley Hotel
606 South Alaska Street
907-745-3330
Rooms with private bath, cable TV. 24-hour
  coffee shop. Lounge, liquor store.

Anchorage:

Alaska's Tudor Motel
4423 Lake Otis Parkway
1-800-550-2234 or 907-561-2234
Kitchenettes, one-bedroom apartments,
  cable TV. Close to self-service laundry.
  Senior discounts.

Captain Cook Hotel
4th Avenue and K Street
907-276-6000
Rooms and suites, plus health club, travel
  agency, gift stores, café, lounge.
  Penthouse-level restaurant with view.
  Central downtown location.

Comfort Inn
111 West Ship Creek
1-800-228-5150 or 907-277-6887
Rooms and suites, free continental
  breakfast. Indoor pool, spa. Along Ship
  Creek, downtown. Airport shuttle.

Hillside on Gambell Motel
2150 Gambell
1-800-478-6008 or 907-258-6006
www.hillside-alaska.com
Rooms with private bath, kitchenettes.
  Coffee, cable TV, data ports, bicycle
  rentals.

Hilton Anchorage
500 West 3rd Avenue
1-800-245-2527 or 907-272-7411
Deluxe accommodations, fitness room, gift
  shops, café. Walking distance to
  downtown attractions.

Long House Alaskan Hotel
4335 Wisconsin Street
1-888-243-2133 or 907-243-6060
54 rooms, free continental breakfast. Close
  to airport; shuttle service.

Microtel Inn & Suites
5205 Northwood Drive
1-888-680-4500 or 907-245-5002
Rooms, suites, free continental breakfast,
  laundry facility. Close to airport; shuttle
  service.

Northern Lights Hotel
598 West Northern Lights Boulevard
1-800-235-6546 or 907-561-5200
Rooms and suites, cable TV, laundry. Close
to restaurants, in midtown Anchorage.

Ramada Limited
207 Muldoon Road
907-929-7000
Rooms and suites, free breakfast buffet,
coffee. Cable TV, data ports, voice mail.
Restaurant, lounge. Shuttle to
downtown or airport.

Regal Alaskan Hotel
4800 Spenard Road
1-800-544-0553 or 907-243-2300
Lakeside rooms with views of floatplanes.
Wildlife displays, historical photos
decorate lobby. Gift shop, restaurant,
lounge.

Sheraton Anchorage Hotel
401 East 6th Avenue
1-800-478-8700 or 907-276-8700
Well-appointed rooms and suites, cable TV,
room and laundry service, fitness room.
Gift store, lounge, penthouse restaurant
with view.

Campgrounds

Tok: See listings in the section on Tok in
Chapter 6, The Alaska Highway.

Glennallen:
Tolsona Wilderness Campground
Mile 173 Glenn Highway
907-822-3865
80 campsites with full or partial hookups,
tenting, creekside location. Showers,
laundry, dump station, modem access,
store.

Brown Bear Rhodehouse
Mile 183.5 Glenn Highway
907-822-3663
Camping, cabins, motel with restaurant,
lounge. Display of grizzly bear photo
collection.

Moose Horn RV Park
Mile 188 Glenn Highway
Full hookups and dry camping, close to The
Hub and visitor center.

Northern Lights Campground & RV Park
Mile 189 Glenn Highway
907-822-3199
Campsites with partial hookups, pull-
throughs, tent sites. Rest rooms, phone,
wooded setting, close to visitor center
and shopping.

Palmer:
Finger Lake State Recreation Site
Bogard Road
Campground with water, rest rooms, trails,
fishing, boat launch.

The Homestead RV Park
Half a mile toward Palmer from Parks and
Glenn Highways junction
907-745-6005
Campsites with a view. Showers, walking
trails, area tours, evening entertainment, Thursday night square dances.

Matanuska River Park
Mile 17.5 Old Glenn Highway
80 sites for RVs or tents, fire rings, showers,
dump station.

Mountain View RV Park
Off Old Glenn Highway on Smith Road
1-800-264-4582 or 907-745-5747
83 sites with full hookups, pull-throughs,
    laundry, rest rooms, pay phone.

Anchorage:
Anchorage RV Park
7300 Oilwell Road
1-800-400-7275 or 907-338-7275
196 sites with full hookups, pull-throughs.
    Showers, laundry, water, dump station.
    Quiet wooded setting just outside city.

Hillside on Gambell RV Park
2150 Gambell
1-800-478-6008 or 907-258-6006
www.hillside-alaska.com
71 campsites with full or partial hookup.
    Free showers, coin laundry, water, pro-
    pane. Freezer available for your fish.

Restaurants

Tok: See listings in the section on Tok in
Chapter 6, The Alaska Highway.

Glennallen:
Brown Bear Rhodehouse
Mile 183.5 Glenn Highway
907-822-3663
Steaks, broasted chicken, seafood, pizza.

Caribou Café Family Restaurant
Downtown Glennallen
907-822-3656
Open daily; lunch and dinner specials.

The Hitchin' Post
Mile 190 Glenn Highway
Next to Moose Horn RV Park
Breakfast, burgers, ice cream.

Palmer:
Colony Kitchen
Mile 40.5 Glenn Highway
Across from fairgrounds
907-746-4600
Breakfast all day; steaks, burgers,
    salad, pie.

Gold Miner's Hotel & Restaurant
918 South Colony Way
1-800-7ALASKA or 907-745-6173
Family dining with full menu.

The Inn Café
326 Elmwood Avenue
907-746-6118
Fine dining in historic Colony Inn.

La Fiesta
132 West Evergreen Avenue
907-746-3335
Authentic Mexican cuisine.

Round House Café
606 South Alaska Street
907-745-3330
24-hour café with home-style cooking, pies.

Slack's Sugar Shack Bakery
340 West Evergreen Avenue
907-745-4777
Breads, pastries, cookies, donuts.

Anchorage:
Arctic Roadrunner
5300 Old Seward Highway
907-561-4016
Burgers, fries, shakes.

Blondie's Café
333 West 4th Avenue
907-279-0698
Breakfast, lunch specials, family dining.

Club Paris
417 West 5th Avenue
907-277-6332
Popular downtown steakhouse since 1957.

Corsair Restaurant
944 West 5th Avenue
907-278-4502
Fine dining, Alaska seafood specialties.

Dianne's Restaurant
550 West 7th Avenue
907-279-7243
Soups, salads, sandwiches, lunch specials.

Downtown Deli & Café
525 West 4th Avenue
907-276-7116
From sourdough pancakes to reindeer stew,
   and more.

Elevation 92
1007 West 3rd Avenue
907-279-11578
Dining with a Cook Inlet view.

Elmer's Pancake & Steak House
711 East Fireweed Lane
907-258-2913
Family dining; specials.

Glacier Brewhouse
Corner of 5th Avenue and H Street
907-274-BREW
Brew pub featuring wood-grilled seafood,
   pizzas, grilled meats.

Gwennie's Old Alaska Restaurant
4333 Spenard Road
907-243-2909
Alaska decor, Alaska-size meals.

Harry's Restaurant & Bar
101 West Benson Boulevard
907-562-5994
Fresh seafood, 20 beers, in midtown.

Hogg Brothers Café
1049 West Northern Lights Boulevard
907-276-9649
Inventive breakfasts, "hogg-size" meals.

Humpy's Great Alaskan Alehouse
610 West 6th Avenue
907-276-2337
43 brews on tap, live music nightly.
   Downtown.

Jens' Restaurant
701 West 36th Avenue
907-561-5367
Fine dining, featuring pepper steak,
   seafood, lamb, veal.

Josephine's
401 East 6th Avenue
In Sheraton Anchorage
907-343-3160
Fine dining on the 15th floor. Dinner and
   Sunday brunch, excellent views.

Lucky Wishbone
1033 East 5th Avenue
907-272-3454
A local favorite for chicken and burgers.

Mesa Grill Restaurant & Lounge
720 West 5th Avenue
907-278-3433
For a taste of America's Southwest.

Phyllis's Café and Salmon Bake
Corner of 5th Avenue and D Street
907-274-6576
Specializing in seafood.

Simon & Seafort's Saloon & Grill
420 L Street
907-274-3502
Seafood, prime rib, desserts; great view of
Cook Inlet.

Sourdough Mining Company
5200 Juneau Street
907-563-2272
Seafood, ribs, sourdough bread. Family
dining. Free evening show.

HAINES HIGHWAY

Haines Junction, Yukon, to Haines, Alaska: 152 miles (245 km)
Travel Opportunities: *Chilkat Bald Eagle Preserve; Tlingit culture; Fort Seward.*

Haines is an all-Alaska town, but it's disconnected from the rest of the state highway system by miles and miles of water on one side, and miles and miles of Canada on the other. Alaskans on the highway system literally have to leave the country for the roundabout drive to this Alaska town. And international cooperation makes it possible. Built in 1943, just after principal construction of the Alaska Highway, this single spur road crosses land belonging to a state and two provinces.

The paved 152-mile Haines Highway is a southbound road off the Alaska Highway at Haines Junction (985 miles, or 1,635 km, north of Dawson Creek). The highway cuts through the Canadian and Alaska wilderness as Yukon Route 3, B.C. Route 4, and Alaska Route 7. It borders sparkling lakes and rivers, and crosses mountain passes, portions of a historic trade route used by First Nations people for centuries.

Haines also is accessible via the Alaska Marine Highway System, which connects the town of 1,429 people with other Southeast and Southcentral Alaska coastal communities by ferry. Some travelers choose the mostly water route to get to Alaska, boarding their vehicles onto the ferry system at Bellingham, Washington, the southernmost port, and disembarking at Haines, thus skipping the 1,000 miles or more of driving through Canada. (See Chapter 9, Alaska Marine Highway System.)

Set beneath an alpine range that includes impressive peaks such as 3,610-foot **Mount Rapinsky** and 1,760-foot **Mount Riley**, Haines was settled in the early 1900s and incorporated in 1910. Presbyterian missionaries arrived, hoping to convert, serve, and educate the Native population. Like other towns on the route to the goldfields, Haines grew wild in the atmosphere of greed and hurry.

Evidence of Alaska's first permanent military post is still present at **Fort Seward**, which has long since been decommissioned. Still, its clean-cut parade grounds are encircled by former officer's quarters, now private homes and businesses.

Long before the arrival of any military or gold miners, this beautiful coastal region supported people for thousands of years. Nearly all of today's Southeast Alaska was traditional land for the **Tlingit Indian people**. In the Haines area, local tribes include the **Chilkat** and **Chilkoot**, which may be best known for intricately woven blankets and raven's tail robes, as well as carvings in totems and masks.

Salmon and the small, greasy fish known as hooligan have traditionally been important to the Native diet, as have goat, sheep, and deer, which are hunted for meat and hide. And centuries-old stories are still passed from one generation to the next. In Haines, you can be part of the hearing. A workshop in the old hospital of Fort Seward is home to the **Alaska Indian Arts** carvers and weavers. Drop by to watch them at work. Or come to watch dance demonstrations, or enjoy the salmon dinner held from 5 P.M. to 8 P.M. daily at the **Totem Village Tribal House** on the Fort Seward parade grounds. For reservations, call 907-766-2000.

The **Haines Museum and Cultural Center**, on Main Street near Beach Road, exhibits typical offices and living quarters from early-day Haines. You can also learn there about the valley's natural history, the Tlingit people and their traditions, the founding of Fort Seward, and the influences of early missionaries and gold miners. Call 907-766-2366.

Just outside town, at the **Southeast Alaska Fairgrounds**, visit the set used in the filming of the Disney movie *White Fang*, based on the Jack London novel. Many locals were enlisted for the production.

Along the Haines Highway, the 48,000-acre **Chilkat Bald Eagle Preserve** attracts thousands of visitors each year who arrive in late fall to observe the great numbers of eagles. Their rendezvous is determined by the salmon—a late-season run of chum makes the Chilkat River one of the last places where the eagles can easily feed before the water freezes. So they congregate here—sometimes 3,500 and more—and roost in the cottonwood trees along the riverbank. The birds engage in unique social behavior, fighting for a single scrap of fish when thousands more fish are within reach. Their dramatic airborne fights are wondrous to behold.

Depending on when you visit the preserve, the highest concentration of eagles usually is found between 18 and 22 miles (29–35.5 km) northwest of Haines on the Haines Highway. Make sure your camera batteries don't fail you now. Don't expect to see large groups of eagles in spring or summer, but you should see some individuals or pairs because the preserve is the year-round home to several hundred birds. Learn all about the birds, their behavior, and their favorite habitat at the **American Bald Eagle Foundation interpretive center** in Haines at 2nd Avenue and the Haines Highway. Knowledgeable staffers can answer your questions, and they offer videos, books, and other printed materials.

If you've come to fish, you'll find plenty in these rich waters. Book a charter for halibut or salmon fishing. Lakes and streams also support hooligan, trout, and Dolly Varden. Keep your license current, and check in with the Alaska Department of Fish and Game for regulations at 907-766-2625. Other recreation includes flightseeing, biking, rafting, canoeing, and hiking.

For more information on events and activities in Haines, stop by the visitor center at 2nd Avenue and Willard Street. Call the Haines Convention & Visitors Bureau at 1-800-458-3579 or 907-766-2234, or visit their website at www.haines.ak.us.

Lodging

Captain's Choice Motel
108 2nd Avenue North
907-766-3111
39 rooms with view of Lynn Canal. Room
   service, tour booking, car rentals.
   Walking distance to restaurants. Shuttle
   service.

Dalton Street Cottages
116 6th Street
907-766-3123
Kitchenettes with private entrance and
   bath, smoke-free. Phones, hot tub. Up
   to four persons per cottage. Downtown
   Haines.

Eagle's Nest Motel
Mile 1 Haines Highway
907-766-2891
13 rooms, kitchenettes. Car rental, courtesy
   van.

Fort Seward Condos
On historic fort grounds
907-766-2425
Furnished apartments with kitchens, two-
   night minimum. Historic building with
   view of Lynn Canal.

Fort Seward Lodge
On historic fort grounds
1-800-478-7772 or 907-766-2009
10 rooms with private or shared bath,
   ocean-view kitchenettes. Restaurant,
   lounge. Courtesy van.

Hotel Halsingland
On Fort Seward grounds
1-800-478-5556 or 907-766-2000
50 rooms, private bath, cable TV, phones,
   car rental. Seafood restaurant, lounge.
   Historic building with canal views.

Mountain View Motel
Near Fort Seward grounds
1-800-478-2902 or 907-766-2900
9 rooms, kitchenettes, views. Walking
   distance to restaurants.

Thunderbird Motel
2nd Avenue and Dalton Street
1-800-327-2556 or 907-766-2131
20 rooms, kitchenettes. Walking distance to
   restaurants, shops.

Campgrounds

Haines:
Alaskan Eagle RV Park
755 Union Street
1-888-306-7521 or 907-766-2335
60 sites with full hookups, cable TV,
   laundry, restaurant. Discounts for local
   tours, fishing charters.

Bear Creek Camp and Youth Hostel
1 mile (1.5 km) south of Haines on Small
   Tracts Road
907-766-2259
Cabins, bunks, tent camping. Kitchen,
   showers, laundry, bedding. Bicycle and
   hot tub rentals.

Haines Hitch-up RV Park
Haines Highway and Main Street
907-766-2882
Full and partial hookups, dry camping. No
    tenting. Laundry, gift shop.

Oceanside RV Park
Front and Main Streets
907-766-2444
Full hookups overlooking Lynn Canal.
    Walking distance to showers, shopping,
    laundry.

Port Chilkoot Camper Park
Next to Fort Seward
1-800-478-2525 (Alaska, British Columbia,
    Yukon) or 907-766-2000
Full and partial hookups, showers, laundry,
    dump station. Close to town.

Salmon Run RV Campground
Almost 2 miles (3 km) north of ferry on
    Lutak Road
907-723-4229
Forested campsites with fire rings, tables,
    showers, trails, boat launch. Inlet and
    mountain views.

Northeast of Haines:
Swan's Rest RV Park
On Mosquito Lake Road, off Mile 27 Haines
    Highway
907-767-5662
12 sites with full hookups, cabin available.
    Showers, laundry, rest rooms, fishing
    and boat rental.

Chilkat Charlie's RV & Tent Park
Mile 33 Haines Highway
907-767-5510
8 sites with full hookups, next to 33 Mile
    Roadhouse.

The state maintains four campgrounds near
Haines, offered on a first-come, first-served
basis:

Chilkat State Park
7 miles (11 km) south of Haines on Mud Bay
    Road
32 pull-through sites, 3 beachfront tent
    sites. Water, toilets, fishing, boat
    launch, hiking, log cabin interpretive
    center.

Portage Cove State Recreation Site
About 1 mile (1.5 km) south of Haines on
    Beach Road
Tent camping for backpackers and
    bicyclists, no overnight parking. Water
    pump, tables, fire rings, toilets.

Chilkoot Lake State Recreation Area
10 miles (16 km) north of Haines, off Lutak
    Road
32 spaces, lake views, water, toilets, fishing,
    boat launch, log cabin interpretive
    center.

Mosquito Lake State Recreation Site
On Mosquito Lake Road, off Mile 27 Haines
    Highway
7 spaces, fire rings, tables, toilets, fishing,
    boat launch.

Restaurants
Alaskan International Café
755 Union Street
At Alaskan Eagle RV Park
1-888-306-7521 or 907-766-2335
Salmon bake.

Bamboo Room Restaurant
2nd Avenue and Dalton Street
907-766-2800
Breakfast, lunch, dinner; espresso, halibut
   fish and chips. Seniors' and children's
   menus. Sports bar.

Chilkat Restaurant & Bakery
5th Avenue and Dalton Street
907-766-2920
Breakfast, lunch, dinner; pastries.

The Commander's Room Restaurant &
   Officer's Club Lounge
On Fort Seward grounds
907-766-2000
Seafood and other Alaska specialties;
   historic building.

Fort Seward Restaurant & Saloon
Mile 0 Haines Highway
1-800-478-7772 or 907-766-2009
Steak and seafood; breakfast, lunch,
   dinner.

Grizzly Greg's Pizzeria & Deli
Main Street and 2nd Avenue
907-766-3622
Espresso, sandwiches, soups, pizza.

Klondike Restaurant
Dalton City
On the grounds of Southeast Alaska State
   Fair
907-766-2477
Open summers only.

Lighthouse Restaurant & Harbor Bar
Main and Beach Streets, near small boat
   harbor
907-766-2442
Espresso, breakfast, lunch, dinner.

McWall's Café
Main and Union Streets
907-766-2488
Breakfast, lunch, dinner. Open
   summers only.

33 Mile Roadhouse
Mile 33 Haines Highway
907-767-5510
Breakfast, lunch, dinner.

Wild Strawberry
2nd Avenue, off Haines Highway
907-766-3608
Breakfast and lunch; espresso.

KLONDIKE HIGHWAY 2

From Alaska Highway to Skagway: 99 miles (159 km)
Travel Opportunities: *White Pass & Yukon Route railway; Skagway; Gold Rush*
Cemetery; Slide Cemetery; Arctic Brotherhood Hall; Dyea and trailhead to
Chilkoot Pass.

Klondike Highway 2 is a fairly new road (built in 1978) that covers very old
ground. This route over **White Pass** is an ancient one used by the coastal Tlingit who
traveled to trade with inland tribes. During the 1898 Klondike Gold Rush, White Pass
and nearby Chilkoot Pass were the two major overland routes to the goldfields.
   Klondike Highway 2 heads south to Skagway from the Alaska Highway at Mile 874

The White Pass & Yukon Route's steam locomotive is still in operation.

(1,407 km), about a dozen miles south of Whitehorse. The high-elevation lakes and rocky cliffs along this highway rank it among the most impressive topographically. At White Pass, the wind is fast and chilly, even in the middle of summer.

You will cross from the Yukon into Alaska at the international border about 7 miles (11 km) before you reach Skagway, so be prepared for U.S. Customs and Immigration. Remember to turn your watch back an hour—you'll be in the Alaska Time Zone.

Skagway

Skagway is one of two Alaska communities on the northern end of the Inside Passage that are served by the Alaska Marine Highway System. Haines is the other. It's possible to board your vehicle in Bellingham, Washington, and take the ferry all the way along the protected waters of Southeast Alaska, then rejoin the road system at Haines or Skagway. (See Chapter 9, Alaska Marine Highway System.)

Walking through Skagway is like stepping into a colorized postcard from 1898, when businesses like these also lined the streets and served the gold seekers who were headed to Dyea and over Chilkoot Pass. This northernmost town on the Inside Passage was the gateway to the Klondike, and in the two years between 1897 and 1899, the primary reason to be here was to get rich quick—by either mining the ground or mining the pockets of the miners. Skagway boomed into a city of 20,000 in a few months' time.

The **Chilkoot Trail** was a steep and treacherous route over Chilkoot Pass to the

A historical photo depicts the summit of the White Pass during the Gold Rush of 1898. Stampeders were not allowed to cross without a year's worth of supplies.

goldfields. Photos often depict a dark line of men (and a few women) hiking an arm's length from each other as they climbed the snowy steps to the pass. Today the 33-mile (53 km) route remains a challenge, even to hikers dressed in the latest outdoor gear. If you're planning to try the Chilkoot, check first with the **Klondike Gold Rush National Historical Park** visitor center at 2nd and Broadway in Skagway. The center is housed in the restored White Pass & Yukon Route railway depot. Ask about guided tours of the historic downtown, or programs in the auditorium. Call 907-983-2921.

The **White Pass & Yukon Route** narrow-gauge (36-inch) railway offers trips in railcars pulled by a steam locomotive, letting day-trippers retrace the steps of gold-rush stampeders. Call 1-800-343-7373 or 907-983-2217 to arrange a ride.

The **Arctic Brotherhood Hall** on Broadway between 2nd and 3rd, its false front decorated with thousands of pieces of driftwood, looks the same today as it did a century ago. The **Trail of '98 Museum** inside the hall holds personal artifacts from the gold rush, and items that have been donated by local people since 1961. Call 907-983-2420.

The saloons, restaurants, gift shops, and soda fountains of Skagway are all wrapped in historical storefronts. A horse-and-buggy tour operator is dressed in the garb of old. The storefront windows along Main Street are trimmed with the hats, gloves, and doodads that would have pleased your grandma. The big difference between then and now, besides the plumbing and telephone lines, lies in the harbor: Enormous cruise ships bring their passengers to Skagway to soak up a little atmosphere of the Days of '98.

A century ago, outlaw **Soapy Smith** reigned here, along with his gang of con artists and thugs who took advantage of the weak, the innocent, and even the dead. One story tells of the terrible avalanche that killed dozens of men on the Chilkoot Trail. Soapy set up a "morgue" near the site, and he and his men dug up bodies, took them into his morgue, and stripped them of their valuables before the real authorities arrived. His reign ended when he was confronted by a man named **Frank Reid**, who shot Soapy several times and was mortally wounded himself.

The graves of both men, in the **Gold Rush Cemetery**, are visited by thousands of people every year. To get to the cemetery, go north on State Street, then follow the signs. Reid's grave bears these words: "He gave his life for the honor of Skagway." Every July 4, the city remembers those days with an event called Soapy Smith's Wake. Another cemetery holds the remains of victims from that Chilkoot avalanche.

You can drive to what used to be **Dyea**, a town of thousands, where nothing but a derelict dock remains. From the parking area, you can walk to the Chilkoot trailhead. I hiked up a few yards, had my picture taken, and came back down.

Lodging

Gold Rush Lodge

6th Avenue and Alaska Street
907-983-2831
Smoke-free rooms, private bathrooms.
Cable TV and Showtime. Free continental breakfast. Walking distance to downtown Skagway historic district.

Sgt. Preston's Lodge

6th Avenue and State Street
907-983-2521
30 rooms on street level. Cable TV and phones. Courtesy van. Close to bank and post office.

Skagway Inn

7th Avenue and Broadway Street
1-800-478-2290 (from Alaska) or
    907-983-2289
12 rooms in historic district. Breakfast, van service. Reservations for White Pass & Yukon Route, shows, tours.

Westmark Skagway

3rd Avenue and Spring Street
1-800-544-0970 or 907-983-6000
www.westmarkhotels.com
195 deluxe rooms, nonsmoking available. Cable TV, dining room, lounge. Close to shopping and entertainment.

The White House

Near downtown
907-983-9000
www.skagway.com/whitehouse
Rooms with private baths in 1902 family-run inn. Complimentary breakfast.

Wind Valley Lodge

Klondike Highway at 22nd Avenue
907-983-2236
30 rooms with private bath, nonsmoking available. Cable TV and phones, guest laundry. Wheelchair access. Shuttle service. Two-Diamond rating, AAA.

Campgrounds

Garden City RV Park
State Street between 15th and 17th Avenues
907-983-2378
Level sites with full and partial hookups,
    pull-throughs. Laundry, rest rooms,
    coin-operated showers.

Pullen Creek RV Park
2nd Avenue near Alaska State Ferry dock
1-800-936-3731
Partial hookups. Showers, dump station.
    Walking distance to shopping and
    attractions.

Skagway Mountain View RV Park
12th Avenue and Broadway Street
1-888-778-7700
Wooded sites with partial hookups, pull-
    throughs, cable TV access. Picnic tables,
    firewood. Showers, laundry, rest rooms,
    dump station. RV wash facilities. Tour
    reservations. Near downtown historic
    district.

Restaurants

The Corner Café
4th Avenue and State Street
907-983-2155
Three meals a day, specializing in pizza.
    Free delivery.

Dee's Café
2nd Avenue across from railroad depot
907-983-2200
Charbroiled salmon, halibut, burgers,
    steaks.

Deli Delights
4th and State Streets, in Fairway Market
907-983-2220
Sandwiches and other carryout food.

Panda Express
21st and State Streets
907-983-3328
American and ethnic Chinese cuisine.

Skagway Brewing Co.
3rd Avenue and Broadway Street, in Golden
    North Hotel
907-983-2451
Microbrewery, restaurant, pub; established
    1897.

Sweet Tooth Café
3rd Avenue and Broadway Street
907-983-2405
Breakfast, lunch, dinner. Homemade
    donuts, soups, bread, fries. Takeout
    available.

$\mathcal{P}$ARKS HIGHWAY

Anchorage to Fairbanks: 358 miles (576 km)
Travel Opportunities: *Iditarod Trail Sled Dog Race Headquarters, Wasilla;*
Independence Mine; Talkeetna; Denali State Park; Denali National Park and
Preserve; Fairbanks.

The (George) Parks Highway connects the state's largest and second-largest cities, Anchorage and Fairbanks, in a 358-mile south-to-north trek from the Southcentral coast into Alaska's great Interior. It is among the newest of the highways (completed in 1972) and sees heavy summer use, often by motorists on their way to Denali National Park and Preserve.

To reach the Parks Highway from Anchorage, take the Glenn Highway north for 35 miles (56 km) and turn north (left) at the junction. Even though this place is the official start of the Parks Highway, roadside mileposts will reflect total mileage from Anchorage. (For details on Anchorage-area attractions, lodging, campgrounds, and restaurants, see the section on the Glenn Highway, in this chapter.)

Just north of the Glenn Highway and Parks Highway junction is **Wasilla**. Once a sleepy little stop along a two-lane road, Wasilla has experienced a population boom in the past two decades, and the two-lane Parks Highway widens into four lanes as it passes through town. Wasilla is a good last-chance, full-service shopping stop before you begin your lengthy road trip north. Although many small, family-operated stores and service stations lie ahead, Wasilla offers a variety of goods, services, fast-food restaurants, grocery stores, and so forth. Almost the entire shopping district lies at roadside.

To learn more about local history, visit the **Dorothy Page Museum & Historical Townsite**, 323 Main Street, in Wasilla. Exhibits focus on the development of the Iditarod Trail Sled Dog Race, area homesteading, and settlement in the Mat-Su Valley. Admission is charged. For information, call 907-373-9071.

At the Knik-Goose Bay Road traffic light in Wasilla, you can turn west and follow the road for a little more than 2 miles (3 km) to the impressive log building that is **Iditarod Trail Sled Dog Race Headquarters**. Inside are the administrative offices of the famous 1,000-mile race across Alaska, as well as a mini-museum, video theater, and gift shop. Admission is free. A mount of a champion sled dog named Andy is on display here, too. A leader for five-time Iditarod champion Rick Swenson, Andy is a testimonial to the athletic ability of Alaska sled dogs. For a nominal fee, you can take a dogsled ride in summer as the teams pull wheeled carts instead of sleds. At a replica of a checkpoint cabin, learn more about this phenomenal race. Call 907-376-5155 or visit the Iditarod website at www.iditarod.com.

Transportation buffs will enjoy a visit to a museum north of Wasilla off the Parks Highway at Mile 47 (75.5 km). Follow the signs for another mile to the **Museum of Alaska Transportation & Industry**. Here you'll see early-day snowmobiles, vehicles, airplanes, trains, and more. Call 907-376-1211.

As you drive the Parks Highway, you'll occasionally pass through little enclaves where people choose to live far away from big cities. **Willow** is such a town. It has its own post office, library, convenience store, gas station, café, lodge, and dozens of little homes sprinkled throughout the surrounding forests and around lakes. Roadside fishing opportunities exist all along this stretch of the Parks Highway. Even if you don't fish, it's fun to pull over and watch the anglers.

A popular attraction for campers and fishers is **Nancy Lake State Recreation Area**, at Mile 66.5 (107 km) Parks Highway, developed with 30 campsites, water, toilets, a trail, and a boat launch. Just past Willow at Mile 71 (114.5 km) is the westbound

Talkeetna, Alaska, can be found at the dead end of a spur road off the Parks Highway. It is believed that creators of the television show Northern Exposure *based their fictional town upon this locale.*

turn for Willow Creek State Recreation Area, located at the end of the **Willow Creek Parkway**, about 5 miles (8 km) from the highway. Here's another example of a label that doesn't quite fit. This "parkway" is a gravel road that's occasionally so full of washboard that you can hear your motor mounts coming loose. It's wise to slow down on this road. There will still be plenty of salmon in the river when you get there. The area is nicely developed with RV parking, water, outhouses, tent camping, trails, and river access.

Just north past the entrance to Willow Creek Parkway is the eastbound turnoff for Hatcher Pass Road and access to **Independence Mine**. (See details in the section on the Glenn Highway, in this chapter.)

Take a side trip to **Talkeetna** for a taste of old Alaska. Almost 99 miles (159 km) north of Anchorage, make the right turn onto a spur road that leads to Talkeetna. This is an excellent drive along a paved 14-mile (22.5-km) road that dead-ends in a historic gold-mining town. Incredible views of Mount McKinley are possible on clear days. At certain times of the year, Talkeetna is overrun with mountain climbers who have journeyed here from all over the world. Local bush pilots fly the climbers and their gear to the base camp of Mount McKinley for ascents up North America's tallest peak.

Poke around Talkeetna on foot. A car only gets in the way. At the end of Main Street, you'll find tent camping or RV sites for dry camping. Outhouses are nearby.

Several of Talkeetna's buildings are on the National Register of Historic Places. Although it's small, the town features museums, two roadhouses, a modern National Park Service ranger station, a post office, motels, a country store, and many gift shops. Each December, Talkeetna hosts the Bachelor Society Ball; in summers, it's the Mountain Mama Contest, where women can prove their mettle by chopping wood and hauling water while packing a baby doll in a carrier on their backs. The town hosts the Talkeetna Blue Grass Festival in early August. Call 907-495-6718 for information.

Here you can arrange a jet-boating adventure, a flightseeing trip, a float trip, a day or more on the water fishing for big salmon. In Talkeetna, you'll find a number of outfitters, some of them with storefronts along Main Street. Ask for directions at the visitor information cabin by the sign that says "Beautiful Downtown Talkeetna."

On clear days, a crowd gathers at the **Mile 135 (237 km) wayside** on the Parks Highway. From here, you'll gain an incredible view of 20,320-foot **Mount McKinley** and the lesser surrounding mountains, which would receive more notice were they not flanking McKinley. Neighboring peaks include Mount Foraker, rising to 13,395 feet (4,082 m); Mount Hunter, at 14,580 feet (4,444 m); and Mount Silverthrone, at 13,220 feet (4,029 m); plus three others with summits that exceed 12,000 feet (3,658 m). Portable toilets and litter barrels, plus interpretive signs and the chance to see The High One, make this a popular stop along the Parks.

The boundary of **Denali State Park** lies about 132 miles (213 km) north of Anchorage. This park straddles the highway and offers 325,460 acres filled with recreational opportunities: fishing, hiking, biking, camping, canoeing, floating. Three state-operated campgrounds are in the park: Byers Lake, Lower Troublesome Creek, and Denali View North. Thirty-seven miles (59 km) of developed trails thread above and below tree line in a panoramic landscape. For more information, call the Alaska Division of Parks and Outdoor Recreation in Palmer at 907-745-3975, or visit the website at www.dnr.state.ak.us/parks/index.htm.

A popular landmark at Mile 188.5 (303 km) is a private business that has long been a curiosity as well as a milepost: a three-story igloo. The giant geodesic structure originally was built as a hotel but never served that purpose. Ask about its history when you stop at **Igloo City Resort** for gas or gifts. The igloo marks roughly the halfway point between Anchorage and Fairbanks.

At Mile 210 (338 km), near Cantwell, an eastbound turnoff leads to the Denali Highway, which connects the Parks Highway with the Richardson Highway. (See the section on the Denali Highway, in this chapter.)

The crown jewel of North America, Mount McKinley rises within the 6-million-acre **Denali National Park and Preserve**. And while views of The Mountain tease motorists during their northbound drive, the park entrance doesn't arrive until Mile 237 Parks Highway (382 km), about 4.5 hours north of Anchorage.

An extended visit to Denali National Park takes some advance planning, because reservations are necessary for campsites, for hotel rooms, and for seats on the shuttle buses that travel on the only road that penetrates the park. You can easily drop in and check out the visitor center, walk around the local trails, enjoy a picnic, and take off. But overnight stays are more complicated. The nationwide reservation phone number is 1-800-622-7275; in Anchorage, call 907-272-7275.

Most visitors to the park stay in hotels along the Parks Highway just a few miles farther north, where development of restaurants, gas stations, hotels, gift shops, and tour operators has clustered in what is known as **McKinley Village**, outside the park's boundaries. There are plenty of places to stay nearby, yet outside the park. Only one hotel is in operation within the park itself: the Denali National Park Hotel, which includes a gift shop and restaurant. The hotel and the modern visitor center are operation centers as people come and go on hikes, catch rides to sled-dog demonstrations, head out on guided nature walks, or leave for the bus ride to the end of the 87-mile (140-km) park road. Private vehicles are not allowed beyond Mile 30 (48 km) on that road, so if you want the best chance to see wildlife, you have to take the shuttle bus. Wildlife-watching (and mountain-watching) remain the top draw. Chances are you might see a bear, caribou, moose, ptarmigan, fox, Dall sheep, or snowshoe hare.

The **Alaska Railroad** depot lies within the park, too, and shuttle buses transport passengers to their waiting hotels. The place is abuzz with activity—and the scenery, close and far away, is awesome. Out on the Parks Highway, the Nenana River races below the road's edge. Look for whitewater rafters down there any time of day. Overhead, small airplanes and helicopters engage in viewing Denali from the top down.

About a half-hour farther north on the Parks Highway, the coal-mining town of **Healy** lies in the northern foothills of the Alaska Range. This is the next place along the road to find a meal, accommodations, and fuel. A small community, Healy is growing as more visitors to Denali National Park want to leave the crowds behind when they find a hotel room.

From here, the Parks Highway continues north through the boreal forests of Alaska's Interior. Set between the Alaska Range and the Brooks Range, this vast region charts the coldest colds and the hottest hots in the state. From Healy to Nenana, you'll find occasional services, gift shops, and gas stations, but little other development.

The section of the Parks between Nenana and Fairbanks wends through the Tanana uplands, round-topped tall hills (they would be called mountains elsewhere) that border the **Tanana Valley**. As you cross these hills, passing lanes are available for faster traffic. Be sure to stay to the right if your vehicle pulls hills slowly. Every few miles, pullouts offer clear views, from the top down, of the braided Tanana River and its tributaries. Local forests are mostly spruce and birch and aspen.

On clear days, North America's tallest mountain, Mount McKinley—or Denali, as it's also known—is visible from a paved pullout at Mile 135 on the Parks Highway.

About 5 miles (8 km) before entering Fairbanks on the Parks Highway, you'll note signs that lead west to **Ester Gold Camp**. Ester was once a vibrant gold-mining community; today it's a historic site where a handful of people live. But every evening in the summer, Ester Gold Camp is filled with more visitors than residents. After a buffet dinner of Alaska specialties at the camp, the old Malemute Saloon fires up with melodrama, readings of Robert Service poetry, music, and more. The floor is sawdust, and the peanut shells can fall where they may. Call 1-800-676-6925 or 907-479-2500, or visit www.alaskabest.com/ester.

For information on Fairbanks history, attractions, events, lodging, campgrounds, and restaurants, see the section on Fairbanks in Chapter 6, The Alaska Highway.

Lodging

The Mat-Su Chapter of the Bed and Breakfast Association of Alaska has information on rooms, apartments, and cabins from Glennallen to Anchorage to Denali. Call 1-800-401-7444 or visit the association's website at www.alaska.net/~akhosts.

Wasilla:

Alaskan View Motel
2650 East Parks Highway
907-376-6787
24 rooms, Alaska decor in log building.
Cable TV, mountain and inlet views.

Kozey Cabins
351 East Spruce (1 mile from town)
907-376-3190
www.alaskaone/kozeycabins
Furnished cabins, with kitchens and baths.

Bush pilots out of Talkeetna land on Ruth Glacier daily, allowing visitors to step out of the plane and onto a glacier.

The Alaska Railroad wends through the Alaska Range.

Lake Lucille Inn
1300 West Lake Lucille Drive
907-373-1776
54 deluxe rooms, suites. Athletic facility,
   whirlpool, gift shop. Floatplane and
   boat docks, boat rentals.

Mat-Su Resort
1850 Bogard Road
907-376-3228
Deluxe rooms, cabins with view, cable TV,
   refrigerators. Restaurant, lounge.
   Floatplane dock, paddleboats.

Valley Country Store & Motel
Mile 40.5 Parks Highway
907-357-7878
Rooms, RV camping, pull-throughs, dump
   station, fuel.

The Windbreak
Mile 40.5 Parks Highway
907-376-4209
Rooms, plus café serving breakfast, lunch,
   dinner.

Denali Park:
Denali Backcountry Lodge
Kantishna
1-800-841-0692 or 907-783-1342
www.denalilodge.com
30 units, dining, cocktails. Inside the park.
   Train shuttle service.

Denali Cabins
Mile 229 Parks Highway
1-800-450-2489 or 907-683-2642
www.alaskan.com/denalicabins
43 cedar cabins with private bath. Hot tubs,
   dining. South of park entrance, train
   shuttle service.

Denali Grizzly Bear Cabins and
   Campground
Mile 231 Parks Highway
907-683-2696
21 kitchenette units, laundry. Pets allowed.

Denali Park Hotel
Mile 238 Parks Highway
1-800-276-7234 or 907-279-2653
www.denalinationalpark.com
100 units, dining, cocktails. Train shuttle
   service.

McKinley Chalet Resort
Mile 238 Parks Highway
1-800-276-7234 or 907-279-2653
www.denalinationalpark.com
345 units, restaurant, cocktails. Train
   shuttle service.

McKinley Village Resort
Mile 238 Parks Highway
1-800-276-7234 or 907-279-2653
www.denalinationalpark.com
150 units, dining, cocktails. Train shuttle
   service.

Denali Bluffs Hotel
Mile 238.5 Parks Highway
1-800-488-7002 (in Alaska) or 907-
   683-7000
www.denalibluffs.com
Views, TV, phones, coffee, laundry, van
   service, dining. Close to park entrance,
   train shuttle service.

Denali Crow's Nest Log Cabins
Mile 238.5 Parks Highway
907-683-2723
www.alaska.net/crowsnest
39 units with view. Hot tub, restaurant,
   lounge. Train/airport shuttle service.

Denali Princess Lodge
Mile 238.5 Parks Highway
1-800-426-0500 or 907-683-2800
280-unit hotel along river with mountain
    views. TV, phones, hot tubs, tour desk,
    theater. Restaurants, lounges. Train
    shuttle service.

Denali Windsong Lodge
Mile 238.5 Parks Highway
1-800-208-0200 or 907-245-0200
www.alaskaparks.com
Mountain views, full baths, satellite TV.
    Near dining. Just north of park entrance,
    train shuttle service.

Healy:
Sourdough Cabins & Gift Shop
Mile 239 Parks Highway
907-683-2773
51 units, laundry, pets allowed. Train
    shuttle service.

Denali North Star Inn
Mile 249 Parks Highway
907-488-1505
100 rooms, plus gift shop, salon services,
    sauna, exercise room, tour desk, lounge.
    Train shuttle service.

Stampede Lodge
Mile 249 Parks Highway
1-800-478-2370 or 907-683-2242
29 units, restaurant, lounge. Train shuttle
    service

Totem Inn
Mile 249 Parks Highway
1-800-478-2384 or 907-683-2420
50 units, plus laundry, dining, cocktails.
    Train shuttle service.

Fairbanks: See listings in the section on
Fairbanks in Chapter 6, The Alaska
Highway.

Campgrounds
Wasilla:
Best View RV Park
Mile 35.5 Parks Highway
1-800-478-6600 or 907-745-7400
64 sites with full hookups, pull-throughs,
    tenting area. Mountain views. Free
    showers; laundry, dump station.

Iceworm RV Park & Country Store
Mile 50 Parks Highway
907-892-8200
Sites with full hookups, pull-throughs,
    showers, dump station.

Denali Park:
**Denali Grizzly Bear Cabins and
    Campground**
Mile 231 Parks Highway
907-683-2696
40 RV sites with full hookups and pull-
    throughs, tent sites. Showers, laundry,
    water, dump station.

Denali RV Park and Motel
Mile 245 Parks Highway
1-800-478-1501 or 907-683-1500
90 RV sites with hookups and pull-
    throughs. Showers, water, dump station.

McKinley RV and Campground
Mile 248.5 Parks Highway
1-800-478-2562 or 907-683-2379
77 RV sites with full hookups and pull-
    throughs, tent sites. Fireplace/grills.
    Showers, water, dump station.

Ester:

Ester Gold Camp

3660 Main Street

1-800-676-6925 or 907-479-2500

www.alaskasbest.com/ester

16 RV sites, 3 tent sites, showers, dump
  station.

Fairbanks: See listings in the section on
Fairbanks in Chapter 6, The Alaska Highway.

Restaurants

Wasilla:

Legends at Settlers Bay

Mile 8 Knik-Goose Bay Road

Adjacent to Settlers Bay Golf Club

907-376-5298

Fine dining and great views.

Mat-Su Resort

1850 Bogard Road

907-376-3228

Restaurant, lounge open daily for lunch
  and dinner; weekend breakfasts.

Mead's Coffeehouse

405 East Herning

907-357-KOFE

Soup, salad, breads, pasta. Computers to
  check your e-mail.

Mile 49 Café

Mile 49 Parks Highway

907-373-2663

Breakfast all day, lunch and dinner.

The Windbreak

Mile 40 Parks Highway

In Windbreak Hotel

907-376-4484

Breakfast, lunch, dinner.

Denali Park:

Also check the Denali Park lodging listings,
above, for hotels with restaurants and
lounges.

The Perch

Mile 224 Parks Highway

1-800-322-2523 or 907-683-2523

Breakfast, lunch, and dinner featuring
  steak, seafood, Alaska specialties.
  Outdoor seating available.

Ester:

Ester Gold Camp

3660 Main Street

1-800-676-6925 or 907-479-2500

Dinner entrees featuring Alaska specialties.

Fairbanks: See listings in the section on
Fairbanks in Chapter 6, The Alaska Highway.

$\mathcal{R}$ICHARDSON HIGHWAY

Valdez to Fairbanks: 364 miles (568 km)
Travel Opportunities: *Valdez; pipeline terminus on Prince William Sound;
Thompson Pass; Worthington Glacier; pipeline pump stations; Delta Junction;
North Pole; Fairbanks.*

The original name for this historic route was the Valdez to Fairbanks Trail. Work
on the road began in 1903, after the Tanana Valley gold strike near Fairbanks. In 1904
the government pushed development along by requiring every man along the

After an afternoon of sea kayaking in the waters near Valdez, a group of women help each other with beaching their kayaks.

length of the road to work two days per year on the project or pay a tax of $8.

Valdez (val-DEEZ) is an ice-free, deepwater port on an arm of Prince William Sound. It is the terminus of the trans-Alaska pipeline. From Valdez, crude oil continues its journey south via massive tanker ships. Tours of the **Alyeska Marine Terminal** are available through Valdez Tours at 907-835-2686.

Valdez is on the Alaska Marine Highway System, with the ferry terminal located near Hazelet Avenue and Fidalgo Drive. Waterfront businesses along the small-boat harbor offer cruises, salmon fishing charters, and kayak rentals. Stan Stephens Cruises offers daily departures from Valdez to see **Columbia Glacier** in **Prince William Sound**; call 1-800-992-1297. Full- or half-day rafting trips can be booked through Keystone Raft & Kayak Adventures at 907-835-2606. Anadyr Adventures leads sea kayaking, hiking, and sailing excursions; call 907-835-2814 or visit www.alaska.net/~anadyr.

This little city gets more snow than anywhere else in Alaska. In the winter of 1999–2000, some 380 inches of snow fell on the town. A paralyzing 596.9 inches fell in the winter of 1994–1995. That's almost 50 feet of snow—enough to bury a house, or at least cave in its roof during many months when there is rare chance of any snow melting. Snow, and what to do with it, is the reason Valdez is laid out as it is. Side streets end in cul-de-sacs with rights-of-way for snowplows to push snow out of the streets and into a dump area behind the homes. Note that most roofs are metal, and angled so that snow slides off into yards, not onto walkways or driveways.

You'll find lots of opportunity to view wildlife in and around Valdez, so keep your telephoto lens or field glasses handy. Make noise while hiking or biking so you don't surprise the bears. It's common to see eagles, sea otters, harbor seals, humpback whales, and orcas. Shorebirds and waterfowl move through seasonally.

The **Valdez Museum**, at 217 Egan Drive, features rotating exhibits as well as displays and photos on town history, the gold rush, cultural history, and the Exxon Valdez oil spill that tainted Prince William Sound in 1989. Call 907-835-2764. A host of restaurants and gift shops and a couple of grocery stores are easy to find on the simple street grid of Valdez.

Each year Valdez hosts the **Prince William Sound Community College/Edward Albee Theater Conference**, which attracts top writers and actors, and continues to gain in national prominence. For more on Valdez and its attractions and events, contact the Convention & Visitors Bureau at 1-800-770-5954 or 907-835-2984, or visit the city's website at www.alaska.net/~valdezak.

Traveling north from Valdez on the Richardson Highway, you'll encounter breathtakingly beautiful canyons and waterfalls, and the looming **Worthington Glacier**. A visitor information wayside at **Thompson Pass**, elevation 2,678 feet (816 m), provides information about the nearby glacier. The route to Thompson Pass remains a daunting climb, even in modern vehicles, but a century ago and more, the trail included numerous switchbacks to make it easier for the horse-drawn double-ender sleighs that traveled in winter and the wagons that crossed the pass in summer.

Record snowfall on the pass in the winter of 1952–1953 measured 974.5 inches. And yet Thompson Pass is not the highest on the Richardson Highway. That honor goes to Isabel Pass, at 3,000 feet. It was named for the wife of Fairbanks founder E. T. Barnette, who traveled with his wife, Isabelle (yes, it's spelled differently than the pass), over this route several times, summer and winter.

Eighty-three miles (134 km) north of Valdez, the Edgerton Highway splits off to the east, leading to Chitina. From Chitina, the McCarthy Road continues to the town of McCarthy, and access to the former mining town of Kennicott. (See the section on the Edgerton Highway, in this chapter.)

Watch for views of the trans-Alaska pipeline along the Richardson Highway, and pullouts for pump stations with signs that explain the operation of these sites.

Farther north, 115 miles (185 km) from Valdez, **Glennallen** marks the junction of the Richardson and Glenn Highways. (See the section on the Glenn Highway, in this chapter.) For 14 miles, the Richardson and Glenn Highways now share the same route—until Mile 129 (207.5 km) on the Richardson, at Gakona Junction, where the Glenn veers northeast toward Tok. (This section of the Glenn is widely referred to as the Tok Cutoff.)

From Gulkana to Paxson, you'll be driving on the Richardson toward the Alaska Range and great picture-taking possibilities. The Gulkana River near **Sourdough**, Mile 147.5 (237 km), is popular with anglers, canoeists, and river rafters. Gulkana River paddlers usually put in at Paxson, almost 30 road-miles ahead, and then float the 50 river-miles down to Sourdough for takeout. Managed by the Bureau of Land

Management, the Gulkana was designated a Wild and Scenic River in 1980. A BLM campground at Sourdough offers 60 campsites near the boat launch.

Farther north at **Paxson** is the turn onto the Denali Highway, which travels west to meet the Parks Highway near Denali National Park (see the section on the Denali Highway, in this chapter). Here in the foothills of the Alaska Range, the views are broad and mountainous, and plenty of camping opportunities exist, either in developed campgrounds or simply along the road wayside, where it is permissible to dry camp overnight. Paxson is home to 33 people. Services include lodging, meals, fuel, and fishing guides.

At **Delta Junction**—266 miles (428 km) north of Valdez and 98 miles (157 km) south of Fairbanks—the Alaska Highway joins the Richardson Highway. The two highways share the ride for the rest of the way into Fairbanks, passing by the community of North Pole on the way. For details on attractions, lodging, and restaurants in Delta Junction, North Pole, and Fairbanks, see the last portion of Chapter 6, The Alaska Highway.

Lodging

Valdez:

Downtown Inn
1113 Galena Drive
1-800-478-2791 or 907-835-2791
31 rooms with private or shared baths, free
   continental breakfast.

Keystone Hotel
144 Egan Drive
907-835-3851
www.alaska.com/keystonehotel
107 rooms.

Pipeline Inn
112 Egan Drive
907-835-4444
16 rooms, restaurant, lounge.

Totem Inn
144 East Egan Drive
907-834-4430
Rooms, with refrigerators, microwaves,
   coffee. RV campground with full
   hookups. Central location.

Village Inn
100 Meals Avenue
907-835-4445
www.alaska-vacations.com/vi_lh/wi.html
79 rooms, restaurant, lounge.

Westmark Valdez
100 Fidalgo Drive
1-800-544-0970 or 907-835-4391
97 deluxe rooms, restaurant, lounge. On the
   waterfront.

Delta Junction, North Pole, and Fairbanks: See listings under the respective town names in Chapter 6, The Alaska Highway.

Campgrounds

Valdez:

Bayside RV Park
Off Egan Drive on Chitina Drive
1-888-835-4425 or 907-835-4425
94 RV sites with full and partial hookups,
   cable TV. Bookings for cruises and
   charter fishing trips.

The landmark cutout of Santa stands outside of his distinctive house along the Richardson Highway at North Pole.

Bear Paw Camper Park
101 North Harbor Drive
907-835-2530
120 sites with full or partial hookups, tent
  camping, cable TV, phone, laundry.

Eagle's Rest RV Park
630 East Pioneer Drive
1-800-553-7275 or 907-835-2373
Campsites with full or partial hookups,
  pull-throughs, tent camping. Showers,
  laundry, dump station. Walk-in freezer
  space and fish-cleaning table. Tickets
  for local tours.

Totem Inn
144 East Egan Drive
907-835-4443
27 campsites with partial hookups, laundry,
  phone.

Delta Junction, North Pole, and Fairbanks:
See listings under the respective town
names in Chapter 6, The Alaska Highway.

Restaurants
Valdez:
Alaska Halibut House
208 Meals Avenue
907-835-2788
Lunch and dinner.

Captain's Table
100 Fidalgo Drive
In the Westmark Valdez
907-835-4391
Fine dining.

Chinook Books & Coffee
126 Pioneer Drive
Adjoining bookstore, gift shop
907-835-4222
Breakfast and lunch.

Fu Kung Chinese Restaurant
207 Kobuk Street
907-835-5255
Chinese food; beer and wine.

Lisa's Kitchen
Fairbanks Drive next to Pinzon Liquors
907-835-5633
Mexican dishes.

Mike's Palace
201 North Harbor Drive
907-835-2365
Greek, Italian, Mexican, American.

No Name Pizza
1212 Egan Drive
907-835-4419
Eat in or take out.

Pioneer Drive Pizza

310 Pioneer Drive

907-835-2066

Pizza, sandwiches, salads.

Pipeline Club

112 Egan Drive

907-835-4444

Steaks, Alaska seafood. Lounge,
  entertainment.

Rose Cache

321 Egan Drive

907-835-8383

Lunch, dinner in English tearoom setting.

Totem Inn

144 East Egan Drive

907-835-4443

Hearty breakfasts, lunches, dinners.

Tsaina Lodge

Mile 35 Richardson Highway

907-835-3500

Healthful foods, juices, espresso, wine list.

***Delta Junction, North Pole, and
Fairbanks:*** See listings under the respective
town names in Chapter 6, The Alaska
Highway.

$\mathcal{S}$EWARD HIGHWAY

Anchorage to Seward: 127 miles (204 km)
Travel Opportunities: *Potter Marsh; Turnagain Arm; Alyeska Ski Resort at
Girdwood; Portage Glacier and Exit Glacier; Seward and Resurrection Bay.*

The Seward Highway was named
for Secretary of the Interior Frederick
Seward, a key figure in the purchase
of Alaska from Russia in 1867.
(Remember "Seward's folly" from
your history class?) Looking at a map
of Alaska, you'll see that the Seward
name gets around. The Seward
Highway is on the **Kenai Peninsula**;
the Seward Peninsula is in Northwest
Alaska; and then there's Fort Seward
in Southeast Alaska.

The views along this highway are
so stunning that the road has been
designated an official scenic byway

*McHugh Creek Park is a beautifully
developed mini-park overlooking Turnagain
Arm off the Seward Highway. The Seward has
been designated a National Scenic Byway.*

within the nation's transportation system. From Anchorage heading south, it cuts into the foot of the mountains along the edge of Cook Inlet's Turnagain Arm. Wending between the mountains and the water, motorists may see Dall sheep, whales, eagles, and running salmon. Rest stops and recreation areas are abundant. Most of what you're driving through is public land, either **Chugach State Park** or **Chugach National Forest**. Only a handful of small communities existed before development of the parks.

Just south of Anchorage, the road borders **Potter Marsh**, a portion of the Anchorage Coastal Waterfowl Refuge. A boardwalk trail winds above the wetlands, with interpretive signs. Here, and in other places along the Seward Highway, you'll see some unusual areas of sunken land where the ground dropped by several feet during the huge 1964 earthquake. In these coastal areas, still-standing dead trees were killed when the land dropped and their roots were flooded with saltwater from Turnagain Arm.

Continuing south on the Seward, **Turnagain Arm** flanks the right side of the road. The water is not the cerulean blue that one might imagine at oceanside, but rather a flat gray from the many tons of glacial silt that is carried in streams pouring from the mountains. The silt buildup has created a mudflat all around Anchorage's coastal areas, and the extreme tide at this point (sometimes surpassing 30 feet) means that for part of every day, the view is of gray mudflats. At other times, it's a vision of loveliness—especially when the returning water creates a bore tide, sometimes a foot high or more, which floods the arms of Cook Inlet on either side of Anchorage. In Turnagain Arm, sightings of the bore tide often cause motorists to pull over and watch in awe. In a bore tide, the volume of returning water is so great that a low wall of water forms the leading edge of the incoming tide. Signs warn about the dangers of walking on the mudflats. Even though the surface looks firm, it's possible to become trapped in the silty mud—a perilous spot when the tide is about to turn.

Turnagain Arm was given its name by Captain James Cook. In his search for the Northwest Passage, Cook ventured down this body of water, mistakenly believing it was a river. When Cook saw the retreating tide taking the water out from beneath his ship, he realized his error and advised his men to hurriedly "turn again."

Thirty-seven miles (59.5 km) south of Anchorage, turn left at the spur road into **Girdwood** for world-class skiing at **Alyeska Ski Resort**. This picturesque little town beneath 3,939-foot (1,200.5-m) Mount Alyeska has been on the map since a minor gold rush in the early part of the 20th century. It was only in the last half of the century that Girdwood discovered its economic potential as a ski resort.

Although known internationally, Girdwood and Alyeska retain a small-town feel. Adding to the area's amenities is the recent construction of **Westin's Alyeska Prince Resort**, along with an enclosed tram that travels up the mountain to the Seven Glaciers Restaurant. The views are spectacular. At ground level, take Crow Creek Road to Crow Creek Mine, where you can pan for gold or enjoy a picnic among the old buildings and artifacts. **Crow Creek Mine** is a national historic site.

At Portage, 47 miles (76 km) south of Anchorage, the Alaska Railroad offers passenger service to **Whittier** via an 11-mile (17.5 km) ride through Bear Valley and several tunnels. Whittier was originally a military post, valued for its ice-free, deepwater location on **Prince William Sound**. Today the harbor is home port for dozens of pleasure vessels and several cruise operations. If you book your cruise in Anchorage, operators often make the arrangements for travel by bus to Portage, where the bus is loaded onto a railroad flatcar bound for Whittier. Whittier is a port on the Alaska Marine Highway System, connected with Valdez and Cordova by ferry. The state's newest road, completed in June 2000, parallels the railroad tracks between Portage and Whittier.

Portage was ravaged in the 1964 earthquake. You can still see remnants of homes and business structures in the abundant fireweed along the road. Dead trees in this area are a testament to that terrible event, too.

Just a few miles south of the ruins of Portage, look for **Big Game Alaska**, where you can view bison, elk, eagles, moose, caribou, and musk oxen in a natural setting. This drive-through park is open 7 days a week. Call 907-783-2025.

The turnoff to **Portage Lake** also is just a short distance south of Portage, at a point 48 miles (77 km) south of Anchorage. Turn east and follow the road for 5.5 miles (9 km) to the lake, which is within Chugach National Forest. At lakeside you'll find food and gift shopping at Portage Glacier Lodge and natural history information at the **Begich-Boggs Visitor Center**. In the center's theater, watch the video Voices from the Ice, about glaciers and the wildlife of this area. Kids will have fun touching fur samples and bones from various animals and learning more about them. Photos tell the story of a gold rush that boomed here a century ago.

Because Portage Glacier has been in retreat for decades, it's difficult to see it from the visitor center. But you can travel to the face of the glacier by tour boat, operated by Gray Line of Alaska; call 907-783-2983.

The Seward Highway rounds the end of Turnagain Arm, which is fed here by the Placer River. Sometimes, especially during late winter and early spring, a dozen or more moose may be seen resting here among the sparse trees.

A "Welcome" sign greets drivers at the gateway to the Kenai Peninsula, and the road now rises and falls as it wends its way through the pristine Kenai Mountains above and below tree line. At the fork in the road 89 miles (143 km) south of Anchorage, continue straight. The town of **Seward** lies another 38 miles (61 km) ahead. (The right-hand fork marks the start of the Sterling Highway, which leads to Soldotna, Kenai, and Homer. See the section on the Sterling Highway, in this chapter.)

About 4 miles (6.5 km) north of Seward, you can follow the signs and turn west for several miles to reach **Exit Glacier.** Trails lead the way to this very accessible glacier. You can even walk up to its face, but be wary—multiple signs warn of the danger.

Portage Glacier is in retreat, but close-up views are still possible by boat through a concession called Portage Glacier Cruises.

The oceanside community of **Seward** lies at the end of the Seward Highway, 2.5 hours south of Anchorage. Settled in 1903, Seward was founded as a shipping port and in 1915 became the southernmost terminal on the Alaska Railroad. Seward is a port along the Alaska Marine Highway System (see Appendix 1).

At the edge of **Resurrection Bay**, protected waters off the Gulf of Alaska, Seward is the home of the **Alaska SeaLife Center**, located along the waterfront. Educational exhibits bring viewers close to seabirds and to marine mammals such as sea lions, seals, and otters. The center also serves as a research laboratory, designed so biologists can work as visitors look on. Call 907-224-6300 for ticket information, or visit www.alaskasealife.org.

As the gateway to **Kenai Fjords National Park**, Seward has a small-boat harbor that is filled with pleasure craft as well as commercial fishing vessels and tour boats. The **Kenai Fjords National Park Visitor Center** at the harbor has information on the birds and animals that inhabit the park; call 907-224-3175. Cruise operators offer full-day or half-day tours for wildlife-watching or glacier-viewing or both. Usually a meal is served on board. At the harbor, you can also find fishing charters. Seward's Silver Salmon Derby and Jackpot Halibut Tournament are hot competitions.

At the **Seward Information Cache**, on the corner of 3rd Avenue and Jefferson Street in a circa-1916 railroad car, volunteers can direct you on a walking tour of the town's historic downtown. Seward was among the coastal communities severely damaged in the 1964 earthquake. The Community Library, at 5th Avenue and Adams

Moose, normally solitary animals, can be seen along the Seward Highway in spring, when they "yard up," or gather in small groups, to forage for food.

The Alaska Railroad train is headed south from Anchorage as visitors walk the Potter Marsh boardwalk, which is marked with interpretive signs about the birds and fish that inhabit this protected wetland.

Street, shows a film about the earthquake every Monday, Wednesday, and Friday at 7 P.M. Photos from that time are on display in the **Resurrection Bay Historical Society Museum** at 3rd Avenue and Jefferson Street.

Stop in at the **Chugach Heritage Center** for performances of *So They Say*, a live show that entertains as well as teaches about the cultural history of this area. The center also offers Native art demonstrations, displays, and a gift shop. It's near the Alaska SeaLife Center, at 501 Railway Avenue. Call 907-224-5065.

Two unusual annual events represent the spirit of Seward: challenge mixed with fun. Each July 4, scores of runners assault **Mount Marathon**, the peak just at the town's back. It's a grueling race to the top and back down, and city streets are choked with spectators. Then, in late February, it's time for the **Polar Bear Jump-off**, an American Cancer Society fund-raiser. Challengers dress in absurd costumes, then jump off the boat dock—to raise money for cancer research.

Check at the Chugach National Forest district office at 334 4th Avenue for information on hiking and biking. Call 907-224-3374. For more information on Seward, contact the Seward Convention & Visitors Bureau at 907-224-8051 or visit www.seward.net/chamber.

Lodging

Anchorage: See information at the end of the section on the Glenn Highway, in this chapter.

307 deluxe rooms, suites. Fitness center, shops, tour desk, tramway sightseeing. Lounges, cafés.

Indian:
Bird Ridge Motel
26 miles (42 km) south of Anchorage
907-653-7302
Rooms near excellent fishing.

Moose Pass:
Summit Lake Lodge
81 miles (130 km) south of Anchorage
907-595-1520
Rooms, plus gift shop, restaurant, lounge.

Girdwood: You may book Girdwood accommodations through All-Season Booking Service at 907-222-7669 or www.girdwood.net.

Seward:
A Creekside RV Park & Motel
6.5 miles (10.5 km) north of Seward on Bear Lake Road
907-224-3647
Rooms with private bath, nonsmoking available. Tour booking, fishing charters, watercraft rentals.

Alyeska Accommodations
1-888-783-2001 or 907-783-2000
Chalets and condos, kitchenettes with a view.

Westin Alyeska Prince Resort
1-800-880-3880 or 907-754-1111
www.alyeskaresort.com

Alaska's Seward Resort
1-800-770-1858 or 907-224-5559
www.usarak.army.mil/framwr/seward.htm
Motel rooms, cabins, RV sites. Fishing
    charters. Exclusive use by current and
    retired military personnel, their guests,
    and families, as well as federal
    employees, their guests, and families.

Box Canyon Cabins
Mile 1 Old Exit Glacier Road
907-224-5046
Log cabins for four to six people. Kitchens,
    baths, phones.

Breeze Inn
At Small Boat Harbor
1-888-224-5237 or 907-224-5238
86 rooms, nonsmoking available. Gift shop,
    coffee and espresso bar, restaurant,
    lounge.

Camelot Cottages
Mile 3.2 Seward Highway
1-800-739-3039 or 907-346-3039
www.alaska.net/akcabins
Cabins, kitchenettes, hot tub, laundry.

The Farm Inn
3 miles (5 km) from Seward on Salmon
    Creek Road
907-224-5691
Rooms, cottages, bungalow, kitchenettes,
    private baths. Cable TV, barbecue,
    freezer space for your fish.

Harborview Inn
804 3rd Avenue
1-888-324-3217
Rooms with view, wheelchair access. Cable
    TV, phone/data ports. Walking distance
    to tours, train, downtown.

Hotel Edgewater
5th Avenue and Ballaine Boulevard
1-888-793-6800 or 907-224-2700
Well-appointed rooms with cable TV,
    nonsmoking available. Overlooks
    Resurrection Bay.

Hotel Seward
221 5th Avenue
1-800-656-7330 or 907-224-2378
Rooms and executive suites, nonsmoking
    available, cable TV, movies. Half-block
    to Alaska SeaLife Center.

Murphy's Motel
911 4th Avenue
907-224-8090
Rooms with a view.

New Seward Hotel & Saloon
Downtown Seward
907-224-8001
35 rooms, kitchenettes, videos, phones.
    Charter fishing and Kenai Fjords tours
    available. One block to Alaska SeaLife
    Center.

River Valley Cabins
Mile 1, Old Exit Glacier Road
907-224-5740
Log cabins: family cabin for four to six
    people; six cabins for two to three
    people. Baths, phones, continental
    breakfast.

Seward Windsong Lodge
0.5 Mile, Exit Glacier Road
1-800-208-0200
Rooms with cable TV, VCRs, phones.
    Forested setting.

The Taroka Inn Motel
3rd Avenue and Adams Street
907-224-8975
Rooms with private baths, kitchens, cable
    TV, data ports. Downtown.

The Van Gilder Hotel
308 Adams Street
1-800-204-6835 or 907-224-3079
Accommodations in a National
    Historic Site.

Campgrounds

Anchorage: See information at the end of
the section on the Glenn Highway, in this
chapter.

Bird Creek:
Bird Creek State Recreation Site
26 miles (42 km) south of Anchorage
19 campsites, picnic tables, water, toilets.
    Close to great salmon fishing.

Girdwood:
Crow Creek Mine
3 miles (5 km) up Crow Creek Road
907-278-8060
Historic gold mine offers sites for dry
    camping and tenting.

Portage:
Williwaw Creek Campground
Mile 4 Portage Glacier Road
1-877-444-6777 for reservations
38 campsites, picnic tables, water, toilets.
    Deck for viewing spawning salmon, late
    July to mid-September. Nature trails.
    Campground operated by Bureau of
    Land Management.

Seward:
A Creekside RV Park & Motel
6.5 miles (10.5 km) north of Seward on Bear
    Lake Road
907-224-3647
Streamside RV sites with full or partial
    hookups. Free shower, courtesy van,
    tour booking service.

Bear Creek RV Park
6.5 miles (10.5 km) north of Seward on Bear
    Lake Road
907-224-5724
Full and partial hookups. Showers, laundry,
    rest rooms, dump station, store. Fishing
    and glacier tours, courtesy van.

Restaurants

Anchorage: See information at the end of
the section on the Glenn Highway, in this
chapter.

Indian:
Bird Ridge Café & Bakery
26 miles (42 km) south of Anchorage
907-653-7302
Home-style cooking, pastries, beer, wine.

Girdwood:
Alpine Diner & Bakery
Mile 90 Seward Highway, at turnoff to
    Girdwood
907-783-2550
Italian cuisine, hamburgers, baked goods.

The Bake Shop
At Alyeska Ski Resort
907-783-2831
Homemade soups, sourdough pancakes,
    breads, pizza.

Chair 5 Restaurant
Alpine Street, off Alyeska Highway
907-783-2500
www.chair5.com (features live views of
    Girdwood via the Mount Alyeska
    webcam)
Seafood, pizza, microbrews.

Double Musky Inn
On Crow Creek Road
907-783-2822
Cajun specialties, Alaska seafood; funky
    Alaska decor.

Westin Alyeska Prince Resort
At Mount Alyeska
1-800-880-3880 or 907-754-1111
www.alyeskaresort.com
Choose from several restaurants for the
    dining experience of your choice; casual
    to fine dining.

Portage:
Portage Glacier Lodge
Across from visitor center
907-783-3117
Soups, sandwiches. Eat in or take out.

Moose Pass:
Summit Lake Lodge
81 miles (130 km) south of Anchorage
907-595-1520
Restaurant, lodge, lounge, gift shop.

Seward:
Breeze Inn
At small boat harbor, adjacent to motel
1-888-224-5237 or 907-224-5238
Dining with a view; seafood specialties.

Ray's Waterfront
Overlooking Seward Boat Harbor
907-224-5606
Seafood specialties.

Resurrection Roadhouse
0.5 Mile, Exit Glacier Road
1-800-208-0200
Good food, casual atmosphere with a view,
    microbrews.

$\mathscr{S}$TEESE HIGHWAY

Fairbanks to Circle City: 162 miles (261 km)
Travel Opportunities: *Chena Hot Springs; Gold Dredge No. 8; Fox; Eagle Summit;*
Central, Circle Hot Springs, and Circle City.

If the Steese Highway were ever renamed, it should be the Gold Road, for this is the historic transportation corridor between some of the state's richest goldfields near Central and Circle City, and Fairbanks, the boomtown that was built on the discovery of gold. In fact, the road edges Pedro Creek, near the very place where Italian immigrant Felix Pedro discovered gold in 1902, launching yet another gold rush.

Somewhere on the east side of Fairbanks, the Steese Highway is born. The signs are vague, but almost immediately it splits into the Old Steese and, a block away, the

New Steese. The older road is retired from heavy-duty service and now merely meanders through residential areas. But the New Steese is a four-lane highway that tends toward a gentle roller-coaster ride with the occasional missing two feet of track. Just remember that the insidious permafrost works against the road builders' best efforts.

These early miles of the Steese are heavily used by Fairbanks residents who live in the surrounding hills or along Chena Hot Springs Road. Take this 56-mile spur road east to its dead end and you'll land at **Chena Hot Springs Resort**. Winter or summer, you can soak in 100-degree pools of mineral water that seem to suck the tension out of every pore. The resort offers nicely appointed rooms or rustic cabins. Swim in an enclosed pool area, or soak in outdoor hot tubs. Call 907-452-7867 or visit www.chenahotsprings.com.

Back on the Steese Highway, press on past Chena Hot Springs Road to experience some of the area's best tourism sites, as well as unparalleled views of the Tanana Valley and beyond.

View Fairbanks from atop **Engineer Hill**, 6.5 miles (10.5 km) north of town. At the top, turn west on Hagelbarger Road to the pull-out parking area immediately on your right. This is the place to get the best bird's-eye view of Fairbanks. On clear days, the Tanana Valley is spread at your feet and, beyond it to the south, the Alaska Range.

Return to the Steese Highway and travel north (left) off Hagelbarger. During your descent down Engineer Hill, portions of the **trans-Alaska pipeline** will be visible on your right. At Mile 8.5 (13.5 km), a spacious parking area with interpretive signs allows visitors to roam around and walk up to the pipeline. A **visitor information center** there (in a log cabin) is usually staffed, and free brochures are available. A sign cautions, "Please do not climb on the pipeline." Near here, the Steese Highway reduces from four lanes to two, but remains paved for many more miles.

A mile later, turn left to access **Gold Dredge No. 8**, a piece of mining history that has been restored for visitors. Operated by Gray Line of Alaska, the attraction includes tours aboard this floating gold-processing ship. You can pan for gold yourself, and eat hearty at a miners' buffet lunch. For ticket information, call 907-451-6835.

If you plan to stay on the Steese Highway, the upcoming intersection, at Mile 11 (18 km), may be confusing. The Steese makes a sharp right. If you go straight, you'll be on the Elliott Highway and bound for the Brooks Range.

One other option at this intersection is well worth your time, particularly if you're hungry or thirsty. Turn left and you'll be driving through the "main street" of beautiful downtown **Fox**, where few people live, but many come to eat and drink. The grocery store and gas station on this corner is the last place to fuel up for many miles, so top off here if you haven't done so in Fairbanks.

Other notable businesses include **The Howling Dog Saloon**, your classic funky Alaska bar. Pizza and other bar grub are available, as well as a full bar selection of beverages. There's live music on weekends, too. **The Fox Roadhouse** may not look like a historic building from the outside, but step inside and you'll discover that the original roadhouse has been completely encased by the newer exterior. The roadhouse offers lunches, dinners, and bar selections. Farther down the road, **The Turtle Club** is a Fairbanks-area favorite for casual dining and large portions of prime rib. Reservations are suggested.

Thirty-eight miles (61 km) from Fairbanks is the site of an old gold-mining town that's long gone. Left behind is a monster gold dredge, just over a hill from the highway, and a historic lodging, dining, and drinking establishment named **Chatanika Lodge**. Call 907-389-2164 for a room reservation. They'll tell you more about the days when this was a bona fide community, with a postmaster and plenty of people, and that derelict gold dredge across the way was hard at work.

Just around the bend, the University of Alaska Fairbanks conducts research on the aurora borealis from **Poker Flat Rocket Range**, a remote site marked by a mounted rocket at the entrance. As you can imagine, it's not open for drop-in visitors.

Up ahead, a series of summits and interesting switchbacks makes driving the Steese an on-your-toes proposition. For one, you run out of pavement. However, the gravel surface is well graded in summer, and the snowy surface is plowed often in winter. Views of the river valleys from above are breathtaking, and as you drive over the mountain range, above tree line, with few guardrails along the road, you can experience something like vertigo.

The road leads over Cleary Summit and Twelve-Mile Summit with access to the **Pinnell Mountain National Recreation Trail**, managed by the Bureau of Land Management. For maps of this trail and others in the area, contact the BLM at 907-474-3202 or www.ak.blm.gov/ndo.

At Mile 107.5 (173 km), you'll cross **Eagle Summit**, the tallest of them all at 3,685 feet (1,123 m) above sea level. For those accustomed to trees and roadside businesses, the trek up and over Eagle Summit will come as a surprise in its nakedness. The road threads over rolling mountains and above tree line with nothing between you and the distant valley floor except fresh air. At the top, the view is nearly dizzying, with nothing but undulating country on all sides. Here is where dozens of people drive on June 20 or 21, summer solstice, to observe and photograph an unobstructed view of the midnight sun. Their photographs, taken over several hours with timed exposures, will show an orange orb gently touching down to the horizon line before beginning its slow ascent.

In the village of **Central**, 127 miles (205 km) northeast of Fairbanks, most of the folks are gold miners, or have been miners, or at least know miners. This little town of log cabins includes a couple of restaurants and some roadside lodging.

The trans-Alaska pipeline is visible right along the road, north of Fairbanks on the Steese Highway.

The people of Central raised money to open the town's mining museum, which has limited hours due to a volunteer staff. Ask about it in any of the local businesses. It's worth a stop.

At the end of an 8-mile, unpaved spur road that leads southeast out of Central is **Circle Hot Springs.** You'll find a delightful old wooden hotel surrounded by log structures of every size and age. But the centerpiece of it all is the Olympic-size, naturally heated outdoor swimming pool. Summer or winter, the pool attracts people who come to warm their bones in water that emerges from the ground so hot, it has to be mixed to cool it for swimmers. People were coming here long before gold miners discovered the hot springs in the late 1800s. Native Alaskans already knew about the soothing warmth of the water.

In winter, the below-zero air above the pool turns the steam into ice fog that settles on everything near it, turning the pool area into a fairyland of frosted outdoor furniture. Swimmers can float in inner tubes, and the parts of them that are above water likewise become frost-covered, down to the smallest hairs on their arms, until they slip underwater again. You can even hold your wet hair straight up or sideways, and it will freeze that way. Winter guests often have the privilege of seeing the aurora borealis color the skies overhead.

Circle Hot Springs Resort includes a restaurant and saloon, and rooms range from deluxe accommodations on the first floor to dormitory-style hostel quarters in the attic. RV parking is available, too. Almost a century ago, pioneers Frank and Emma Leach worked this ground, and watered their superb gardens with hot-springs water.

Located off a spur road of the Steese Highway, Circle Hot Springs is open year-round for outdoor swimming in an Olympic-sized pool. Outside temperature was –30°F on this particular day.

Their graves are on a nearby hill, and it is said that they still haunt the place. In the game room, we even dealt an extra hand of poker for Emma, in case she showed up.

Beyond Central, the Steese Highway consists of nearly 34 unpaved miles (54 km) of winding road through the boreal forest. At the end of the road, you'll find **Circle City**. The claim to be the Paris of the North seems to have been overused during the gold rushes of the late 1800s. That was the claim for Dawson City, but Circle City came up with it first, based on all the theaters and other signs of refinement that accompanied the boom here.

Located along the Yukon River, Circle was misnamed by miners more than a century ago when they mistakenly thought they were on or near the Arctic Circle. They figured out their mistake soon enough, but the name stuck. Before the 1898 gold rush to the Klondike, Circle was the center of mining activity, and the town boomed to 10,000 people in a matter of months. There were saloons and dance halls, theaters, two-story hotels, and streets filled with people.

Looking at Circle now, it's hard to believe. A smattering of cabins has collected along the waterfront, more homes have been built away from the water, and several businesses supply the needs of local folks and the visitors who are intent on driving to the Yukon River. But the Paris of the North? Today it takes a great stretch of the imagination.

A sign at the river with another end-of-the-road message is among the most-photographed images in the area.

Lodging/Campgrounds/Meals

Central:

Central Motor Inn and Campground
Mile 127.5 Steese Highway
907-520-5228
Motel rooms, tent sites, and RV camping.
  Showers and laundry facility.
  Restaurant, cocktail lounge.

Crab's Corner
Mile 128 Steese Highway
907-520-5599
Rooms, food, gas, groceries, liquor.

Circle Hot Springs:
Circle Hot Springs Resort
Mile 8 Circle Hot Springs Road
907-520-5113
Hotel rooms, cabins, restaurant, saloon,
  shops, year-round outdoor pool.

Circle City:

Circle Riverview Motel
End of the Steese Highway
907-773-8439
Rooms, TV and VCR, laundry facilities.
  Restaurant, general store, saloon.
  Summer charters for jet boat rides on
  Yukon and Charley Rivers.

H.C. Company Store
End of the Steese Highway
907-773-1222
Gas, groceries, snacks, tire repair.

Yukon Trading Post
End of the Steese Highway
907-773-1217
Free dry camping along the Yukon River.
  General store, café, saloon, fuel.

$\mathcal{S}$TERLING HIGHWAY

From Seward Highway to Homer: 143 miles (230 km)
Travel Opportunities: *Kenai Lake at Cooper Landing; fishing the Kenai and Russian Rivers; deep-sea charter fishing at Anchor Point or Homer; day trips to Seldovia and Halibut Cove.*

The Sterling Highway leaves the Seward Highway at a fork 90 miles (145 km) south of Anchorage. It wends west and south through a sparsely populated wilderness area and passes through a handful of small towns on the way to its dead end in another small town, Homer. Lofty mountains shoulder the two paved lanes, and nearby lakes and streams run clean and cold. Most of the land is included in the 1.9-million-acre **Kenai National Wildlife Refuge**. Moose and bear numbers are strong, and you might see Dall sheep, caribou, loons, eagles, and trumpeter swans. Offshore, watch for sea otters, seals, puffins, and numerous birds.

Flightseeing operations offer bird's-eye views of unbelievable beauty. Hiking, canoeing, and rafting are other recreation offerings on the Kenai Peninsula. Nature photography ranks high on the list as well. Beautifully adorned subjects lie all around you. Distant glaciers flow from the **Harding Ice Field**, and along the road the gem-green **Kenai Lake** flows into a magnificent river of the same color and name.

The biggest towns along the Sterling Highway are **Cooper Landing**, Mile 11

(17.5 km); Sterling Highway, 101 miles (162.5 km) south of Anchorage; **Sterling**, at Mile 44 (71 km); **Soldotna**, at Mile 58 (93 km); and the end of the road at **Homer**, Mile 142.5 (229 km). The combined population of all Kenai Peninsula towns is about 46,000 people (including Seward, on the Seward Highway). In each town, you'll find gas, food, campgrounds, services, fishing licenses, hotels, and opportunities to line up a guide or gather some local knowledge.

What the Kenai Peninsula may be best known for worldwide is its prime fishing. Sportfishers travel great distances to fish the **Kenai River**, to wade into turquoise-colored waters in the hope of wrestling with a king, the salmon that can grow into the size and weight of a 7-year-old child. (The world-record king salmon of 97.4 pounds was taken from the Kenai River in 1985.) Equally attractive is another world-class, roadside sportfishing stream, the **Russian River**. On this river, the prized fish is the red salmon.

Every day of every summer, campgrounds near these rivers are jammed with RVs and cars as anglers head for the water. This is a camping experience like none other. Don't expect peace and solitude when the salmon are running. Anglers stand shoulder to shoulder and work in cooperation to flip out their lines to drift with the current without tangling with those of their neighbors. The cry "Fish on!" is the signal to reel in your line and get out of the way until a lucky angler nets his or her fish.

Charter fishing operations at Anchor Point, Deep Creek, Ninilchik, and Homer lead clients to unforgettable deep-sea halibut fishing. Getting a 100-pound lunker off the bottom and over the side of the boat takes more than finesse. It's just sheer muscle-fishing. The biggest halibut caught in Cook Inlet weighed about 465 pounds.

Six peninsula towns offer prizes for the biggest salmon or halibut in annual fishing derbies (combined, the prizes equal about $100,000). For recorded sportfishing information, call the Alaska Department of Fish and Game in Soldotna at 907-262-2737. The Soldotna Visitor Information Center is across the bridge in Soldotna, and offers information on wildlife viewing, fishing, and other outdoor recreation. Call 907-262-9814 or visit www.soldotnachamber.com.

Fishing in a new region always carries with it a hefty learning curve, so consider whether you want to devote the time necessary to learning how these fish behave. Hiring a guide is often the best option. They know the best holes, the best time of day, and the regulations. It's likely, too, that a guide will haul you away from the crowds in a boat or floatplane. Most places can arrange to have your fish smoked or frozen and shipped home when you're ready to receive it.

The biggest town on the Kenai Peninsula lies on the shores of Cook Inlet and shares the same name as the peninsula: **Kenai**. Located on the Kenai Spur Highway, westbound from Soldotna, the city is home to fishing and oil industry workers, tourism operators, and other people in support services.

A **visitor information log cabin** is at the corner of Kenai Spur Highway and Main Street Loop. Pick up a walking map for Old Town Kenai, and learn about its early

A proud halibut fisherman poses by his day's catch at Ninilchik.

One of the oldest Russian Orthodox churches in the state, dating back to 1894, can be found in Kenai's Old Town.

Kenaitze Indian and Russian residents. The Holy Assumption of the Virgin Mary Russian Orthodox Church has stood here since 1894. The Dena'ina Athabascans have lived and hunted in this region for thousands of years.

From Kenai and its neighboring town, **Nikiski**, the view across Cook Inlet is panoramic: Mount Spurr, Mount Redoubt, and Mount Iliamna are the cone-shaped volcanoes on the horizon—and they are *not* dormant. Two of these beauties have erupted in the last 15 years, spewing fine ash that rained down on Southcentral Alaska for hundreds of miles. For more information on north

The Sterling Highway affords the only way to access west Kenai Peninsula communities by road.

peninsula events, activities, and attractions, contact the Kenai Visitors and Convention Bureau: 907-283-1991 or www.visitkenai.com.

Private campgrounds may be found near or in the towns that dot the length of the Sterling Highway and the Kenai Spur Highway. The state maintains several recreation areas and sites along these roads, too, and **campsites** are plentiful at Clam Gulch, Deep Creek, Ninilchik, Kenai, Nikiski, and Johnson Lake, and in Homer at Kachemak Bay State Park. Another dozen less-developed grounds also offer campsites, rest rooms, and water. For full details, call the Division of Parks and Outdoor Recreation's Soldotna office at 907-262-5581.

The Kenai is steeped in the ancient **Kenaitze Indian culture** and in that of the Russians whose two centuries of influence are still visible in the blue-domed churches at Kenai and Ninilchik. Native surnames often possess an echo of Russia, as do place-names such as Kalifornsky, Nikiski, Kasilof, and Ninilchik. At the village of Ninilchik, the Russian Orthodox church majestically overlooks Cook Inlet from atop a bluff. Visitors are welcome to photograph the church, but remember that this is a place of worship. The local people ask that you do not enter the cemetery. Throughout the Kenai, shops offer handmade Native crafts and Russian gift items, as well as the more typical Alaska souvenirs.

The Sterling Highway ends at the sea at **Homer**, a town that's a wonderful mix of artist colony, commercial fishing seaport, small-town Alaska, and tourist destination. Homer is a port of call on the Alaska Marine Highway System; for information, call 1-800-382-9229.

The **Alaska Maritime National Wildlife Refuge Visitor Center** is right at the entrance to town at 50 Sterling Highway. The 3.5-million-acre refuge extends along much of the Alaska coastline. Call 907-235-6961.

More than 100,000 shorebirds migrate through this part of the state annually. Each May the city hosts the **Kachemak Bay Shorebird Festival**, drawing hundreds of birders to witness thousands of sandpipers, turnstones, dowitchers, and dunlins. Eagles are year-round residents.

You can learn more about the natural and cultural history of this area at the **Pratt Museum** in Homer, on Bartlett Street off Pioneer Avenue. Artifacts from prehistory to homesteaders, information on marine mammals, and guided ecology tours are among the offerings. The items for sale at the art gallery and gift shop include Alaska-made crafts and collectibles. Call 907-235-8635.

Fine art galleries featuring the work of local and guest artists may be found throughout town and on the **Homer Spit**, a 4.5-mile finger of land that extends into Kachemak Bay. Homer is a creative place, so take a gallery trek. Along the Homer Spit, you can walk along an elevated boardwalk and watch happy anglers posing with the day's catch of halibut. You can book a salmon or halibut charter, or arrange a day boat trip across the bay to visit the tiny villages of **Seldovia** and **Halibut Cove**. Central Charters Booking Agency can help line up a fishing charter, wildlife tour, sightseeing, and accommodations; call 1-800-478-7847 or 907-235-7847. Or call Homer-Alaska Referral, operated by longtime Homer residents Floyd and Gert Seekins, at 907-235-8996.

On the spit are RV and tent camping, hotel rooms, gift shops, art galleries, pleasure boats, and commercial fishing vessels. Have a cold drink at the Salty Dog Saloon; enjoy a meal with an amazing view at Land's End; walk the beach with your kids and examine what high tide has delivered. The spit, with its festival-like atmosphere, is a gathering place for revving up or winding down. Rest your eyes on the horizon. You've reached the end of the road.

Lodging

Cooper Landing:
Gwin's Lodge
Mile 52 Sterling Highway
907-595-1266
Cabins, rooms, full RV hookups, restaurant, bar.

Soldotna:
Alaska Lodging and Adventures
West Mackey Lake
907-252-3692
www.ptialaska.net/akcabins
Fully equipped cabins, private baths, TV, phones. Canoes, fish-processing facilities.

Eagle Island Lodge
35555 Spur Highway
1-877-262-9900 or 907-262-4050
Log cabins, RV and tent camping. Sauna, tackle and gift shop, salmon bake, smokehouse. Fishing charters, boat rentals.

The Riverside House
44611 Sterling Highway
1-877-262-0500 or 907-262-0500
www.riverside-house.com
Rooms, RV parking, restaurant, lounge, nightclub.

Kenai:
Kings Inn
20352 Kenai Spur Highway
907-283-6060
51 rooms, laundry, room service. Restaurant, lounge. Freezer space for your fish.

Uptown Motel
Mile 47 Spur View Drive
907-283-3660
Rooms adjacent to Louie's Steak & Seafood restaurant.

Homer: The Kachemak Bed and Breakfast Association will help you find Homer-area bed-and-breakfast accommodations. Call 907-235-6677 or www.homer-lodging.com.

Almost Home Accommodations
1269 Upland Court
907-235-2553
www.alaskaone.com/almosthome
Furnished cabins, fishing charter/lodging packages.

Anchor River Inn
Just north of Homer at Anchor Point
1-800-435-8531 or 907-235-8531
20 rooms, store, gift shop, restaurant, lounge.

Bay View Inn
Top of the hill at entrance to town
1-800-478-8485 or 907-235-8485
Rooms, suites, kitchenettes; nonsmoking facility. Views.

Best Western Bidarka Inn
575 Sterling Highway
907-235-8148
Full-service hotel, restaurant, sports bar, charters.

Driftwood Inn & RV Park
135 West Bunnell Avenue
1-800-478-8019 or 907-235-8019
Historic beachfront inn with full hookup campsites.

Heritage Hotel Lodge
147 East Pioneer Avenue
1-800-380-7787
32 rooms, suites in log hotel. Walking
   distance to downtown restaurants,
   entertainment, museums.

Land's End Resort
4789 Homer Spit Road
907-235-0400
Beachfront rooms, mountain and bay
   vistas, Chart Room Restaurant.

On the Sterling Highway, one business specializes in selling antlers—just as they were shed, or carved into a specialty piece.

Homer's boat harbor is an active place, with tour boat operations, pleasure vessels, and commercial fishing boats coming and going.

Lighthouse Village
Homer Spit
907-235-7007
Cabins and cottages, viewing deck,
    restaurant, charters, boat storage.

Ocean Shores Motel
3500 Crittenden Drive
1-800-770-7775 or 907-235-7775
www.akoceanshores.com
Seaside rooms, private beach, walking
    distance to town.

Campgrounds
Cooper Landing:
Kenai Princess RV Park
Mile 47.5 Sterling Highway
907-595-1425
35 sites, power, tables. Shower, laundry,
    water, dump station. Groceries. Next to
    Kenai Princess Lodge. Turn at Mile 47.5
    (76.5 km), then drive 2 miles (3 km) on
    Bear Creek Road.

The **U.S. Forest Service** manages the
following campgrounds near Cooper
Landing:

Crescent Creek Campground
Turn off at Mile 45 Sterling Highway and
    follow Quartz Creek Road
RV parking and tent sites. Water, toilets,
    fishing.

Quartz Lake Campground
Turn off at Mile 45 Sterling Highway and
    follow Quartz Creek Road
RV parking and tent sites. Water, toilets,
    fishing.

Cooper Creek Campground
Mile 50.5 Sterling Highway
RV parking and tent sites. Water, toilets.

Russian River Campground
Mile 53 Sterling Highway
RV parking and tent sites. Water, toilets,
dump station. Excellent salmon fishing
in season.

The **U.S. Fish and Wildlife Service** has
developed several campgrounds between
Cooper Landing and Sterling:

Skilak Lake
21 miles (33.5 km) west from the junction of
Sterling and Seward Highways is the first
turnoff for Skilak Lake Road, a loop
along which there are three
campgrounds. Two developed
campgrounds are on Skilak Lake; a third
lies nearby on Hidden Lake. All three
have fire pits, toilets, water, and boat
ramps.

Kenai-Russian River Campground
Mile 55 Sterling Highway, near boundary of
Kenai National Wildlife Refuge
Developed campsites, with water, and
toilets. Near excellent fishing.

Alaska State Parks manages the following
recreation sites and campgrounds near
Sterling:

Bing's Landing, Mile 79 (127 km)
Izaak Walton, Mile 81 (130 km)
Morgan's Landing, Mile 85 (136.5 km)
Scout Lake, Mile 85 (136.5 km)
Funny River, Mile 10 (16 km) Funny River
Road

Soldotna:
Big Eddy Campground
End of Big Eddy Road off Kenai Spur
Highway

907-262-7888
Full hookups, showers, laundry, rest
rooms. Full-service fish processing,
charters, boat rentals. A thousand feet
of riverbank fishing.

Eagle Island Lodge
35555 Spur Highway
1-877-262-9900 or 907-262-4050
Log cabins, RV and tent camping.
Tackle and gift shop, fishing charters,
sauna, salmon bake, smokehouse. Boat
rentals.

The Riverside House
44611 Sterling Highway
1-877-262-0500 or 907-262-0500
www.riverside-house.com
RV park, hotel, riverview dining, lounge,
nightclub.

Kenai:
Captain Cook State Recreation Area
Miles 36—29 Kenai Spur Highway
Campsites, fishing, hiking, picnic shelter,
boating.

Kenai RV Park
Corner of Highland and Upland Streets
907-398-3382
18 sites with hookups, tent camping,
showers, laundry, rest rooms. One block
from Kenai visitor center.

Homer:
Homer Spit Campground
At the end of the road
907-235-8206
Oceanfront camping for RVs, with partial
hookups, tent camping, showers, dump
station. Gift shop, charter bookings,
trailer rentals.

Hornaday Memorial Park
Off Bartlett and Fairview Avenues
City campground with 33 sites, views of the
    bay, water spigot, rest rooms.

Ocean RV Park
455 Sterling Highway
907-235-3951
Full and partial hookups, pull-throughs,
    tent camping. Panoramic views.
    Showers, rest rooms, gift shop. Special
    charter rates.

Alaska State Parks manages the following
campgrounds between Ninilchik and
Homer:

Ninilchik View Campground
North end of Ninilchik
Mile 134 Sterling Highway
RV parking and tent sites. Water, toilets,
    dump station. Fishing.

Ninilchik Campground
Mile 135 Sterling Highway
RV camping and tent sites. Water, toilets,
    fishing.

Deep Creek State Recreation Area
Mile 138 Sterling Highway
164 sites near excellent fishing.

Stariski Campground
Mile 151 Sterling Highway
Partial hookups, tent camping. Water, picnic
    shelter, wheelchair-accessible toilets.

Anchor River State Recreation Area
Mile 157.5 turnoff to Anchor River Beach
    Road
5 campgrounds with more than
    150 campsites.

Restaurants
Cooper Landing:
Gwin's Lodge
Mile 52 Sterling Highway
907-595-1266
Restaurant, bar, cabins, rooms, RV
    hookups.

Soldotna:
China Sea Buffet Restaurant
Soldotna Mall, half a mile north of the
    bridge
907-262-5033
All-you-can-eat buffet, salad bar.

Coffee Concepts
35228 Kenai Spur Highway
907-260-3255
Sandwiches, soups, gourmet coffees,
    muffins.

Golden International Restaurant
Mile 91.5 Sterling Highway
907-262-7862
Chinese and American food.

Jersey Subs
44224 Sterling Highway
907-260-3393
Hot and cold submarine sandwiches.

Odie's
Across from Soldotna Mall
907-262-5807
Big breakfasts, box lunches anytime,
    breads, desserts.

Pizza Pete's
35433 Kenai Spur Highway
907-262-7797
Italian, Greek, Mexican, steaks, seafood.

The River Side House
44611 Sterling Highway
1-877-262-0500 or 907-262-0500
Riverview dining, lunch and dinner;
   lounge, nightclub.

Sal's Klondike Diner
Mile 95.5 Sterling Highway
907-262-2220
Alaskan and Yukon burgers, breakfast
   anytime. Sack lunches to go.

Through the Seasons Restaurant
Sterling Highway
907-262-5006
Seafood, pasta, steaks, desserts.

Kenai:
Don Jose's
205 Willow Street
907-283-8181
Authentic Mexican food.

Louie's Steak & Seafood
Mile 47 Spur View Drive
Adjacent to Uptown Motel
907-283-3660
Fine Alaska seafood.

Veronica's Coffee House
604 Peterson Way
907-283-2725
Food, coffee, live music on weekends, in
   historic building in Old Town.

Homer:
Alaska's Italian Bistro
4241 Homer Spit Road No. 1
907-235-6153
Soups, sandwiches.

Boardwalk Fish & Chips
Homer Spit Road
907-235-7749
Burgers, fresh halibut, and the works.

Don Jose's
127 Pioneer Avenue
907-235-7963
Authentic Mexican food.

Fresh Sourdough Express Bakery & Café
1316 Ocean Drive
907-235-7571
Breakfast, lunch, dinner; box lunches,
   desserts, espresso, bakery.

Homestead Restaurant
East End Road and Fritz Creek
907-235-8723
Lunches and dinners; views of
   Kachemak Bay.

Pioneer Building Pizzeria
265 East Pioneer Avenue
907-235-3663
All-you-can-eat pizza and ice cream.

Rainbow Wok Café
4480 Homer Spit Road
907-235-3873
Sandwiches, soups, salads.

Smith Family Restaurant
412 East Pioneer Avenue
907-235-8600
Family dining, full menu.

𝒯aylor Highway

Part of the Klondike Loop
From Alaska Highway to Eagle: 160 miles (257 km)
Travel Opportunities: *Town of Chicken; Fortymile gold-mining country; Jack Wade*
No. 1 gold dredge; Eagle; Fort Egbert; Yukon River; riverboat Yukon Queen III.

The Taylor is the highway for stouthearted drivers who promise to pay close attention to the road; let your navigator take the pictures for you to enjoy later. Unpaved and narrow, the Taylor climbs and descends, turns and doubles back, changing its mind multiple times in a matter of miles as it wends through and above some of the most spectacular country in east-central Alaska. For those who want a taste of what the Alaska Highway used to be like, this is the road.

The Taylor Highway takes off northward from Tetlin Junction on the Alaska Highway, about a dozen miles east of Tok. The Taylor is part of the **Klondike Loop**, the route over a series of three highways that connects Tok and Whitehorse via Dawson City. (See the sections on the North Klondike Highway and the Top of the World Highway in Chapter 7, Western Canada's Northbound Byways.)

The Taylor provides access to two distinctive Alaska towns, Chicken and Eagle, both of which are steeped in gold-mining history. The towns are inaccessible by road in winter, however. The Taylor is one of the few Alaska highways that is not maintained throughout the winter, meaning that the state does not plow it, making it good for dog-mushing and snowmobile traffic, but not much more.

Chicken is the town that the late author Ann Purdy made famous in *Tisha*, her novel based on her own life. The book details the adventures of a young teacher who moves to Chicken, falls in love with the place and her Athabascan Indian students, and settles down to make it home. Chicken, she is told, was given this name because miners couldn't correctly spell the name of the local chickenlike bird, the ptarmigan.

It's easy to pass by the best parts of Chicken if your eyes look dead ahead. At about Mile 66 (106 km) from Tetlin Junction, follow the Airport Road turnoff to the historic Chicken business district. Chicken offers a couple of restaurants, a saloon, a gift shop and bookstore, and a gas station. The Goldpanner hosts RV parking and 2 P.M. daily tours of Chicken, including a stop at Tisha's Schoolhouse.

At Mile 86 (138 km), you'll see the ruins of the old **Jack Wade No. 1** gold dredge, which sits right at roadside and makes for a wonderful photo opportunity.

At Mile 96 (154 km), you'll encounter the only fork in the highway. At this point, you may choose to continue north on the Taylor Highway to its dead end at the town of Eagle on the Yukon River. Or you may turn east and connect with the **Top of the World Highway** to continue along the Klondike Loop.

If you turn east, 12 miles (19 km) of travel will take you to the Alaska–Yukon border—and after another 66 miles (105 km) of driving adventure on a winding, unpaved road, you'll land in Dawson City, Yukon. Along the way, you'll catch a glimpse of why they named it the Top of the World Highway. At Dawson City, you can connect with the North Klondike Highway as you proceed along the Klondike Loop.

Each late February, over the course of three weekends, more than 700 snowmobilers dominate the Taylor and Top of the World Highways during a fun run between Tok and Dawson City that's called the **Trek Over the Top**. Trekkers travel 200 miles (322 km) one way in a day, stopping to refuel in Chicken. They spend a couple of days seeing Dawson and visiting Diamond Tooth Gerties for entertainment and one-armed bandit fun, then jump back on their machines for the return trip. Since all of the traffic is headed in one direction, and there's no concern of meeting a car or RV on a nasty bend, the snowmobilers pull out all the stops and enjoy the ride. For more information, call Eric Zalitis, the Canadian coordinator in Dawson City, at 867-633-2154, or visit the website at http://trek.dawsoncity.net/home.html.

The **Fortymile caribou herd**, which numbers 20,000-plus animals, migrates across the Taylor Highway twice a year: from east to west during March and April, and from west to east during October and November. Watch for moose and bears, too.

At the end of the Taylor Highway is **Eagle**. Imagine this sleepy little town as the hustle-bustle community it was in 1897. The city was crawling with gold miners, traders, merchants, and soldiers; commerce often was conducted with gold. This was a regular stop for the fleet of steam paddleboats that traveled the Yukon, delivering passengers and supplies. Here, too, was **Fort Egbert**, a military installation that brought order to the gold boomtown.

A mature community when Fairbanks was still merely a forested bend on the Chena River, Eagle was then the seat of the Third Judicial District, with Judge James Wickersham on the bench. The judge would play a major role in Eagle's decline, however, when he made a deal with the founder of Fairbanks, E. T. Barnette, to move the judicial seat from Eagle to Fairbanks. The old courthouse has been restored to its days of yore, as have the old customs building and the adjacent Fort Egbert. Another Eagle landmark is the wind-powered water well that was dug in 1903 and continues to serve. From the waterfront, the sternwheeler *Yukon Queen III* offers daily trips between Eagle and Dawson City.

At the river, you may see rafters preparing for a float trip from Eagle to Circle City. Planning for this trip takes some extraordinary effort in shuttling vehicles and rafts, as Circle is hundreds of miles away by road at the end of the Steese Highway. But most say it's worth it for the experience of floating through this stretch of the **Yukon-Charley Rivers National Preserve**. The National Park Service offers informational talks, videos, publications, and books, along the river near Fort Egbert. Other rafters or canoeists may be arriving from a Dawson City-to-Eagle excursion. (Having crossed an international border on the water, they need to check in with U.S. Customs at Eagle.)

Eagle is still a part of the active Fortymile Mining District, and gold-mining operations continue in this region. You may meet a gold miner or support crew member during your stay here, as the town is the nearest point of civilization for many of these folks. They'll come into town for mail, gossip, and a change of menu, as well as to stock up on supplies.

For more information on what Eagle has to offer, contact the Eagle Historical Society and Museums at 907-547-2232.

Lodging/Meals

Eagle Trading Co. Motel
Along the Yukon River, in Eagle
907-547-2220
Rooms, laundry, public showers. Store, fuel, café. Hunting and fishing licenses.

Falcon Inn
220 Front Street, Eagle
907-547-2254
Rooms with private baths, hot breakfast. Walking distance to museums. Along the Yukon River.

Campgrounds

The Bureau of Land Management oversees three camping areas along the Taylor Highway. They are open seasonally, mid-April to October, based on road openings. For more information, contact the Northern Field Office in Fairbanks at 907-474-2302 or visit the bureau's website at www.ak.blm.gov/ndo.

West Fork Campground
Mile 48.5 Taylor Highway
Developed campsites on 20 acres, with wheelchair-accessible toilets. Fishing.

Walker Fork Campground
Mile 82 Taylor Highway
Developed campsites on 60 acres. Water, toilets, hiking trails, fishing, gold panning.

Eagle Campground
Mile 160 Taylor Highway
Developed campsites on 80 acres, with toilets.

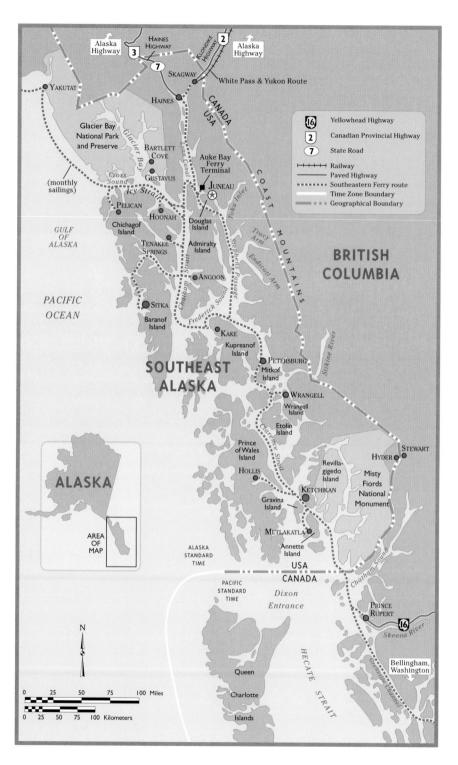

Alaska Highway

HAINES Highway

Alaska Highway

3

7

SKAGWAY

2

Alaska Highway

White Pass & Yukon Route

YAKUTAT

HAINES

CANADA
USA

Glacier Bay National Park and Preserve

BARTLETT COVE

Auke Bay Ferry Terminal

16   Yellowhead Highway

2   Canadian Provincial Highway

7   State Road

├┼┼┼┼┤ Railway

━━━━ Paved Highway

▪▪▪▪ Southeastern Ferry route

━━━━ Time Zone Boundary

▪▪▪▪ Geographical Boundary

Glacier Bay

GUSTAVUS

JUNEAU

(monthly sailings)

Cross Sound

Icy Strait

COAST

Lynn Canal

Taku Inlet

PELICAN

Chichagof Island

HOONAH

Douglas Island

Tracy Arm

MOUNTAINS

GULF OF ALASKA

TENAKEE SPRINGS

Admiralty Island

Stephens Passage

Endicott Arm

BRITISH COLUMBIA

PACIFIC OCEAN

ANGOON

Chatham Strait

SITKA

Baranof Island

Frederick Sound

Stikine River

SOUTHEAST ALASKA

KAKE

Kupreanof Island

PETERSBURG

Mitkof Island

WRANGELL

Wrangell Island

Etolin Island

Prince of Wales Island

HOLLIS

Revilla-gigedo Island

Clarence Strait

HYDER

STEWART

Misty Fiords National Monument

KETCHIKAN

Gravina Island

METLAKATLA

Annette Island

Chatham Sound

ALASKA

AREA OF MAP

ALASKA STANDARD TIME

USA
CANADA

PACIFIC STANDARD TIME

Dixon Entrance

PRINCE RUPERT

16

Skeena River

N

Granville Channel

Bellingham, Washington

HECATE STRAIT

Queen

Charlotte

Islands

0   25   50   75   100 Miles

0   25   50   75   100 Kilometers

Chapter 9

Alaska Marine Highway System

$\mathcal{T}he$ Inside Passage marine route from Washington to Alaska gained fame in the late 1890s when Klondike miners and their gold arrived in Seattle and ignited a gold rush. The news spread quickly, and people came to believe that riches awaited in the north—and that all it took was to jump on a steamer headed up the Inside Passage.

The thrill of traveling by ship on the Inside Passage has taken on a new slant today. Even occasional dreary weather cannot suppress the extraordinary beauty of a trip on these protected waters between mainland and islands. As you travel, you are free to walk the decks, sleep when you're tired, buy a meal when you're hungry, and visit with the people around you. There's nothing else to do but enjoy yourself as incredible vistas slowly slide by.

Two ferry systems operate in these waters. BC Ferries, an arm of British Columbia's transportation system, owns a fleet of more than 40 vessels of all sizes, which cruise among the islands and mainland ports of the province. From Victoria to Prince Rupert, with many stops between, BC Ferries operates more than 25 routes. It connects with the Alaska Marine Highway System at Prince Rupert.

The Alaska Marine Highway System ferries, affectionately called the "blue canoes," stick to a routine schedule for picking up and dropping off passengers at coastal communities, almost like a vast city bus system. The vessels of the fleet also vary in size and in their specialized routes.

The southeastern portion of the Alaska system operates all the way from Bellingham, Washington, on the southern end, to Prince Rupert, B.C., then farther northward to the cities of Alaska's Inside Passage, up to Skagway.

The southcentral/southwestern portion of the Alaska system operates on a separate schedule with an entirely different fleet. That portion includes Cordova, Valdez, Whittier, Seward, Homer, Kodiak, and some ports in the Aleutian Islands. The two parts of the Alaska system are connected only in summers by the M/V *Kennicott*, the newest and largest vessel in the fleet, which crosses the Gulf of Alaska once a month in what is called an "inter-tie trip."

People come aboard the Alaska state ferries on foot, sometimes for a day trip to a nearby town. Or they arrive in campers, ready to drive their rigs into the hold and then head upstairs to a stateroom and a warm bed. Others carry their belongings on their backs. Travelers without a stateroom are welcome to bunk under the stars on the vessel's top deck. This is freedom at its finest—come one, come all—and presents plenty of opportunity to make friends with someone from a local village or someone from the other side of the planet.

Major ports of call in Southeast Alaska are Ketchikan, Wrangell, Petersburg, Sitka, Juneau, Haines, and Skagway. Between them, shorter trips link Metlakatla, Hollis, Kake, Angoon, Tenakee, and Hoonah.

These ports each claim a unique personality: Petersburg, the fishing town with Norwegian roots; Sitka, the former capital of Russian America, as Alaska was known before its purchase by the United States; Native villages that welcome visitors eager to know more about Tlingit, Haida, and Tsimshian culture; Juneau, Alaska's capital— and, like most Southeast Alaska towns, inaccessible by road. Skagway and Haines, the northernmost ports in Southeast Alaska, are connected to the Alaska Highway by spur roads. (See the sections on the Haines Highway and Klondike Highway 2 in Chapter 8, Alaska's State Highways.) Consider a southbound trip on the marine highway as a way to return home after your northbound drive up the Alaska Highway.

The cost for passage depends on distance between ports, whether a stateroom is reserved, length of your vehicle, and other factors. You can customize your trip so that you can disembark and tour the towns of your choice before continuing on your journey.

Here are some contacts for more information on marine travel in Alaska and along the Inside Passage:

Alaska Marine Highway System
1-800-642-0066 or 907-465-3941
www.dot.state.ak.us/external/amhs/guide.
    html

BC Ferries
1-800-448-7181 or 907-456-7888
www.bcferries.com

Southeast Alaska Tourism Council
1-800-423-0568
www.alaskainfo.org

Further Reading

Canada

Berton, Pierre. *The Klondike Fever*. New York: Carroll & Graf, 1985.

———. *The Klondike Quest: A Photographic Essay 1897–1899*. North York, Ontario: Stoddart Publishing, 1997.

Bruhn, Karl. *Best of B.C.: Lake Fishing*. Vancouver, B.C.: Whitecap Books, 1998.

Coull, Cheryl. *A Traveller's Guide to Aboriginal B.C.* Vancouver, B.C.: Whitecap Books, 1996.

Madsen, Ken, and Graham Wilson. *Rivers of the Yukon: A Paddling Guide*. Whitehorse, Yukon: Primrose Publishing, 1990.

Neering, Rosemary. *A Traveller's Guide to Historic B.C.* Vancouver, B.C.: Whitecap Books, 1993.

Schofield, Janice J. *Discovering Wild Plants: Alaska, Western Canada, the Northwest*. Bothell, Washington: Alaska Northwest Books, 1989.

Short, Steve, and Bernie Palmer. *Best of B.C.: Exploring Canyons, Glaciers, Hotsprings, and Other Natural Highs*. Vancouver, B.C.: Whitecap Books, 1992.

Wolf Creek. *The Klondike Gold Rush: Photographs from 1896–1899*. Whitehorse, Yukon: Wolf Creek, 1997.

Zuehlke, Mark. *The Alberta Fact Book*. Vancouver, B.C.: Whitecap Books, 1997.

———. *The B.C. Fact Book*. Vancouver, B.C.: Whitecap Books, 1995.

———. *The Yukon Fact Book*. Vancouver, B.C.: Whitecap Books, 1998.

Alaska

Alaska Geographic. *Denali*. Anchorage: Alaska Geographic Society, 1995.

———. *Kenai Peninsula*. Anchorage: Alaska Geographic Society, 1997.

———. *Southeast Panhandle*. Anchorage: Alaska Geographic Society, 1997.

Alaska Northwest Books. *The Alaska Almanac: Facts About Alaska*, 24th ed. Portland, Oregon: Alaska Northwest Books, 2000.

———. *The Alaska–Yukon Wild Flowers Guide*. Bothell, Washington: Alaska Northwest Books, 1990.

Armstrong, Robert. *Guide to the Birds of Alaska*, 4th ed. Seattle: Alaska Northwest Books, updated 2000.

Brown, Tricia, ed. *Alaskan Wilderness* (Discovery Travel Adventures). London: Discovery Channel Inc., 1999.

Brown, Tricia, and Roy Corral (photography). *Children of the Midnight Sun: Young Native Voices of Alaska*. Seattle: Alaska Northwest Books, 1998.

———. *Fairbanks: Alaska's Heart of Gold.* Portland, Oregon: Alaska Northwest Books, 2000.

Ewing, Susan. *The Great Alaska Nature Factbook.* Seattle: Alaska Northwest Books, 1996.

Hunt, William R. *North of 53°: The Wild Days of the Alaska–Yukon Mining Frontier, 1870–1914.* New York: Macmillan, 1974.

Jettmar, Karen. *The Alaska River Guide: Canoeing, Kayaking, and Rafting in the Last Frontier, 2nd ed.* Seattle: Alaska Northwest Books, 1998.

Kelley, Mark, and Sherry Simpson. *Alaska's Ocean Highways: A Travel Adventure Aboard Northern Ferries.* Seattle: Epicenter Press, 1995.

Littlepage, Dean. *Hiking Alaska.* Helena, Montana: Falcon Publishing Co., 1997.

Maschmeyer, Gloria (text), and Alissa Crandall (photography). *Along the Alaska Highway.* Bothell, Washington: Alaska Northwest Books, 1992.

Morgan, Lael. *Good Time Girls of the Alaska–Yukon Gold Rush.* Seattle: Epicenter Press, 1998.

Murie, Margaret E. *Two in the Far North, 2nd ed.* Seattle: Alaska Northwest Books, 1997.

Murphy, Claire Rudolf, and Jane G. Haigh. *Gold Rush Women.* Seattle: Alaska Northwest Books, 1997.

Piper, Ernie. *Alaska Sportfishing.* Anchorage: Alaska Geographic Guides, 1997.

Ritter, Harry. *Alaska's History: The People, Land, and Events of the North Country.* Seattle: Alaska Northwest Books, 1993.

Satterfield, Archie. *Chilkoot Pass: A Hiker's Historical Guide.* Seattle: Alaska Northwest Books, updated 1998.

Sherwonit, Bill. *Alaska's Bears: Grizzlies, Black Bears, and Polar Bears.* Seattle: Alaska Northwest Books, 1998.

Simmerman, Nancy (photography), Helen Nienhueser, and Johnson Wolfe. *55 Ways to the Wilderness of Southcentral Alaska, 4th ed.* Seattle: The Mountaineers Books, 1994.

——— and Tricia Brown. *Wild Alaska: The Complete Guide to Parks, Preserves, Wildlife Refuges, & Other Public Lands, 2nd ed.* Seattle: The Mountaineers Books, 1999.

Smith, Dave. *Backcountry Bear Basics: The Definitive Guide to Avoiding Unpleasant Encounters.* Seattle: The Mountaineers, 1997.

———. *Alaska's Mammals.* Seattle: Alaska Northwest Books, 1995.

Distance Charts

Distances in Western Canada and the U.S.

In **Miles** *and* Kilometers

	Cache Creek, BC	Calgary, AB	Dawson City, YT	Dawson Creek, BC	Edmonton, AB	Fairbanks, AK	Fort Nelson, BC	Great Falls, MT	Prince George, BC	Seattle, WA	Watson Lake, YT	Whitehorse, YT
Anchorage, AK	**2135** / 3416	**2160** / 3456	**515** / 824	**1608** / 2573	**1975** / 3160	**363** / 581	**1281** / 2136	**2473** / 3960	**1678** / 2685	**2435** / 3896	**967** / 1611	**724** / 1158
Cache Creek, BC		**438** / 701	**1722** / 2755	**527** / 843	**545** / 872	**2013** / 3221	**800** / 1280	**753** / 1205	**277** / 443	**294** / 470	**1139** / 1822	**1411** / 2258
Calgary, AB			**1747** / 2795	**549** / 878	**108** / 291	**2037** / 3259	**835** / 1336	**315** / 504	**635** / 1016	**738** / 1181	**1164** / 1862	**1436** / 2298
Dawson City, YT				**1195** / 1912	**1562** / 2499	**393** / 629	**900** / 1501	**2078** / 3325	**1390** / 2318	**2022** / 3235	**586** / 976	**327** / 523
Dawson Creek, BC					**367** / 587	**1488** / 2395	**282** / 451	**867** / 1387	**250** / 400	**821** / 1314	**612** / 979	**886** / 1418
Edmonton, AB						**1855** / 2968	**630** / 1050	**500** / 800	**442** / 737	**790** / 1264	**979** / 1566	**1253** / 2005
Fairbanks, AK							**1206** / 1930	**2353** / 3765	**1728** / 2781	**2313** / 3701	**875** / 1400	**601** / 962
Fort Nelson, BC								**1335** / 2225	**532** / 851	**1027** / 1712	**330** / 528	**604** / 966
Great Falls, MT									**790** / 1317	**681** / 1090	**1615** / 2692	**1731** / 2731
Prince George, BC										**571** / 914	**737** / 1228	**983** / 1639
Seattle, WA											**1272** / 2120	**1707** / 2781
Watson Lake, YT												**274** / 438
Whitehorse, YT												

To read, choose a place name at the bottom of a column and scan upward to meet the corresponding horizontal line.

Distances within Alaska

In **Miles** and Kilometers

	Circle	Delta Junction	Eagle	Fairbanks	Glennallen	Haines	Homer	Prudhoe Bay	Seward	Skagway	Tok	Valdez
Anchorage	**520**	**338**	**501**	**363**	**187**	**775**	**226**	**847**	**127**	**832**	**328**	**304**
	832	541	802	581	299	1240	362	1355	204	1331	525	486
Circle		**260**	**541**	**162**	**411**	**815**	**746**	**1972**	**646**	**872**	**368**	**526**
		416	866	259	658	1304	1194	3155	1034	1395	589	842
Delta Junction			**281**	**98**	**151**	**805**	**564**	**587**	**464**	**603**	**108**	**266**
			450	157	242	1288	902	939	742	965	173	426
Eagle				**379**	**324**	**620**	**727**	**868**	**627**	**579**	**173**	**427**
				606	518	992	1163	1389	1003	926	277	683
Fairbanks					**249**	**653**	**584**	**489**	**487**	**710**	**206**	**364**
					398	1045	934	783	779	1136	330	582
Glennallen						**589**	**413**	**738**	**313**	**636**	**141**	**115**
						942	661	1181	501	1018	226	184
Haines							**1001**	**1142**	**901**	**359**	**447**	**701**
							1602	1827	1442	574	715	1122
Homer								**1073**	**173**	**1058**	**554**	**530**
								1717	277	1693	886	848
Prudhoe Bay									**973**	**1199**	**695**	**853**
									1557	1918	1112	1365
Seward										**958**	**454**	**430**
										1533	726	688
Skagway											**504**	**758**
											806	1213
Tok												**254**
												406
Valdez												

Index

(*Note:* Page numbers in italics indicate photographs; "t." indicates table.)

Tricia and Perry Brown, and Barney, traveling over the White Pass, Yukon.

Tricia Brown is a veteran Alaska writer who has been publishing articles and books on Alaska subjects for twenty years. She is the author of a travel guide to Fairbanks, an award-winning children's book on Alaska's Native cultures, and two books on dog mushing. She also is the editor of *Alaskan Wilderness* and *Wild Alaska: The Complete Guide to Parks, Preserves, Wildlife Refuges & Other Public Lands*.